New Blood in Co

New Blood in Contemporary Cinema

Women Directors and the Poetics of Horror

Patricia Pisters

EDINBURGH
University Press

Edinburgh University Press is one of the leading university presses in the UK. We publish academic books and journals in our selected subject areas across the humanities and social sciences, combining cutting-edge scholarship with high editorial and production values to produce academic works of lasting importance. For more information visit our website: edinburghuniversitypress.com

Edinburgh University Press Ltd
The Tun – Holyroad Road, 12(2f) Jackson's Entry, Edinburgh EH8 8PJ

First published in hardback by Edinburgh University Press 2020

Typeset in Monotype Ehrhardt by
Servis Filmsetting Ltd, Stockport, Cheshire

A CIP record for this book is available from the British Library

ISBN 978 1 4744 6695 0 (hardback)
ISBN 978 1 4744 6696 7 (paperback)
ISBN 978 1 4744 6697 4 (webready PDF)
ISBN 978 1 4744 6698 1 (epub)

Contents

Figures

Acknowledgements

'Writing is always an incomplete completion and a complete incompletion', writes Elisabeth von Samsonow in her book *Anti-Electra*. I want to repeat this statement because I have never felt the incomplete completion that this book is as such a complete incompletion, because the topic keeps growing. This project began as a chapter in an edited volume celebrating the twenty-fifth anniversary of Barbara Creed's *The Monstrous-Feminine*, and I am therefore grateful to the editors of that volume and particularly Jeanette Hoorn, who put me back on the horror track. During the research for my contribution about female directors and horror aesthetics, I discovered so many interesting films directed by women that I soon decided that it should be a book-length project. During my research, however, I kept discovering new directors and new films, and every day I found new names, new titles, new interviews and references. I collected information from many different sources ranging from online lists of best horror films, best female-directed films, most scary mothers, etc. to cross-references in articles, talking to curators, film fans and colleagues as well as searching online platforms such as Netflix and MUBI, buying, renting or borrowing DVDs and obtaining temporary online links by approaching film critics, festivals, distributors and archives. What began as a small project grew in size and scope. I kept discovering and rediscovering material, never covering everything but always finding new gaps. Female directors from around the globe are appropriating and transforming the rules of the genre game, and by the time this book comes out many new films will have seen the (dark or bloodshot) light of day. Many more books will be necessary to cover the global extension of this relatively recent development in cinema to which I hope to make a small contribution.

I am indebted to many people. First, I wish to thank Cinepoetics, the Centre for Advanced Film Studies at the Freie Universität Berlin, especially Michael Wedel and Hermann Kappelhoff, who invited me to take up a fellowship which made it possible to write most of this book during the summer and autumn of 2019 in Berlin. Eileen Rositzka, Regina Brückner, Jan-Hendrik Bakels, Michael Ufer, Matthias Grotkopp, Hannes Weeselkämper, Danny Gronmaier, Katharina Störrle, Jasper Stratil,

Daniel Illger, Zoé Schlepfer, Kasper Aebi and others of the Cinepoetics team created a welcoming atmosphere and organised many conversations about the poetics of film during the bi-weekly film colloquia and other events. Additionally, dialogues with co-fellows David Rodowick, Özgür Çiçek, Christine Lötscher, Anna Steininger and colleagues from King's College London, Erica Carter, Catherine Wheatley, Victor Fan and Sarah Cooper, added to the inspiring academic spirit. I also wish to thank Christine Reeh for inviting me to the Konrad Wolf Film University of Babelsberg in Potsdam to meet with students; and Milena Gregor and the Arsenal Cinema for hosting a lecture about my research findings, followed by a screening of Lucille Hadžihalilović's *Evolution*. I also want to thank Les Films du Worso for giving permission to use an image from that film on the cover of this book. Furthermore, I am grateful to Gillian Leslie at Edinburgh University Press for her long-standing support and enthusiasm regarding this project, and to Richard Strachan and Rebecca Mackenzie for the production and design process. Thanks also to Michael Katzberg for pointing out the 'devilish details' in the text. I also wish to thank Dan Oki and Maja Vrančić for all their support during a short writer's residency at KURS Art 'n' Culture in Split, where part of the book was conceived.

At the Media Studies department of the University of Amsterdam I want to thank my colleagues for many years of gratifying teamwork and collaboration, specifically Julia Noordegraaf and Erik Laeven for taking care of many administrative tasks in my absence; and I also wish to welcome all the Media Studies babies born during the baby boom of 2019. At the Amsterdam School for Cultural Analysis I want to acknowledge Eloe Kingma and Esther Peeren for co-directing ASCA in the years before my research sabbatical in a wonderful collaborative spirit. I am indebted to Eugenie Brinkema for passionately sharing articles and horror suggestions and Inez van der Scheer for keeping me alert and critical. In addition, much thanks goes to Ansuya Blom and Marleen Gorris for the public conversations about their work. For their suggestions and assistance in finding and accessing films, I want to express my gratitude to Minah Jeongh, Lonnie van Brummelen, Gitta Kruisbrink, Yfke van Berkelaer, Annemiek de Jong (from Distributor Cinemien), Anne van der Pol (from Distributor Cineart), Chris Oostrom and Phil van Tongeren (from Imagine Festival), Mitch Davies (from Fantasia Festival), and Han* and the Final Girls Festival in Berlin. Dana Linssen and Jan Pieter Ekker deserve much appreciation for inviting me to create a video essay about Mati Diop's *Atlantics* for the International Film Festival Rotterdam. Last but certainly not least, I wish to express my gratitude to my friends and family, especially Rocco Enzo for joining me in Berlin during the summer months and Gertjan ter Haar for bearing with the nomadic lifestyle of being in between houses and in between cities in times of transition and change.

Introduction
Virginia's Unruly Daughters and
Carrie's Crimson Sisters

Red Flags on the Red Carpet

At one time, I truly disliked horror films. In the late 1980s Brian De Palma's *Carrie* (1976) was shown on television. I did not want to watch it, but my friends and sister convinced me that I should stay in the living room and watch with them. It was a nerve-wracking experience. I had no way of distancing myself from this poor girl covered in blood on her prom night, and from her humiliation and the unbridled fury unleashed from within. I did not see the point of the gruesome images, shocking suspense and the fear and disgust that Noël Carroll identified as the dominant emotions of the horror genre in his seminal book *Philosophy of Horror* (1990). Some years later, however, after I had discovered the powers of cinema, studied film at university and worked in a film-oriented book shop named Cinequanon in Amsterdam, I had a change of heart. In a small corner of the store there was a cult video section. One day a most angelic-looking boy entered, asking me with the kindest shy smile: 'Excuse me, but do you have *I Drink your Blood and Eat your Skin*?' Baffled by the contrast between his timid and friendly looks and the ferociousness of the title he requested, I handed over David Durston's 1970 cult film.

There and then I decided to give the horror genre another try. In the meantime both Carol Clover's *Men, Women and Chain Saws* (1992) and Barbara Creed's *The Monstrous-Feminine* (1993) had appeared. Since I had also begun to teach, I designed a course on horror film around these feminists' interpretations of the genre, and took my students to the carnivalesque Night of Terror in the Tuschinski theatre.[1] Beginning to understand that there is much more to the horror genre than just plain violence and disgust, I learned to appreciate the explicit exploration and exploitation of themes that in other genres often remain 'what lies beneath', our hidden desires and deepest fears, especially in relation to questions of gender. While the films discussed by Clover and Creed were all male authored and the audiences at horror festivals was also predominantly masculine, the genre is also about opening-up and rezoning traditional gender boundaries, albeit often at the expense of women, as Clover argued in her analysis of tropes and themes of the slasher and possession films of the 1970s and 1980s. According to Creed's psychoanalytic reading of the genre, women are not just damsels in distress, victims of the male monsters, as classic horror cinema would have it, but they often inspire fear and have castrating powers. And even the classic gendered positions of female victims and male monsters can be appropriated differently, as Rohna Berenstein argued in her take on the classic horror film in *Attack of the Leading Ladies* (1996), where she shifted the attention to spectatorship and cult appropriation.

Twenty-five years after these seminal feminist readings of the 1990s, I was asked to contribute to a volume rereading Creed's monstrous femininity (Chare, Hoorn and Yue 2019).[2] After the theoretical reappreciation of the genre in the 1990s, horror films received relatively less attention, even if they continued to be made with increasing self-reflexivity with regard to the genre itself, as epitomised by Wes Craven's *Scream* (1996) and its sequels *Scream 2* (1997), *Scream 3* (2000) and *Scream 4* (2011). Since the new millennium, however, there seems to have been another revival of the horror genre, both in terms of production and in terms of theoretical attention. Thomas Alfredson's *Let the Right One In* (2008) brought the vampire film into the art house theatre, as did the genre of French extreme cinema (Kerner and Knapp 2016; Del Rio 2016) or the so-called 'feel-bad film' (Lübecker 2015); online platforms such as Netflix made zombies respectable binge material with horror series such as *The Walking Dead* (2010–); and Jordan Peele not only presented an explicitly biting version of racism in his body-snatching *Get Out* (2017) and a social commentary on the fear of outsiders in *Us* (2019), but also made horror 'Oscar-fähig'. Theoretically, the work of Cynthia Freeland on the appeal of cinematic evil (Freeland 2000) redraws attention to the genre, together with Julian Hanich's take on the emotion of horror (Hanich 2010) and Angela Ndalianis's analysis of the 'horror sensorium' (Ndalianis 2012); the more explicitly gendered approaches of Sarah Arnold (2013) and Erin Harrington (2018) consider maternal horror, and Rikke Schubart conceives of female spectatorship of horror as a playful yet serious and insightful way of mastering fear (Schubart 2018).

However, thinking about the most salient changes in respect to the genre and gender, I am in particular struck by the fact that since the first publication of *The Monstrous-Feminine* a great number of women directors have begun to adopt and adapt formal and thematic elements from horror

cinema. While indebted to both the cinematographic and theoretical legacies of their predecessors, this contemporary female-directed 'poetics of
horror' seems to offer additional and new perspectives on gender and
monstrosity that are worthwhile exploring further. Many of the afore-
mentioned studies on horror and gender focus on either horror cinema's
female protagonists, or on the particular pleasures that horror can offer
female spectatorship. And while the work of women directors who use
horror aesthetics in their work has received individual reviews and in-
depth analyses, less academic attention has been given to the growing phenomenon of female-authored horror as an entire body of collective work.
While women directors did make horror films in earlier periods, they were
either the exceptions that confirmed the rule, or their work slipped into
the shadows of film historiography. Since the new millennium, however,
the number of female directors in the genre has grown spectacularly, and
many of them will be discussed in the following chapters.[3]

This focus on women directors is the main consideration of *New Blood
in Contemporary Cinema*. Following quite literally a trail of blood and the
different shades, hues and values of its colour in the poetics of the cinema
of female filmmakers, I investigate both the formal and affective qualities
as well as the particular themes and meanings of horror embedded in
these films. Therefore, my initial definition of horror is that there must
be blood, ranging from the invisible blood of ghosts of the past, to a drop
from a nosebleed or a barely visible scratch, to rivers of ruby-red blood
covering the entire screen. While many of the films in this book feature
typical tropes of the horror genre such as monsters, avenging women,
vampires, witches and ghosts, there are other, sometimes more subdued
forms of horror that we will encounter. Following this trail, I have three
main hypotheses regarding the salient features of 'new blood' that run
through the veins of this book. First, it is striking that in the female-
directed films under discussion, the poetics of horror (as form, aesthetics
and meaning) has opened up to perspectives that present terror and dread
not just from an outsider's perspective (such as female monstrosity seen
through the eyes of male directors) but also and predominantly from the
intimate point of view of the inner experience of the female body, as well as
the inner thoughts and desires and experiences of social violence. Second,
I suggest that the *emotional spectrum* of horror aesthetics goes beyond the
variations of fear (dread, anxiety) and disgust, the traditional emotions
connected with the genre (Carroll 1990; Creed 1993; Hanich 2010), to also
include a whole range of 'ugly feelings' such as jealousy, irritation and paranoia (Ngai 2007) or sadness, mourning and other trauma-related affects.
And finally, a poetics of horror is *not confined to strict genre boundaries* but

can be found appropriated in psychological, social or political dramas as well as other genres (Brinkema 2015); and vice versa, apparent horror aesthetics can incorporate these other genres beneath its surface, or present completely new genre blends that simply cannot be disentangled.

All these developments are part of larger developments in cinema (and quality television series for that matter) and are not necessarily bound to a female gaze.[4] However, by insisting on new scarlet landscapes of female-made horror, I hope to highlight that women have an active part and creative agency in the contemporary film and media landscape, and present their own perspectives within these general premises. Noticeably, they have always had an active part in film history as makers, but as Jane Gaines demonstrates in her book *Pink-Slipped* on women filmmakers in silent cinema (Gaines 2018), their work was often lost, ignored or disremembered in the folds of historiography. The online database on forgotten female pioneers 'features silent-era producers, directors, co-directors, scenario writers, scenario editors, camera operators, title writers, editors, costume designers, exhibitors, and more to make the point that *they were not just actresses*'.[5] In a similar spirit, I argue that 'women and horror' does not simply comprise either victims or scary female protagonists, nor women in the audience who enjoy terror for many different reasons.

By focusing on the agency of female makers, I want to flag their presence in the contemporary cinema landscape so as not to let them slip away again.[6] Even if much has improved for women's rights, in the wake of the #MeToo debates the protest of eighty-two women from the film industry on the red carpet of the Cannes Film Festival in 2018 indicates that gender inequality at many levels of the film industry and in society at large is still an important battle to fight. The Venice Film Festival has featured very few female directors, even in the 2018 and 2019 selections. The response of artistic director Alberto Barbera that he had selected many 'films that reveal a new sensibility geared toward the feminine universe, even if directed by men', is rather condescending (Bakare and Shoard 2019). As Dina Iordanova responded cynically, 'Why indeed would women directors bother to make films when men already address "the female condition"' (Iordanova 2019). Of course male directors can make beautiful films about women, but there is quite a difference between being the object of the gaze and looking for oneself, between speaking or being spoken about.

Therefore, while acknowledging female agency in all parts of the audiovisual production process, the main selection criterion for the corpus of this book was first the question: is this film directed by a woman? And second, does this film, in one way or another, engage in a poetics of horror? Is there blood, or the colour red in the *mise en scène*? Besides the historiographic argument that I have just made regarding the necessity of being seen and acknowledged outside the shadows of history, with this single focus on female directors I emphasise the importance of self-expression. And self-expression does imply that there is a dissimilarity between male and female authorship. So let me now turn to the vexed question 'What then is this bloody difference?' In order to arrive at a non-binary and non-essentialist understanding of gender, I need to raise another ghostly presence, namely the creative legacies of Virginia Woolf.

The Bloody Difference: Virginia Woolf's Unruly Daughters

Let us begin with Orlando, who after all changes sex and can speak from experience about the difference between the sexes. *Orlando* is Woolf's fictional biography from 1928 of an English nobleman born in the six-teenth century during the reign of Elizabeth I who lives across more than three centuries. Sometime in the mid-eighteenth century Orlando changes sex. Woolf describes the event as unexciting: 'The change seemed to have been accomplished painlessly and completely and in such a way that Orlando herself showed no surprise at it . . . Orlando was a man till the age of thirty; when he became a woman and has remained so ever since' (Woolf 2018: 107). Woolf adds that Orlando had become a woman, but in every other aspect remained the same. In Sally Potter's cinemato-graphic adaptation of Woolf's novel (1992), Tilda Swinton, who plays Orlando, expresses these thoughts succinctly after the sex change. While observing her transformed naked body in a long mirror, she address the viewer directly: 'Same person, no difference at all, just a different sex.' Orlando indeed swings her legs over a horse just like she did before and she does not feel any different than a few moments earlier when she was a man, serving as Great Britain's ambassador to the court of the Sultan of Constantinople. Nevertheless, even though there is no *essential* difference, Orlando quickly finds out that society does look differently upon men and women. When she returns from Turkey to England, she discovers that she has lost the great estate of her ancestors, because she is now a woman and has no legal rights to property. She discovers that ladies are not sup-posed to appear in public places alone, that women are thought of as lesser creatures than men, considered 'beautiful romantic animals that may be adorned with furs' (Woolf 2018: 164) or as 'children of a larger growth' (Woolf 2018: 167).

The different attitudes towards women leave Orlando perplexed, and thus she learns a lesson or two when she changes sex: that historically, socially and politically it does make a difference whether one is a man or a woman. It is therefore telling that when in the nineteenth century Orlando finds her lover Shelmerdine, they fall in love because they can cut across the gender divide, and see each other as their opposite sex: ' "You are a woman, Shel!" she cried. "You are a man, Orlando!" he cried' (Woolf 2018: 198). Again, no essential difference, and yet there are differences that need to be acknowledged in certain historical situations. In her film, Sally Potter, who as late as 1992 was the first female director in Great Britain ever to make a feature film, makes these historically gendered positions even more clear when Orlando and Shelmerdine have an intimate lovers' conversation:

> Orlando: 'If I were a man, I might not choose to risk my life for an uncertain cause, I might think that freedom won by death is not worth having. In fact . . .'
> Shelmerdine: 'You might choose not to be a real man at all.'
> Shelmerdine: 'If I was a woman, I might choose not to sacrifice my life caring for my children and my children's children. Nor to drown in the milk of female kindness, but instead, say, go abroad, would I then be . . .'
> Orlando: '. . . a real woman?' (Potter's *Orlando*, part '1850: Sex')

What makes *Orlando* so powerful is that on the one hand his/her sex is completely unimportant for what makes him/her Orlando; gender fluidity, androgyny and sexual ambiguity are utterly normal and desirable. In this sense *Orlando* can be considered as a very contemporary take on transgenderism, which I have not encountered often in the horror-inspired films directed by women (and which will therefore not be addressed explicitly in this book), but which certainly is an important dimension of contemporary views on sexuality.[7] On the other hand, one is constantly reminded of gender positions that the female and male body seem to occupy. Taking *Orlando* as a starting point, by focusing on female authors, I similarly do not claim any absolute or essential difference in the way women make films: cinematographic language is in principle an asexual (or pansexual) language. And yet there are perhaps perspectives on sexuality, on gender but also more generally on existential questions of life and death, and on the world, that female directors can offer. Throughout this book the spirit of Woolf will regularly return through visionary and sometimes violently striking insights from her writings.

Woolf insisted on the acknowledgement of the position of women in society. Most famously and explicitly she addressed these issues in *A Room of One's Own*, a series of lectures that she gave at women-supporting colleges in Cambridge, which were intertwined with the publication of *Orlando* (Woolf 2015a: xx). Asserting the necessity for women to receive education, to have some financial independence and a room where they could write, she begins her essay by invoking the fictitious sister of William Shakespeare, Judith. Woolf sketches out how with the same talents as her brother, Judith would not have had a chance to write anything, let alone be published and taken up in the canon of literature. Instead, forbidden to read, prohibited from writing, forced into marriage and on the run, she would end up killing herself and be completely forgotten. Another striking reference that recurs throughout *A Room of One's Own* is to an anonymously written sixteenth-century Scottish ballad, 'The Ballad of Mary Hamilton', which refers to Mary, a servant to Mary Queen of Scots, who becomes pregnant by the king, and in desperation kills her child and is about to commit suicide. In connection with this ballad Woolf refers to three other Marys in her essay, all equally and generically named somewhere in the shadows of history.[8] Woolf's stories about women's fates are horrifying in themselves, and address the real conditions of women's lives, which remains important to take into account when defining the poetics and aesthetics of horror.

Compared with Woolf's time, women have gained access to education and professions, rights that only slowly opened up to women after 1919, thanks to the struggles of the suffragettes and other feminists of the first wave, like Woolf herself. Potter brings the end of her film *Orlando* from the year 1928 to the year 1992. Unlike in the novel, Orlando now has not a son but a daughter, and on a motorcycle they ride though contemporary London to her former family estate, now turned into a museum. Freed from the past, she sits under the oak tree where at the beginning of the film she was writing. But her young daughter has picked up a video camera, and films nature and her mother's face from her own perspective, emphasising that a new age has given new means of expression to the daughters of Woolf. And yet the current conditions may also seem precarious and not self-evident. In their manifesto *Women Who Make a Fuss* (2014), Isabelle Stengers and Vinciane Despret revive Woolf's legacy by addressing the precariousness of this newly gained access to previously closed domains for women, most specifically academic education. Even though Stengers and Despret themselves entered university as if it had always been possible, they feel the need to address the current situation in higher education 'as women': 'One quickly forgets the history, once a right is acquired and one is living in the general conditions permitting one to benefit from that right' (Stengers and Despret 2014: 13). Conscious of the fact that as academics they are in a privileged position, they argue the need for a call to arms, because something is changing due to the continuing and exploding neoliberalisation of universities:

> We have the impression of helplessly bearing witness to the end of an epoch, one where we could be delighted in seeing young women (and also men) acquire a taste for research and venture out wherever their questions would lead them – that is, to become capable of this freedom which we have both profited from. (Stengers and Despret 2014: 16)

They see that Woolf's *Three Guineas*, which they call a work of resistance, was written at the limit of despair.

Contrary to *A Room of One's Own*, which was more about obtaining room for creative expression, *Three Guineas*, written in 1938, concerns the political agency of women. The book was published with the terror of the war in Spain fresh in mind and the horrors of fascism and Nazism on the rise. At the time Woolf refused to sign a manifesto to 'protect culture and intellectual freedom' in the name of her country, a culture and freedom that were never granted to women. Not that she believed that the Nazi ideology for women of 'Kinder, Küche, Kirche' (children, kitchen, church) had anything to offer, as Stengers and Despret explain. On the contrary, Woolf simply refused to sign all kinds of petitions against the war but instead chose to delay and think. Ultimately Woolf gives away her three guineas, 'using the money that she earned herself, and choosing where to send it' (Woolf 2015a: xxxiv). After long but razor-sharp deliberations about the question asked of her (as 'a daughter of educated men'), 'How in your opinion are we to prevent war?', she decides to give one guinea to strengthen the education of women, another to support professions for women, and the third to the society for peace that solicited her contribution. 'But the three guineas, though given to different treasurers, are all given to the same cause' (Woolf 2015a: 216). Woolf insists that there is no use giving money to keep old patriarchal systems in place, and her descriptions could sometimes be a scene from a horror movie when, for instance, she vividly writes:

> No guinea of earned money should go to rebuilding the college on the old plan . . . therefore the guinea should be earmarked 'Rags, Petrol, Matches'. And this note should be attached to it: 'Take this guinea and with it burn the college to the ground. Set fire to the old hypocrisies. Let the light of the burning building scare the nightingales and incarnadine the willows. And let the daughters of educated men dance around the fire and heap armful upon armful of dead leaves upon the flames. And let their mothers lean from the upper windows and cry "Let it blaze! Let it blaze! For we have done with this 'education'!"' (Woolf 2015a: 120)

Stengers and Despret see in Woolf's delaying attitude, making a fuss about how to prevent the war by pausing and reflecting on the much deeper causes of the war system, a parallel to the struggles of women working in academia today. They refuse to go along with the neoliberalisation of knowledge and the slow disappearance of those places in academia where there is freedom to think, especially in the humanities and social sciences. They call themselves and other women who have gained access to the domains of knowledge and economic independence 'unfaithful daughters' of Woolf, by extending her legacy to 'make a fuss' about the contemporary situation where intellectual freedom and freedom of speech are called upon as abstract values, while the minority positions that are implied by these values are completely obliterated. They ask Woolf's question again:

> What is this society that 'sinks the private brother, whom we have reasons to respect, and inflates in his stead a monstrous male, loud of voice, hard of fist, childishly intent upon scoring the floor of the earth with chalk marks, within whose mystic boundaries human beings are penned, rigidly, separately, artificially?' Think we must. (Stengers and Despret 2014: 26)

Stengers and Despret are also 'unfaithful daughters' because they criticise Woolf's (and by implication also their own) privileged white position, recalling the legacy of women of colour who

> in the middle of the 1980s, could and would not recognize themselves in the manner in which white sisters spoke 'in the name of women,' notably forgetting that if their grandmothers had been subjugated, assigned to a role of wife and mother, they had also had Black slaves subjugated to them. (Stengers and Despret 2014: 31)

According to Stengers and Despret this challenge posed during the second feminist wave by women of colour reminds us of the fact that in Woolf's feminist writings of the first wave, she does not always escape the normative values of her own time and of her own privileged class position, even if she is critical of British imperialism. *Orlando* opens with a shocking reference to British colonialism when Orlando is introduced as a boy at play with a shrunken-head trophy from an unnamed colonial campaign. While Orlando transcends many of the confinements of his times, this is nevertheless a haunting image that signals a need for updated perspectives. Photographer Paul Mpagi Sepuya addresses this problem in his photographs in an issue of *Aperture*, curated by Tilda Swinton, dedicated to present-day Orlandos, many of whom are of various ethnic backgrounds and in all shades, stages and forms of (gender) transformation (Swinton 2019).

Hence, when I propose contemporary female directors as 'unfaithful' or rather 'unruly' daughters of Woolf, I want to take the challenges and lessons of black feminists and women of colour to heart. I will not suggest that all struggles expressed in a poetics of horror in cinema are the same, nor do I intend to appropriate any of the many different fights that find their way onto screens. Rather, I hope to do justice to the variety of voices and perspectives that form the cells in the new blood that runs through contemporary cinema. Therefore, Woolf's writerly voice will regularly give way to the voice of Octavia Butler, whose novels are another important reference in several chapters. And the corpus of films selected for this book, while far from offering a complete picture, indicates the diversity of women across the world who venture into an aesthetics of horror from a variety of perspectives.

A final point to be made about the legacy of Woolf is her suggestion that woman's traditional exclusion from history also makes it possible for her to see differently (Woolf 2015a: xxiv). Again, this must be seen in a non-essentialist way. Here I want to return to the 'unruliness' of Woolf's style. In some short stories and in her first novels, Woolf experiments with opening up the traditional format of the realist novel, focusing instead on the fleeting moments of everyday perception, offering new angles to the ordinary, the overlooked and the obscure (Woolf 2001: xii). In her interior monologues that attempt to capture what is going on in the minds of protagonists and passers-by, 'living, breathing everyday imperfection' is what she liked (Woolf 2001: xiii). In 'Modern Fiction' she questions approaches to fiction and asks: 'Is it not possible that the accent falls a little differently, that the moment of importance came before or after, that . . . a vague general confusion in which the clear-cut features of the tragic, the comic, the passionate and the lyrical were dissolved beyond the possibility of separate recognition?' (Woolf 2001: xiii). She adds that the mind is exposed to an incessant shower of innumerable impressions, 'trivial, fantastic, evanescent, or engraved with the sharpness of steel' (Woolf 2001: xiii), that are worthwhile exploring.

The female directors who feature in this book all somehow make 'the accent fall a little differently' when they write cinematographically. Like Woolf, they very often speak from inner experiences and observations, confusing a range of generic conventions, operating a scale of sometimes baffling, ambiguous emotions. At the end of the day, they are the unruly daughters of Woolf not only because, like her, they often ignore the rules of genre conventions, but also because they make a fuss and have chosen a rowdy and wild genre in which to work in the first place. Kathleen Rowe writes that unruly woman can be found in genres of laughter, where women use laughter as a strategy to rebel and to undermine normative gender behaviour (Rowe 1995). In this book, the disruptive genre of blood is the place of transgression and unruliness. It is striking also that in the horror genre, reference to writing as the first means to self-expression is a frequent tool. Conversely, it has often been noted that Woolf's writing style is cinematic (Abbs 2005; Kuo 2009). It is also known that from 1915 Woolf often went to the cinema, and after having watched *Das Cabinet des Dr. Caligari* (dir. Robert Wiene, 1920) in 1926 she wrote an essay, 'The Cinema', on the potential of cinema to come: 'So much of our thinking and feeling is connected with seeing, some residue of visual emotion which is of no use either to painter or to poet may still await cinema' (Woolf 2008: 175). The meticulous attention to detail and observation of the visible and the invisible, her attention to the slightest or brightest changes in colour, to shades of transforming moods and visible affect, to the whispers and outbursts of the soundscapes of the world; all this informs my approach when I read the works of the female directors central to this book. That is, my analyses will be predominantly informed by a poetics of cinema, and a poetics of horror that derives from the films themselves.

Cinematic Poetics of Horror, Metaphors and Relations: A Note on Theory

My readings will set out from the aesthetic and affective qualities of the films's cinematography, *mise en scène* and other formal and stylistic elements, as well as the stories told and the contexts in which they are told. Because of my focus on authorship and self-expression, I have also often integrated the voice of the directors themselves, gleaned from interviews I found online and in publications. By bringing together my analytic film observations and other voices (of authors, critics and theorists) that resonate with the images, I hope to weave a tapestry of images and sounds, affects and thoughts of the cinepoiesis of this emerging new wave of female cinematography. Because of the emphasis on the films themselves, this book is relatively low on theory, even if there are theoretical and film-philosophical guides along the way. Let me briefly recapitulate some of the theoretical signposts of the horror genre and then elaborate on the notion of poetics that informs my approach.

First, there is the immense body of work on the horror genre itself. Horror films as a genre have been around since the early days of cinema, where there was always a place for nineteenth-century gothic traditions, ghost stories, haunted houses and monsters such as vampires, mad scientists, psychopathic killers and damsels in distress. After the First World War the horror film became popular in German Expressionism, with *Das Cabinet des Dr. Caligari* being its most famous example. In the 1950s many horror films were allegorical translations of fears of the Cold War, when the monster often represented the embodiment of the terror of imminent nuclear war. In the 1970s and 1980s the cinematographic horror genre reinvented itself, partly in reaction to the second wave of feminism. The power of Women's Lib translated into films full of scary, angry or abject women or female monsters. In turn, these developments were theorised, most notably by Carol Clover and Barbara Creed. Both Clover's *Men, Women and Chain Saws* and Creed's *The Monstrous-Feminine* made significant contributions to understanding the deeper gendered psychology of these modern horror films. Clover presented the typical gendered positions in the slasher film, the possession film, and the rape-revenge film, and most famously coined the term the 'final girl' to describe the typical boyish girl who refrains from sexual intercourse and defeats the monster. Creed adapted Julia Kristeva's psychoanalytic notion of abjection to identify the feminine, and especially its reproductive functions, as monstrous. And beyond Freud's classical idea of the woman as castrated, Creed made an argument for the dangerous 'castrating' woman.

Clover observed that the modern horror genre can be seen as a transgressive experience (if only by virtue of the fact that both men and women can equally be penetrated by an axe or knife, typical horror weapons), but ultimately she argued that the genre is not about equality but about a rezoning of the gendered behaviour of masculinity in crisis. This rezoning to redefine the 'new man' is always at the expense of women. Clover argues that:

> Crudely put, for a space to be created in which men can weep without being labelled feminine, women must be relocated to a space where they will be made to wail uncontrollably; for men to be able to relinquish emotional rigidity, control, women must be relocated to a space in which they will undergo a flamboyant psychotic break; and so on. (Clover 1992: 105)

In her feminist reading of the horror genre, Creed also demonstrates how monstrous femininity, which takes shape in these films, is by and large inspired by male fantasies and anxieties about the other sex. In the second part of *The Monstrous-Feminine*, Creed rereads Freud's case of Little Hans, insisting that 'Hans's various phobias and fears all stem from his original anxiety concerning his mother's genitals [which] ultimately represent castration, suffocation, death, the void – themes also common to the representation of the monstrous-feminine in the horror film' (Creed 1993: 102). Creed explains further that 'not knowing anything about the true nature of the female genitals, coition, and the origin of babies ... he constructs a series of phantasies ... in which he is almost always the passive victim of his mother's frightening sexuality' (1993: 103).

Ultimately, these modern horror films, despite their highly gendered nature, are not about female empowerment. If in this book I turn to the current flood of female directors who are appropriating the tropes and styles of horror cinema, then my starting point is the work of Clover and Creed. I investigate if and how women directors could make a difference by proposing a differently accented poetics, shifting the typical horror tropes slightly or radically.[9]

While I will not deny or exclude the importance of phenomenological or cognitive approaches towards spectatorship of the horror genre, approaches that have been taken in exemplary ways by scholars such as Jennifer Barker (2009), Tarja Laine (2011, 2015), Elena Del Rio (2016) and Rikke Schubart (2018), my approach will begin from an aesthetic analysis of the poetics of film. In that sense I concur with Eugenie Brinkema, who argues for a more formal approach to the horror genre, emphasising that horror is a question of design and componentry that 'opens up fields of possibility for thinking horror in unexpected places, within unexpected juxtapositions . . . horror as a problematics of aesthetics, form, design, element, and composition . . . insisting that textual structures and components are not incidental to affective charge but are indeed responsible for it' (Brinkema 2015: 265; see also Brinkema 2014). I am not sure if form is *responsible* for affect and meaning as Brinkema's radical formalism proposes. Rather, I argue that all formal innovations are always connected to content and resonate with wider social developments. Nevertheless, I think that paying attention to the formal aspects of horror aesthetics, and especially thinking about horror beyond genre conventions, is helpful in rethinking its affective meaning beyond gender conventions as well. Allow me to say a few more words about the poetics of horror and then to unfold some further theoretical perspectives which I will bring to the table in connection with horror aesthetics.

One of the best-known approaches to film poetics is David Bordwell's historical poetics of cinema (Bordwell 1989, 2008). In his work he looks both at the formal principles (such as narrative, cinematography, editing styles, the use of music and sound) according to which films are constructed, and at how these principles arose and changed under particular historical circumstances (Bordwell 1989: 371). Bordwell proposes his method explicitly as an alternative and better way of approaching and understanding cinema to what he and other 1980s cognitivists called Grand theory or SLAB theory.[10] Grand theory such as semiotics and psychoanalytic interpretations of cinema allowed ideological critiques, including feminist ones, and I would not want to reject those readings altogether for a formalist reading of the effects of cinematographic principles. Granted,

Bordwell's formalism does allow for meaning and interpretation, but the purely empirical basis on which his formalism works might not be enough to achieve a deeper understanding of the poetics of horror in the work of contemporary female directors. I find the revision of historical poetics, such as what Hermann Kappelhoff has called 'affective poetics', more productive (Kappelhoff 2015; Greifenstein et al. 2018; Wedel 2019).

Informed by Jacques Rancière's aesthetics of the sensible and the resonances between aesthetics and culture, Kappelhoff proposes a more integrated conception of poetics that is always already tied to the (cultural) politics and reality it assumes. A poetics of affect embodied in the regime of cinematographic aesthetics encompasses a 'sensory-physical relation to the world' that is

> determined by forms of perceptual sensations, of affects, and of speaking positions derived from the historically contingent arrangement of a commonly shared world of the senses. Aesthetics, therefore, designates the connection between an arrangement of art and an idea of thinking itself. And in this connection it is related to the historicity of a community, founded solely in the positions and relations in which we determine how we experience our reality, how we communicate with one another about this, how we describe and process it, in short, how we can think our reality. (Kappelhoff 2015: 7)

A poetics of affect is inspired by Deleuze's famous Bergsonian conception of the cinematographic image as movement-images (Deleuze 1986, 1989).[11] Movement-images entangle the experience of the spectator perceiving and sensing the film as film with the surrounding reality. Kappelhoff proposes a revision of the concept of metaphor in this affective poetic sense. Cinematic metaphors emerge from movement-images (which can be expressed in all kinds of audio-visual images) that come into existence as the viewers affectively experience the film and co-create the film's 'reality' in a poiesis of film viewing. Or, as Kappelhoff writes: 'cinematic metaphor as performative action, as sense-making, grounded in the dynamics of viewer's embodied intersubjective experiences with the film and entangled affectively with cinematic movement-images, temporally orchestrated at every level, emerges with the movement experience of film-viewing' (Müller and Kappelhoff 2018: 78). When I speak about the poetics of horror, I address the affective qualities that the images express not only on a purely formal level but also in relation to the refracted historical realities embedded in both the film itself as well as the contemporary context in which its viewing is taking place, and the poiesis of film taking shape.

By addressing a poetics of horror, I investigate how the regime of aesthetics that is proposed by current women directors provides new ideas about the arrangements between the arts, senses, thinking and politics. With this poetics of horror I also seek 'horror sensibilities' beyond the borders of conventional horror characteristics (White 1971) and extend the emotional spectrum of 'ugly feelings' (Ngai 2007; Brinkema 2014). In order to address the implied politics and cultural realities of this poetics, I refer in some of the chapters to film-philosophical conceptions, especially new materialism and racial and critical theory, which I will elaborate on later. Here, I want to remain with the current conception of poetics and add one important perspective that informs my approach.

One of the elements that is striking in relation to the poetics of horror and the emotions and politics that are implied is that not all images are as explicitly readable as the exploitative characteristics of the genre sometimes prescribe. Many images in the films that will feature on the following pages remain ambiguous, mysterious or opaque. In his seminal work *Poetics of Relation*, Edouard Glissant has called this the 'right to opacity' (Glissant 1997: 189). Glissant explicitly argues against the Western ideal of a desire for transparency and whole 'knowledge' (or grasp) of the other, which also implies measuring everything alongside its norms. Again we could refer here to Woolf who in *Three Guineas* also remarked that 'complete understanding could only be achieved by blood transfusion and memory transfusion' (Woolf 2015a: 92), though Woolf was talking about the relation between the sexes. Glissant speaks from a racial and postcolonial point of view in which the Western world (by and large white and male) no longer sees the world reflected in its own image: 'There is opacity now at the bottom of the mirror' (1997: 111).[12]

Driven by the same desire as Woolf not to repeat the 'master narratives' and structures that have created and continue to create great injustice in the world, Glissant proposes to rethink the notion of identity from what he calls 'root identity' into 'relational identity'. He characterises root identity as fixed in the thought of the self of mythic foundations and of conquest and territory, and the other in opposition to the self. Relational identity is produced in the 'chaotic network of relation and not in the hidden violence of filiation' and circulates nomadically (1997: 144). Glissant proposes a poetics of relation that accepts difference without creating a hierarchy, without trying to make the other into the mirror image of the self. He argues:

> We 'know' that the Other is within us and affects how we evolve as well as the bulk of our conceptions and the development of our sensibility. Rimbaud's 'I is another' is literal in terms of history. In spite of ourselves, a sort of 'consciousness

of consciousness' opens us up and turns each of us into a disconcerted actor in the poetics of relation. (Glissant 1997: 27)

But we cannot know the other completely, 'universally' imposed. 'We demand the right to opacity' writes Glissant (1997: 189), adding that 'the opaque is not the obscure, though it is possible for it to be so and accepted as such. It is that which cannot be reduced, which is the most perennial guarantee of participation and confluence' (1997: 191). With this acceptance of not completely knowing or understanding the other, he also creates a space for a generous relation with the other in an always growing and open network of new (and incomplete) relations.

While it can be argued that the modern horror film has certainly attempted to 'exorcise' women 'as a dark continent' in its particular aesthetics, I receive Glissant's call for opacity as a double challenge. On the one hand, I will claim that films made by female directors might shed more light on this dark continent, though never in a completely transparent way; ambiguity will remain part of its aesthetics. On a meta-level, I also take it as my starting point to attempt to establish a poetics of relation through the diversities of a cinematographic poetics of horror extended through the chapters of this book.

Following a Trail of Blood: Carrie's Crimson Sisters

To propose a poetics of horror this book quite literally follows a trail of blood, in all its colours and viscosities, affective qualities and contextual meanings, which runs through all the chapters. The central figure and form of blood is chosen for its seminal association with both the horror genre (violence, guts and gore) and the female body (menstruation, sexuality and childbirth). To justify the prominence of the poetics of blood let me briefly return to the bloody heroine of 1970s horror cinema, Brian De Palma's Carrie, and her 'crimson sister' in Kimberly Peirce's 2013 remake. By way of introduction, a closer look at the male- and female-directed versions of the same story might be revealing and indicative of some of the issues that will be further elaborated in the various chapters.

Carrie, a girl in a soft-pink prom dress drenched in thick red gushes of blood; it is the seminal image of horror at the apotheosis of humiliation and shame that unleashes the shy and bullied heroine's hidden telekinetic powers in the eponymous film. De Palma's film is based on the novel by Stephen King (1974), and features Sissy Spacek as Carrie. Creed argues in the introduction to *The Monstrous-Feminine* that this scene is one of the most striking images of abjection in the modern horror film: the associa-

tion of pig's blood with menstrual blood. As insisted on by the film, girls
'bleed like pigs' when their bodies are ready for reproduction. The bloody
alliance of the non-human and the human, combined with the procreative
and maternal function of the female body, summarises the monstrous
feminine as confrontation with 'the abject'. As already indicated, Creed
transposes Kristeva's psychoanalytic notion of the abject as that 'which
signifies the place where meaning collapses, the place where "I" am not'
(1993: 8), to themes and images in the horror genre. The abject is related
to any notion of an ambiguous border: between the inside and the outside
of the body, such as blood, wounds, vomit and excrement; between mother
and child; between human and non-human; and ultimately between life
and death.

Creed convincingly argues that the horror film can be seen as a 'modern
defilement rite' that 'attempts to separate out the symbolic order from all
that threatens its stability, particularly the mother and all that her universe
signifies' (1993: 14). It is the 'impure' feminine body that signifies the
abject *par excellence*: menstrual blood, intra-uterine spaces as monstrous
wombs, and terrifying mothers as obsessed and mad creatures that will not
let go of their bodily offspring, are all images that find many translations
in horror figures such as alien monsters, possessed women, lesbian vampires and scary witches. In De Palma's film, Carrie White's own mother,
Margaret White (Piper Laurie), who suffers from theomania, is the first
to declare this abjection of the feminine body as she lectures Carrie on the
'sin and weakness of women' (the first sin being intercourse and sexual
pleasure) and God's punishment as 'the curse of blood'. This curse of
blood is first of all translated into another curse, the curse of childbearing.
Blood signifies the abject as it defies the border between the inside and
the outside of the body (at least once a month for fertile women, and for
mothers in labour).

Does it make a difference when these female issues are presented from
a woman's perspective? This vexed question will return throughout this
book. For now, I want to indicate two salient differences between the
two versions of *Carrie* that provide us with a point of origin. First of all,
Peirce's *Carrie* has an added prologue and a different epilogue.[13] Contrary
to De Palma's version, which opens during a gym class and shows Carrie
showering, erotically filmed in slow motion and soft focus, enjoying the
pleasures of the warm water (until she discovers the blood running down
her legs), Peirce's *Carrie* begins with a flashback of Carrie's panic-stricken
mother (Julianne Moore) crawling up a staircase in the throes of giving
birth, leaving a trail of blood, asking God for forgiveness, thinking she is
dying, in shock and discovering that she has delivered a baby. In panic she

tries to kill her offspring with a knife, but finds herself unable to do so. The film also ends with a nightmarish image of a female body in labour. This time it is Sue, Carrie's only friend, who survives the prom massacre, who is pregnant at the end of Peirce's version of the story. We see her body struggling with contractions, when suddenly Carrie's bloody hand shoots out of her body. As in De Palma's version (where Carrie's hand grabs Sue from the grave) this appears to be a horrific nightmare indeed. The 'curse of childbearing' is literalised in this new prologue and epilogue and clearly resonates with Creed's notion of abjection. Nevertheless, these scenes seem to translate the fears and anxieties more from the perspective of a woman, whose experience of having something growing inside her own body can be scary and alienating. This female point of view on pregnancy, often presented in male-authored horror films but until recently not so often addressed by woman themselves, is one of the themes that will return in this book, as well as other bodily experiences such as menstruation and female sexual desire.

Moreover, Peirce's version emphasises the necessity of knowledge in order for women to understand their own bodies, desires, feelings and social and religious doctrines. A second difference, then, is that the new Carrie, now embodied by Chloë Grace Moretz, has much more knowledge, agency and control than her 'twin sister' from De Palma's film. For instance, the new Carrie counters her mother's biblical dogma that all women are sinful ('I am not Eve, mother!', she exclaims, rejecting her mother's accusations). And when she discovers her power to break glass or move objects by mental energy, she begins to read about telekinesis and hones her skills in her bedroom. In this way, Carrie's feminine powers are not just wild, uncontrollable forces of nature that become unleashed under great (social) pressure, but can be learned and practised.[14] Both the internal, subjective female perspective and feminine knowledge, agency and control seem important elements in the female-directed, blood-filled stories of 'Carrie's crimson sisters' that will be addressed in the following chapters.

Drop by Drop: Chapter Overview

The material and case studies in this book are organised according to themes and tropes of the horror genre to evaluate salient features in the approach and poetics of women directors. The focus on the poetics of blood (and the colour red) also guides the topics addressed in each chapter, as each addresses some form of blood, connected to birth, sexuality, violence or death. The horror genre occupies an interesting place in the media landscape. As a genre at the margins of commercial mainstream and popular cinema, it might be significant that women are now more than ever appropriating this generic space to 'fight for visibility' quite literally. Among all the serious fighting and expressions of rage, fear, sorrow and anxiety, the horror genre also allows wonder, humour and (unruly) laughter, because of the sometimes surreal and over-the-top elements that address the absurdist, weird and violent realities that are implied in its aesthetics. Each chapter focuses on a certain 'female reality' refracted in and through particular generic tropes and themes of the horror genre. Each chapter contains references to the 'old blood' of Woolf, but also acknowledges the work of female directors who began making films during the second wave of feminism (many of whom are still working today), before tapping into the 'new blood' flowing from contemporary directors.

As indicated earlier, women have always participated in the film industry beyond being just there 'to-be-looked-at', to recall Laura Mulvey's famous analysis of predominant heroine positions in classic cinema of the 1970s (Mulvey 2009). The first significant wave of female auteurs coincided with the second wave of feminism in the 1970s and 1980s, when not only did feminist theoretical analyses of classic cinema begin to appear, but women also began to make films on a large scale. Therefore the filmic legacies of female auteurs who have not (explicitly) adopted the horror genre as such (their work is usually labelled as 'women's films') will be revisited and reread in light of a poetics of horror. Today's unruly daughters of Woolf also had wild and disruptive 'aunts' and 'stepmothers' in the 1970s and in the following years of emancipation. Their work will be discussed further in separate chapters that will open with a reference film from these filmmakers of that second wave of creative women.

Chapter 1, 'Violence and Female Agency: Murderess, Her Body, Her Mind', zooms in on the trope of the angry, avenging woman, looking at the revisions of the slasher sub-genre and the reinvention of the 'final girl'. After recalling Woolf's assertion that she must 'kill the Angel of the House' if she wants to execute her profession as a writer and have creative agency, this chapter will first pay homage to several films made by women in the 1970s and 1980s, whose heroines take up a knife or gun to become symbolic or real murderesses, such as *Jeanne Dielman* (dir. Chantal Akerman, 1975), *A Question of Silence* (dir. Marleen Gorris, 1982) and *Welcome II the Terrordome* (dir. Ngozi Onwurah, 1995). The chapter will then move to the rage and fury of avenging women in contemporary cinema by looking at *American Mary* (dir. Jen and Sylvia Sotska, 2012) and especially *Revenge* (dir. Coralie Forgeat, 2017), together with the more subdued and ambiguous terrors of domestic violence in *Retrospekt* (dir. Esther Rots, 2018). The chapter concludes by addressing the opacities of a poetics of relation in the television series *Alias Grace* (dir. Mary Harron, 2017), which is based on a historical case of a murderess.

Chapter 2, 'Growing Pains: Breasts, Blood and Fangs', features a new take on vampires, werewolves and other contrived souls, especially in relation to tortured coming-of-age stories that address social pressures and childhood traumas. After a short encounter with Woolf in the company of a vampire, this chapter commences with a return to Stephanie Rothman's psychedelic exploitation film *The Velvet Vampire* (1971) and Kathryn Bigelow's vampire Western *Near Dark* (1987). The vampire as connected to the confusing experiences of coming of age is picked up in *Red Riding Hood* (dir. Catherine Hardwick, 2011), *The Moth Diaries* (dir. Mary Harron, 2011) and, in a less explicit but no less horrific way, *Sarah Plays a Werewolf* (dir. Katharina Wyss, 2017). The myth of eternal life and beauty and the legacy of Elizabeth Bathory are revised in *The Countess* (dir. Julie Delpy, 2009) and acquire a particular twist in the glamour world of contemporary Japan in *Helter Skelter* (dir. Mika Ninagawa, 2012). Claire Denis's *Trouble Every Day* (2001) takes the genre to its ontological extremes. This chapter will also turn to Butler's reimagination of the vampire in her last novel *Fledgling* (2005) and the imagination of alternative relations between the human and non-human, and looks at the new ethics of the vampire in *A Girl Walks Home Alone at Night* (dir. Ana Lily Amirpour, 2014).

Chapter 3, 'Longing and Lust, "Red Light" on a "Dark Continent"', presents a variegated depiction of female sexuality seen from women's own point of view, beginning with Carolee Schneemann's *Meat Joy* (1964), *Fuses* (1967) and *Mary Jane is Not a Virgin Anymore* (dir. Sarah Jacobson, 1997). Woolf's metaphors for the female sex and lesbian desire are brought to the scene in interracial encounters in *She Must Be Seeing Things* (dir. Sheila McLaughlin, 1987), *The Watermelon Woman* (dir. Cheryl Dunye, 1997) and *Pariah* (dir. Dee Rees, 2011). The stereotypical figure of the lustful and man-eating witch is reworked in *The Love Witch* (dir. Anna Biller, 2016) and *Jennifer's Body* (dir. Karen Kusama, 2009). In *Raw* (dir. Julia Ducournau, 2016), female sexuality is addressed in the ferocious and intense setting of students attending a veterinary school. After the explicit poetics of horror of the films of the middle section, this chapter looks at three other films that have a more implied horror embedded within their narration. In *I'm Not a Witch* (dir. Rungano Nyoni, 2017), witchcraft is seen from a totally different non-Western perspective (involving no sexuality), whereas in *In the Cut* (dir. Jane Campion, 2003) we see a combination of poetry, sexuality and a different type of final girl. In the equally poetic *Longing for the Rain* (dir. Lina Yang, 2013), a contemporary Beijing housewife makes love to a ghost that might not be so benign and slowly takes over her life.

Chapter 4, 'Growing Bellies, Failing Mothers, Scary Offspring', addresses so-called 'gynaehorror', the type of horror that deals explicitly with female reproductive bodily functions. I refer here to the work of Erin Harrington and Schubart who have both elaborated on Creed's work on monstrous femininity. After first addressing Woolf's childlessness, the chapter opens with references to the early work of Agnès Varda, *Diary of a Pregnant Woman* (1958) and *One Sings, the Other Doesn't* (1977), before turning to *Olmo and the Seagull* (dir. Petra Costa and Lea Glob, 2014), the female version of *Rosemary's Baby* with *Lyle* (dir. Stewart Thorndike, 2014), and Alice Low's pregnancy-horror film *Prevenge* (2016). Jennifer Phillips's film *Blood Child* (2017) is a chilling story based on true events where a miscarriage is translated into the raising of a ghost child. This chapter also looks at complicated mother–daughter relations in Ngozi Onwurah's *The Body Beautiful* (1991) and Deborah Haywood's *Pin Cushion* (2017); and at mother–son relations in *We Need to Talk About Kevin* (dir. Lynne Ramsey, 2011), Jennifer Kent's *The Babadook* (2014) and especially *Goodnight Mommy* (dir. Veronika Franz and Severin Fiala, 2015). I also discuss some other family relations from hell as depicted in *Mimi* (dir. Lucile Hadžihalilović, 1998), *Dark Touch* (dir. Marina de Van, 2013), *System Crasher* (dir. Nora Fingscheidt, 2019) and *Family* (dir. Veronika Kedar, 2017). Lucile Hadžihalilović's *Evolution* (2015) takes pregnancy to a post-human level and in that sense resonates with some of Butler's writing, especially her short story 'Blood Child', first published in 1995.

Chapter 5, 'Political Gutting, Crushed Life and Poetic Justice', returns to Woolf's *Three Guineas* and political agency and looks at Butler's *Kindred* and *Parable of the Sower*. This chapter has three sections, each addressing different types of political horror. First there is a return to racial and colonial terror in Euzhan Palcy's *A Dry White Season* (1989), and Claire Denis's *Chocolat* (1988) and *White Material* (2009). Then the chapter takes us to the outcasts and powerful lost souls in man-eat-man environments in *The Bad Batch* (dir. Ana Lily Amirpour, 2016), *Tigers Are Not Afraid* (dir. Issa López, 2017) and *Songs My Brothers Taught Me* (dir. Chloé Zhao, 2015). In *Atlantics* (dir. Mati Diop, 2019), the sea off the coast of Senegal raises ghosts from the past and the present. The chapter concludes with a section on eco-horror through the eyes of female directors: *Spoor* (dir. Agnieska Holland, 2017) is an allegory of the backlash against feminism in contemporary Poland, wrapped in a hunting tale. *Little Joe* (dir. Jessica

Hausner, 2019) and *Glass Garden* (dir. Shin Sue-won, 2017) are contemporary Frankenstein stories with idiosyncratic female scientists.

Throughout the film analyses, I always return to the aesthetics and politics of blood, trusting to show that there are many different blood types in the poetics of horror made by women; each drop contains a world of pain, sorrow and rage but also laughter and wonder, consolation and insight; each gush embodies a world of stories to convey, wisdom to impart and emotions to share.

CHAPTER 1

Violence and Female Agency: Murderess, Her Body, Her Mind

Killing the Angel in the House: Finding a Voice of One's Own

In an address entitled 'Professions for Women', given to the National Society for Women's Service in 1931, Virginia Woolf talked about her profession as a writer (Woolf 2008: 140–5). Acknowledging that other female writers such as Jane Austen, George Eliot, and Emily and Charlotte Brontë had smoothed the path before her, and that she did not encounter many material obstacles (she indicates that she did not need to peel potatoes between sentences, nor was anyone in her family upset by the scratching of her pencil), she conveys how she became a journalist by simply writing a book review one morning in her room, and posting it that very afternoon to a journal. The low cost of pencils and paper is one of the reasons why women had easy access to writing in the first place. The next month Woolf received a cheque for one pound, ten shillings and sixpence; her first money earned as a writer. However, she did not need the money to buy bread and butter, but instead purchased a cat.

Woolf makes a point of her privileged situation which means that, in her own words, she little deserves to be called a professional woman. But she then engages with some less smooth operators barring her path to writing professionally, two phantoms that she, historically and materially privileged as she was, had to combat as a female writer. She names the first phantom after a poem, 'The Angel in the House': 'It was she who used to come between me and my paper when I was writing reviews' (Woolf 2008: 141). The figure of the Angel in the House is the stereotype of good feminine behaviour: friendly, charming, unselfish, sacrificing herself for others and pristine. While Woolf was writing her review about a famous male writer, she recalls how 'the shadow of her wings' fell on the pages, and when she picked up her pen to begin writing, the Angel in the House slipped behind her and whispered: 'My dear, you are a young woman.

You are writing about a book that was written by a man. Be sympathetic; be tender; flatter; deceive; use all the arts and wiles of your sex. Never let anybody guess that you have a mind of your own. Above all, be pure' (2008: 141). And then Woolf suddenly turns into a slasher heroine of sorts, picking up the inkpot and flinging it towards this phantom of femininity: 'I turned upon her and caught her by the throat. I did my best to kill her . . . Had I not killed her she would have killed me . . . She died hard' (2008: 141). But as we know, phantoms have a nasty habit of returning. And so Woolf considers killing the Angel in the House part of her professional skills, a skill she somehow acquired and kept putting to use.

The second phantom battle as a writer, Woolf argues, is harder to win. After buying a cat with her first wages, she became ambitious and decided that she wanted a motor car. She decided to become a novelist. One of the techniques of the novelist is to become submerged in the unconscious, to open unchecked areas of the life of a mind. The image that she brings up here is that of an angler on the verge of a deep lake holding out a rod, letting the imagination flow into the deepest and slumbering places of the unconscious. Then the imagination collides with something hard, something that made her stop writing, when 'she had thought of something, something about the body, about the passion which it was unfitting for her as a woman to say. Men, her reason would tell her, would be shocked' (Woolf 2008: 143). Women writers, more than men, Woolf argues, are 'impeded by the extreme conventionality of the other sex' (2008: 143). Woolf admits that this last phantom, which prevents her from telling the truth about her 'own experiences as a body', has not yet been vanquished. Woolf was part of the first feminist wave that demanded the right to vote, to have a proper education, to earn a proper wage and to have 'a room of one's own'. At the time she addressed the assembled women, many occupations had become available to women for the first time, each with their own challenges and obstacles. However, what is particularly interesting in this address is the relationship between feminine creative expression and the obstacles both of the inner voice of a little angel on her shoulder and of the outward social expectations of normative gender behaviour. As is clear from Woolf's statements, some act of (symbolic) violence is needed to break through those barriers to claim one's voice. Moreover, the question of the experience of the body seems to be a crucial and unresolved one in Woolf's time, and certainly in her own intellectual endeavour, with its focus on mental life, even if, as will be discussed in a later chapter, the body is not absent from Woolf's work.

While much has changed in the situation of women, this chapter will revisit the legacies of Woolf by first returning to women directors who began making films in the 1970s and 1980s as part of the second feminist wave. Uncovering the possibilities of cinematographic writing, called for by Woolf in her essay on cinema from 1926 (Woolf 2008: 172–6), and claiming a voice in the cinematic landscape, these female directors also first had to kill their own 'Angel in the House'. Moreover, the question of the experience of the female body begins to emerge more prominently. While the films made by women directors during this period are usually not labelled as horror films, their sudden outbursts of violence suggest some of these films as starting points to investigate the poetics of horror from a feminine point of view. After revisiting some of the issues and themes in the work of feminist filmmakers in the 1970s and 1980s in seminal films including *Jeanne Dielman* (dir. Chantal Akerman, 1975), *A Question of Silence* (dir. Marleen Gorris, 1982) and *Welcome II the Terrordome* (dir. Ngozi Onwurah, 1995) through the lens of a poetics of horror, this chapter will move to more contemporary works by women directors, focusing on Coralie Fargeat's take on the rape-revenge slasher in her film *Revenge* (2018) and on Esther Rots's daring and difficult to watch investigation of domestic violence in *Retrospekt* (2018). The final part of the chapter will introduce a poetics of relation via the rereading of a historical murderess in *Alias Grace* (dir. Mary Harron, 2018). The colour red in this chapter is predominantly the blood of violence: violence perpetrated against women and violence done by women as enraged furies and avenging angels, even if at certain moments not everything that is in their minds will be revealed unambiguously.

A Stab at Silence:
Women Filmmakers in the 1970s and 1980s

Very little is known about the lives of women, Woolf argues in 'Women and Fiction' (2008: 132–9). Once women finally began writing in the nineteenth century, they 'lived almost solely in her home and in her emotions . . . excluded by their sex from certain kinds of experience' (Woolf 2008: 134). During the mid-twentieth century, when women began making films with an explicit eye for female experiences and for the first time within a collective consciousness of women's liberation, this limited room for experience for women was still true, even if in the wake of emancipatory struggles the span of possible experiences gradually became wider. Agnès Varda, as one of the very few female filmmakers of the French New Wave,[1] was inspired by her own pregnancy to make her experimental short film *Diary of a Pregnant Woman* (1958), and opened up the language of film to female experiences translated into aesthetic forms. In the 1970s she ventured into explicitly feminist topics such as the right to abortion and family planning in *One Sings, the Other Doesn't* (1977).

The modern horror film that emerged in the 1970s, usually made by male directors, by and large targeted young male audiences and can be seen as a reaction to this second wave of feminism and the Women's Liberation movement. So before looking at some of the films made by women in this period reread through the lens of a poetics of horror, I first turn to a few reminders of the male-authored modern horror film.

It was Carol Clover who most famously discussed the changes in the modern horror film in relation to gender as a reaction to women's liberation. Alfred Hitchcock's shocking aesthetics in *Psycho* (1960) of the unexpected stabbing of Marion Crane, a woman on her way to meet her lover and escape from her home town, and the gender fluidity of Norman Bates as her psychotic killer remains the cinematographic influence *par excellence* on the modern horror film. In the late 1950s and early 1960s Hitchcock had an excellent nose for changes in society to which his audiences were already sensitive. He addressed the sexual liberation of women and gendered anxieties, as well as all that this inspired. Clover discusses in particular the sub-genres of modern horror films: the slasher, possession and of course rape-revenge films. Compared with classic horror films that present vampires, mad scientists and their out-of-control creatures – zombies and witches – the modern horror genre is much more explicitly concerned with gender issues. Most of these films present heroines who facilitate cross-gender identification, such as the boyish final girl who defeats the hideous (usually) male killer. Many of these films, especially the rape-revenge films that present a woman bent on revenge after being assaulted, 'explicitly articulate a feminist politics' (Clover 1992: 151). However, Clover argues that it is important to note that these films were created by male directors: 'were they made by women, they would be derided as male-bashing' (Clover 1992: 151). Now, they present gruesome stories in such a way that men can have their cake and eat it too: they can identify with both the killer and the victim. Aligned with the victim they can savour sweet revenge, and usually in a very direct way: there is a rape and then revenge, all taking place on the level of the body, without any interference from the law, or any other ethical or political concerns. In this sense, Clover argues, a cruel rape-revenge film such as *I Spit on Your Grave* (dir. Meir Zarchi, 1978) is the uncensored and unrepressed version of more mainstream films that later appropriated the same topics, such as *The Accused* (dir. Jonathan Kaplan, 1988), which presented them in a displaced way by seeking revenge via the court system.[2]

While the cross-gender identification that this 'politics of horror' allows is an important issue in the gender dynamics that translates into audio-visual language and a 'poetics of horror' in the entanglement of its cultural-historical context, this does not mean that the gender balance has now been equalised. Barbara Creed observes in her take on the slasher genre that in these films, 'woman-as-victim' is represented as an abject thing, but man-as-victim is not similarly degraded and humiliated. 'If anything, the death scenes of the male victims offer a form of masochistic pleasure to the viewer because of the way they associate death with pleasure' (Creed 1993: 130). The men are seduced into sexual intercourse before they realise that it will be their last moment of pleasure, whereas the women are sadistically hunted from the beginning without any respite. This power imbalance remains important to note, as it may be determined by the male gaze of the eye behind the camera (and in the audience).

There is one other important observation related to the authorship of these films. As Clover notes regarding *I Spit on Your Grave*, both the humiliating rape scenes as well as the revenge section of the film present the murders simply as acts of cruelty, the killers going about their business 'almost impassively', which makes it 'an oddly external film' (Clover 1992: 119). Here I think it is interesting to turn to the films made in another corner (not to say margin) of the cinematographic landscape in the same time period, also enabled by the Women's Lib movement, but directed by women who begin to speak for themselves. While addressing less explicitly the gore of body politics of the modern horror film, these films do address the gender dynamics of the epoch, and do so by moving the camera to the interior: both feminine spaces (such as the house) and the woman's experience of the body, her life and the world from an inner perspective. And, as we shall see, these films certainly contain 'politics and poetics of horror', albeit in a different and often more covert way.

Chantal Akerman's *Jeanne Dielman, 23 Quai du Commerce, 1080 Bruxelles* (1975) should be mentioned here as one such subdued and quiet horror film. Much has been written about this extraordinary film (Kinder 1977; Perlmutter 1979; Margulies 1996), and here I simply want to highlight how Akerman's poetics of the everyday life of a housewife for the first time made visible some of the daily habits and gestures of countless women everywhere in the world, as well as how these daily silent gestures conceal a violent undercurrent that will need to erupt at a certain point. Jeanne Dielman, a widow living with her son in an apartment in Brussels, played by Delphine Seyrig, is based on Akerman's observations of the women who surrounded her in her youth, her mother and her aunts. Household routines that by and large are never noticed, but that emphasise the enclosed spatial experiences of many women, structure the rhythm of the film: making coffee, peeling potatoes, preparing meatballs, setting the table, making the bed, switching the light on and off while moving from one room to the next, and keeping everything clean and tidy. In an interview for French television after the release of the film, Akerman and Seyrig talked about the uniqueness of 'making art of a woman who does the dishes'.[3] Following Jeanne in her ritualised behaviour over the course of three days, we understand that the strict order and regularity of her occupations give her some kind of control, while keeping her emotions (anxiety, despair, anger – nothing is spelled out in cause–effect chains as it is in classic narration) at bay.

Consequently, when on the last day she gets up one hour too early, her routine is broken and her anxiety and other traumas buried in her subconscious begin to slip out: the potatoes burn, her hair is messy, she forgets to close the lid on the soup tureen where she keeps the money from her sex clients who she receives every afternoon. And so, through these small gestures and signs, suspense is built, seemingly out of nothing. It is within these small gestures and signs that the horror is hidden; we see glimpses of her unconscious, hidden desires and repressed anger, which culminate in the last act. She is dressing in front of her bedroom mirror, and her third client of that afternoon is visible on the bed. There is a pair of scissors resting on the dressing table at the edge of the frame. As she gets up, we see her grasping the scissors. Directly thereafter, still in the mirror, we see her bending over the supine man while plunging the scissors into his chest. It is a sudden burst of violence that can only be imagined, taking into account the repressed resentment of generations of women confined to their house and housework, or to prostitution as the only way of making money, all gathered into this one stab.

The final scene depicts Jeanne sitting silently in her living room. In the predominantly brown and pale blue-grey colour palette of the controlled *mise en scène* of the film (Lakeland 1979), it is only now that we see the colour red, the blood on Jeanne's blouse and hands as a silent scream while she sits quietly at the table; the soup tureen, the symbol of her side job, prominently in sight, is enveloped by neon flashes emanating from a sign outside. On the surface Jeanne may seem like another Angel in the House, but clearly she has a secret, a less angelic life hidden in the depths of her psyche, only betrayed by minute changes in her gestures, where sexuality and the 'experiences of the body' percolate to the surface in the final part of the film, stabbing the hidden and silenced stories of women's lives and causing them to emerge on the surface. Laura Mulvey recalls the film's lasting impact, indicating that the particular *mise en scène* of the repeated and interrupted gestures also have something absurd and comic about

Figure 1.1 *Jeanne Dielman, 23 Quai du Commerce, 1080 Bruxelles*
(Chantal Akerman, 1975).

them as they 'become detached from their absolute and complete ground-
ing in real life, as the scenes become spectacle, the cinema itself affects
their meaning' (Mulvey 2016: 30).

Emphasising this dimension of the absurd, and the strategy of laughter,
brings us to another disruptive film from the women's movement that is
worthwhile recalling as a slasher film of sorts. Marleen Gorris wrote the
screenplay of *A Question of Silence* (1982) with Chantal Akerman in mind
as its director. However, Akerman advised Gorris that she should make
the film herself. This was the inception of another landmark film of the
women's movement that has been widely discussed elsewhere (Smelik
1993, 1998; Rowe 1995) and that I here want to resurrect for its particular unruliness (violence and excessive laughter), explicitly related to the
struggle of women to find their voice and to get rid of angels and other
demons so as to break the silence about women's experiences.[4] The film's
central plotline concerns the brutal and seemingly unexpected murder
of the male owner of a clothing store by three female clients who have
never before met each other. The women, Andrea (Henriëtte Tol), a
single middle-class secretary; Ann (Nelly Frijda), a divorced working-
class woman who works at a snack bar; and Christine (Edda Barend), a
lower-middle-class housewife, all happen to be at the same time and place
to commit their violent act in silent collaboration. At the beginning of
the film they are being taken to prison; we see the murder as fragmented
flashbacks throughout the film. The other storyline is that of a female
psychiatrist, Janine (Cox Habbema), upper-class, married to a lawyer and

without children. She needs to establish whether or not the women are insane or were insane at the moment of the murder. Both the judicial and medical professions can only explain the act as that of mad women, without reason, and thus in no need of another explanation. The women, however, refuse to tell Janine anything that could lead to this conclusion: Andrea rebuts her questions by posing counter-questions that make Janine reflect on her own situation, Ann responds with excessive laughter, and Christine shrouds herself in catatonic silence. During the flashbacks it becomes perfectly clear why cynicism, laughter and silence are the only valid responses to the disrespect and humiliating disregard that these women receive on a daily basis.

In the course of her investigations, the psychiatrist, who has had relatively the best circumstances in accessing a profession and other privileges of her class, slowly but surely awakens to a feminist consciousness. In the end, she realises that her professional opinion is only tolerated in as far as she does not 'make a fuss' and complies with the expectations of her husband and the male judges. Accordingly, she declares the women perfectly sane, which forces the court and the audience to look for other, more sociopolitical explanations. The dimension of a collective feminist consciousness is reinforced by the fact that during the murder there were a few other clients in the shop, silent witnesses, and all women of different ages, classes and ethnic backgrounds. Without making any of these differences explicit, *A Question of Silence* emphasises recognition and solidarity among all women who understand from the inside the repressed frustration and anger of not being seen, not being valued for qualities other than the confined attributes and places assigned to women. That this is not the entire story of women was a necessary and just reproach offered by black feminists to the predominantly white perspectives taken as universal by second wave feminism, which I will address in the next section. But for now, let us remain at the point of the film, which calls for a collective consciousness regarding the feminine condition.[5]

On a narrative level, *A Question of Silence* calls for a solidarity that resonates with the spirit of the time. In terms of the visual poetics of the film, it should be noted that in its aesthetics, a cinematic poiesis of metaphors is put into operation. As in *Jeanne Dielman*, these metaphors first of all work on the level of the *mise en scène*. Jeanne Dielman's apartment is both the real space of the household common to generations of women, and can also be read as her inner space, where slowly the subconscious begins to interrupt the controlled routines and appearances up until its final outburst. In addition, the prostitution as well as the final violence and the blood can be read as a cinematic metaphor in the sense that they make tangible what is going on in the life of a woman, creating an intersubjective understanding of this, built up during the experience of the film as a specifically mediated event. As Anneke Smelik has demonstrated, both in *A Question of Silence* and also Gorris's next film *Broken Mirrors* (1984), the *mise en scène* should be considered 'moving metaphors' of confined spaces: the prison and the brothel each emphasise their limited options in an allegorical way (Smelik 1993: 349). Highlighted by the different cinematographic approach (synthesised music, rapid editing and a handheld camera give these images an eerie quality different from the more realistic style of the other scenes), the murder scene in *A Question of Silence* can be read as a ritual, a ceremonial performance, as has been observed by many feminist film critics (Smelik 1993: 352). While there is not a drop of blood to be seen in this film, the suggested violence is of the slasher-type, albeit it is not axes or saws but instead coat hangers, a grocery trolley, high-heeled shoes and boots which are the murder weapons. Nevertheless, the spaces in the film are also very real spaces, which allows an engagement with the aesthetics of the film that creates its own reality, which speaks of the real historical conditions that surround the film, and which continues to speak to future generations. Christine M., alone and silent in her living room, taken for granted by her husband, the orange-brown curtains closed, a baby crying in his playpen, is an image that translates everything about the loneliness and feeling of utter uselessness and futility that has been the experience of so many generations of women.

Another point I want to reiterate about *A Question of Silence* concerns the final scene. Kathleen Rowe opens her book about gender and genres of laughter with reference to the remarkable end of the film, when all the women in the courtroom (Christine included) begin to laugh uncontrollably. Bursting with laughter, the women are conducted out of the courtroom, while all the other women congregate in front of the building, where Janine decides not to join her deeply embarrassed and angry husband, but remains with the assembled women. Laughter is a form of resistance (Pisters 2010) that has been theorised in feminist discourse as a way to disruptively express anger, which often remains unspoken, 'repressed beneath all of women's depression – all our compulsive smiling, ego-tending, and sacrifice; all our psychosomatic illness, and all our passivity' (Lesage quoted in Rowe 1995: 7). Rowe relates the power of laughter to the Bakhtinian creative destruction of the grotesque and the carnivalesque, which allows transgression of the normative where otherwise there is none, but also to Hélène Cixous's feminist appropriation of the myth of Medusa as a figure of empowerment and resistance, as she describes in 'The Laugh of the Medusa' (Cixous 1980):

> Associated with both beauty and monstrosity, the unruly woman dwells close to the grotesque. But while mythology taints and dooms Medusa, the unruly woman often enjoys a reprieve from those fates that so often seem inevitable to women under patriarchy, because her home is comedy and the carnavalesque, the realm of inversion and fantasy where, for a time at least, the ordinary world can be stood on its head. (Rowe 1995: 11)

In a similar way, the uncontrollable heroines of *A Question of Silence* turn the ordinary world on its head; in doing so, the film not only operates on a symbolic level, but also drags the spectator along for the ride, and creates a bond with its female spectators and with the men who cross-identify in solidarity.

Like *Jeanne Dielman*, *A Question of Silence* presents violence on different levels. First, there is the institutional violence of patriarchy. Here Jean-Luc Nancy's definition of violence as a force that intervenes in a system is useful (Nancy 2005). As Eugenie Brinkema unfolds this notion further, she argues that the generality of such a structural definition of violence enables a 'proper promiscuity of violence', as the system might be a body, a people, a landscape or a field of colour (Brinkema 2019: 63–4). Implicitly (the gestures in *Jeanne Dielman*) or explicitly (the suffocating denigration of women in *A Question of Silence*), the films themselves show this violence of institutional oppression. Then there is the violence of striking back: in both films the executor of systemic violence is in turn executed. Jeanne kills her client; the women in Gorris's film kill the male shopkeeper. Akerman and Gorris represent powerful pioneering female voices who were not afraid to speak the truth passionately regarding the injustices they observed, using the camera as their weapon to take a stab at the silence around gendered violence.

Welcome to the Terrordome: Horrors of Racism

There is one important critique attached to 'Virginia's unruly daughters' in the second wave of feminism, which is the fact that the work of white-feminist filmmakers did not (or perhaps only partially) offer recognition and solidarity for black female spectators and women of colour. Although one of the witnesses in *A Question of Silence* is a black woman, and in *Broken Mirrors*, Gorris's next explicitly feminist film which addresses physical violence against women, one of the girls in the brothel where the film is set is black, their symbolic roles in these films do not allow any deeper understanding of or engagement with their specific situation. In feminist theory of the 1970s, womanhood was conceived as an abstract category, which actually meant white women (Carby 1985). In the introduction to her 1987 novel *Beloved*, Toni Morrison expressed this point clearly:

> In the eighties, the debate was still roiling: equal pay, equal treatment, access to pro-fessions, schools . . . and choice without stigma. To marry or not. To have children or not. Inevitably their thoughts led me to the different history of black women in this country – a history in which marriage was discouraged, impossible, or illegal; in which birthing children was required, but 'having' them, being responsible for them – being, in other words, their parent – was as out of the question as freedom. Assertions of parenthood under conditions peculiar to the logic of institutional enslavement were criminal. (Morrison 2004: x–xi)

In a similar vein, film criticism did not address the issue of race explic-itly, assuming whiteness as the norm. bell hooks, for instance, remarked that in Hollywood cinema there was a certain 'place and function of white womanhood. There was clearly no place for black women' (hooks 1996: 204). While Laura Mulvey criticised classic cinema for the power imbalance between men as bearers of the gaze, and women as the image to-be-looked-at, black female bodies were give even less presence beyond a stereotypical figure relegated to the background. Given the almost complete absence of black women, hooks argues that when Spike Lee presented in his first movie *She's Gotta Have It* (1984) a black woman as the object of the phallocentric gaze, this did not resolve the problem. hooks criticised Lee for mimicking 'the cinematic construction of white womanhood as object, replacing her body as text on which to write male desire with a black female body. It is transference without transforma-tion' (hooks 1996: 209). In so doing, she calls for black women to con-struct themselves as subject and to 'determine the scope and texture of their looking relations'. She demands a black female spectatorship that can resist the normative power structures of looking and gazing, but also the creation of alternative texts in which black women claim their space. Besides black critics, film theorists and oppositional spectators, this was offered by black female filmmakers who made their entrance into the film world.[6]

While in the twenty-first century black female directors such as Dee Rees, Ava Duvernay, Cheryl Dunye, Chinonye Chukwu and many others have a solid and acclaimed presence in cinema, in the 1980s black female directors were less frequently behind the camera. Partly due to the twofold fight of black women on the levels of both race and gender, the road to the camera was even longer than for the white women directors of this period. Kinitra Brooks insists that 'there can be no privileging of the identities of race and gender over each other, for both affect the black woman deeply, reinforcing each other as interlocking oppressions actively working against the self-actualization of black women' (Brooks 2014: 461). However, there certainly were great forerunners; at the time, they were the exceptions that tested the rule. Madeline Anderson is a pioneer black woman director who addressed civil rights issues in her documentaries *Integration Part One* (1960) and *I Am Somebody* (1970), the first televised film by an African-American woman. Julie Dash's powerful *Daughters of the Dust* (1991) was the first film made by an African-American woman to receive general theatrical release; it took her over ten years to produce but has now been preserved in the National Film Registry by the Library of Congress for being 'culturally, historically or aesthetically significant'.[7] Another pioneering woman of colour in the film industry is Euzhan Palcy, whose film *A Dry White Season* (1989) I discuss in Chapter 5.

Within the framework of this chapter on women who strike back and can therefore be considered as slasher heroines of the horror genre, I want to recall the work of another pioneering woman, the Nigerian-British filmmaker Ngozi Onwurah, who made several significant films in the late 1980s and early 1990s. I will return to her short films *Coffee Colored Children* (1988) and *The Body Beautiful* (1990) in later chapters, but here I want to recall her feature film *Welcome II the Terrordome* (1993) as a particularly striking film that addresses the legacies of slavery in connection to contemporary police brutality and continual excruciating racism. At the time of the making of the film, the Rodney King beatings were not far removed; the situation has not improved much lately, as the Black Lives Matter movement in the 2010s attests.

At the centre of the film is a woman in a red shirt, Anjela McBride (Suzette Llewellyn), who lives in a ghetto called Terrordome, an infernal place that is introduced to us at the beginning of the film through the cage-like metal-reinforced windows of a police car that enters Terrordome on patrol. An angry black man holding a sign 'Rise again Malcolm X' shouts at the cops, a black woman jumps on the bonnet screaming for help, but the car steadily moves on, revealing the chaotic streets and shacks of the enclosed neighbourhood. In voice-over, Black Rad (Felix Joseph), Anjela's husband, begins telling the story of a particularly disastrous evening. At first it is business as usual: the police (a black cop and a white cop) only come in to make sure that there continues to be enough drugs and weapons in circulation to keep the gangs fighting and to paralyse normal life as much as possible; men and young boys hustle on the streets, while the radio plays hip-hop songs that recur during the film. Onwurah borrowed the title of her film from a Public Enemy album, and the lyrics and rhythms of the songs give the entire film a brooding and infernally ominous but also rebellious and empowering undertone. As Black Rad indicates, amid all this mess, Anjela is the one who tries to give the children a normal life, teaching them how to read and write, even putting them to bed on time. 'But she is fighting a losing battle', he comments.

It is precisely Anjela, the stable force and anchor of the extended black family at the centre of the film, who will transform into a black slasher heroine reacting with mad grief and rage to the racist violence that the Terrordome embodies. The situation escalates because a white man from a motorcycle gang, Jason (Jason Traynor), becomes jealous of the relationship his white ex-girlfriend Jodie (Saffron Burrows) is having with Black Rad's brother Spike (Valentine Nonyela), whose child she is carrying. Jason summons the police and other white gang friends, and in the havoc and fighting that erupt, Jason attacks Jodie, kicking her in the abdomen to the point that she has a miscarriage. In the meantime, Anjela's son Hector (Ben Wynter) walks out on to the street and witnesses the violent scenes. During the chase that ensues, Hector falls to his death. After Anjela finds him, she shoots Jason dead and continues her killing spree by murdering several other racists, including the black cop. Anjela's grief and anger is not only the intolerable grief and anger of a mother who has lost her child, but also the rage of the historical injustice of slavery that still has its tentacles in contemporary society. It is the only justice available, a poetic

Figure 1.2 *Welcome II the Terrordome* (Ngozi Onwurah, 1993).

justice with dire consequences. Anjela is sent to jail, shackled to her chair with iron chains and hanged.

The prologue and epilogue, however, give the film an empowering frame. The film opens in 1652 on the coast of North Carolina where a group of slaves land to be met by their owners, 'plunging the film into its essence: the sense of dislocation inherent in the experience of the Middle Passage' and recreating the historic scene of the 'Ibo landing', a slave revolt that took place in 1802 when a group of 75 enslaved Nigerian Ibo people mutinied against the slave owners and, after landing, committed suicide rather than serve as slaves (Reynaud 2017). Onwurah recreates the mythic scene of the Ibo landing when she has the chained slaves at the beach in 1652 turn around and drown themselves, returning to the land reborn in the epilogue. The last image of the film is of Anjela breaking her chains in a huge liberating gesture. The same actors appear in the prologue and epilogue as in the body of the film, which renders the past repeated in the present.

Clearly the poetics of horror is everywhere in *Welcome II the Terrordome*, and it presents a very strong case in which questions of gender are superseded by racial power relations. In the end, the black community overcomes its internal differences and unites to 'fight the power'. There is no room for interracial commitments at this stage. Both Spike and Jodie are mistrusted and hated because of their racial transgression, and when Jodie is beaten up, nobody comes to her aid. Onwurah, who has a Nigerian father and British mother (who features in *The Body Beautiful*, discussed in Chapter 4), shows how at the deepest levels of conflict and hatred there is only terror and oppositional fighting. Anjela in *Welcome II the Terrordome* has different horrors to face than the women in *A Question of Silence* and *Jeanne Dielman*. They are only related by the flow of blood that results from the violence of the acting out of their grief and repressed rage.

Rape Revenge: Resilience of Her Body

The films of the second wave feminists discussed in the first part of this chapter are very clear about the dynamics of this rage: women versus men; black versus white. While there is horror and dread, blood and the fury of the colour red, the works discussed so far are not typically described as horror films. So let us now return to the horror genre more proper. Because, if there is any genre or generic structure of aesthetics that allows rage to erupt in its crudest form from the surface of the screen, it is horror. As both Clover and Creed have shown, in particular, enraged avenging women have shaped the modern horror sub-genre of the rape-revenge film. The women who wield their castrating retaliatory powers are typically not punished; the slasher genre shows them 'to be justified in their actions' (Creed 1993: 123). It is a crude and cruel form that can be explained psychoanalytically, as Creed has demonstrated by proposing these images as forms of male anxiety; or evaluated as mythical pre-Oedipal images that propose gender fluidity and a one-sex model argued for by Clover. However, the 'pureness' of the horror genre in its directness of violence of assault, attack and counter-attack also allows for a more formal reading. In this and the following section, I will look at contemporary female-directed films that address violence against and by women that is embedded in their poetics of horror and formal aesthetics: Coralie Fargeat's *Revenge* (2018) is filmed in the tradition of the rape-revenge slasher where there is no doubt about right and wrong and where we remain on the outside of the characters on a bloody rollercoaster of crime and punishment. Esther Rots's *Retrospekt* (2018), on the other hand, brings us entirely inside the traumatised mind of its female protagonist and here all violence refracts into a million pieces, with a very different set of negative emotions that enlarge the affective spectrum of the horror film.

In my approach I will engage with what Brinkema has called 'the feel of horror' that follows from a formal and material reading of the films. As indicated before, I am not as radically formal in my approach as Brinkema, as I want to read form and content, the experience of the film interwoven with the experience of reality as being intertwined. However, I find her definition of the feel of horror (which perhaps is closer to what Sergei Eisenstein called in *The Film Sense* 'the fourth dimension' of the feeling of a shot or a film as a whole) very useful and refreshing in getting to those readings. In her essay 'Sticky, Nimble, Frantic, Stuck: *A L'Intérieur* and the Feel of Horror' Brinkema proposes to 'consider the feel of horror in the sense in which an object is said to have a certain feel' (2019: 65). Rather than focusing on the phenomenology of emotions in the spectator, she looks at the feel or touch of formal arrangements of the mechanical components of instruments or objects. She explains:

> For example, as in the node of the responsiveness of keys to touch, as in the soft or slow or hard or fast action of a particular piano: a slow or loose action feels mushy, floppy, slack to the touch, compared to the brittle, crisp and sharp feel of a particularly sensitive instrument in which response is governed by rapidity. (2019: 65)

The interplay of the different components also adds to the overall feel. While this formal approach implies a synaesthetic sensitivity, the focus on the particular aesthetics it implies allows new readings of a poetics of horror. In fact, while Brinkema argues against a general 'deterritorialized

Deleuzian affect' (2019: 65), her approach does follow the materiality of Deleuze's film concepts in their impersonal affective qualities, and a Deleuzo-Guattarian diagrammatics in the forces that these qualities carry within their structure. My point, however, is not a theoretical argument. Rather, I take the 'feel of horror' as a starting point for my reflections on contemporary violence to and by women, as seen through the eyes of women directors, hence relating the feel of horror to its contents and politics.

While Cindy Sherman's *Office Killer* (1997)[8] could be mentioned as another early feminist adaptation of the slasher genre, Coralie Fargeat's *Revenge* is a genre film that follows the formal elements of the rape-revenge slasher with bravura. Fargeat pitched the film as somewhere between *Kill Bill* (for the rebirth of an abused woman) and *Deliverance* (for the relation to the natural elements within the rape-revenge setting).[9] However, the film also compares in interesting ways to *I Spit on Your Grave*, briefly introduced above.[10] After all, in both films the avenging woman is called Jennifer/Jen. In *I Spit on Your Grave* Jennifer Hills (Camille Keaton) is a writer who retreats to a lake house to work on a novel and, as Clover demonstrated, as a woman of the city she seems to inspire frustration in the men from the countryside. The first half of *Revenge* introduces Jennifer (Mathilda Lutz) as a blonde bimbo who comes with her rich lover Richard (Kevin Janssens) to a luxurious desert house. At first glance, it does not seem that in the forty years after the second wave of women's liberation there has been much progress. On the contrary, from being a writer, symbolising the emancipation of women that the group of men in the film are terrified of (Creed 1993: 131), the female character has now transformed into an empty-headed seductress who seems to be 'asking for it', at least according to one of her assailants. Is it possible then to distinguish a feminine directorial look within the confines of a genre that stays with the 'outside' point of view that is typical of this sub-genre? There are a few elements in Fargeat's film that I want to highlight to indicate that her treatment of the body, of nature and of violence and blood are different, following the rhythms, colours and sounds of a journey into the extreme.

The desert house is literally eye candy, full of bright colours and playful sunlight, even if some elements foreshadow what is about to happen, most notably a bright green apple missing a bite that slowly begins to turn brown in the first half of the film, while ants eat their way inside. At the beginning of the film, Jen is confident about her body; she knows how to dress and attract roving eyes. Actress Mathilda Lutz explained that in playing this part of her character she was reminded of Marilyn Monroe, who confessed in her biography that even when she was alone she was always pretending to be looked at by someone; the male gaze was always watching her. Fargeat comments on the way contemporary culture creates a space where women are constantly invited to be in the image. Mulvey's famous to-be-looked-at-ness is still omnipresent, as evident in the #MeToo discussions and the power structures that uphold a culture where rape is normalised or goes unpunished. When some friends of Richard, Stan and Dimitri, arrive too early for the men's annual desert hunt, they also cannot keep their eyes off Jen, and when Richard leaves for a few hours to get their hunting permits, Stan feels entitled to rape her. Contrary to *I Spit on Your Grave*, the rape scene itself is not shown in all its humiliations. When Richard returns, he first wants to buy Jen off by sending her to Canada with a cheque (Jen has a dream of being 'noticed in LA'); when she refuses and threatens to call his wife, the alpha male in him gets angry and he throws her off a cliff. He treats her like a disposable product without any value, less than a can of beer. For him, she has never been there.

Jen falls on to a broken tree spike, and from this moment onwards she transforms into a superheroine. Again we see here a difference from Jennifer in *I Spit on Your Grave*, whose castrating revenge actions 'are imbued with a sense of ritual: Jennifer takes a religious pledge prior to the deaths, she wears white robes and appears to have acquired superhuman powers' (Creed 1993: 129). In all the ritualistic gestures she seems absent from herself, more like a psychotic mad woman than a heroine who finds her own power independently of the look of the other. However, this is exactly what Fargeat's Jen uncovers. Her transmutation, helped by some peyote and a beer can that brands an image of a phoenix onto her stomach, is spectacularly over the top, but it is empowering, precisely because the grotesqueness of the violence is dealt with in such an extreme way. Again it is interesting to hear Mathilda Lutz explaining that for this reborn Jen she was thinking along animalistic lines, making her movements cat-like, crawling and creeping like a panther, adapting her speed and slowness, while her sense perceptions adapt like a predator; in short she enters a becoming-animal. Instead of mimicry and image (that of Marilyn Monroe conscious of always being looked at), she now embodies something animal-like on an affective and kinaesthetic level, beyond or beneath the realm of the image. Elsewhere I have elaborated extensively on this idea of becoming-animal (Pisters 2003: 141–74), but here I just want to remark that Jen's becoming-animal is not only related to her transformed bodily appearance, in which her pink I Love LA shirt is burned and replaced by a black warrior outfit, her body covered in wounds and dust, and her blond hair turned brunette. It is also the pace of her movements in contact with the surrounding nature of the dusty desert and her alertness that express this becoming-animal. Shot in Morocco, the desert is an 'any-space-whatever', which allows the transcendence of the particular. Jen is alone in the desert and wounded; the three men hunt her down with loaded guns and travel in a Range Rover, on a quad bike and a motorcycle. What are the odds for our horror heroine?

As Fargeat has indicated in interviews, she wanted to get a different take on violence; the real violence of rape and assault against women needed to be countered by an element of phantasmagoria that even allows humour and laughter as a strategy to cope with reality and to make it something that can be watched by both men and women. A focus on the crescendo of blood that creeps into the film and culminates in a final, exorbitant, baroque bloodbath gives an indication of Fargeat's poetics of gore. In the first half of the film, there is no (visible) blood. The first time we see blood is from an ant's perspective: in extreme close-up we see an ant crawling in the sand, then being suddenly hit by dark red drops of blood from which the ant retreats, its legs almost immobilised by the viscosity of the fluid. It's Jen's blood, her body skewed across a trench, ants crawling on her legs, on her wounds, and while she seems to bleed to death, she is miraculously still alive, indicated by the fluidity of her blood that still runs.

Her hunt for the men brings an even greater amount of blood. The bright daylight and blazing sun have been replaced by cold desert darkness when she sets out. Jen first finds Dimitri near a lake; they begin to fight, and she pokes his eye with a stick and he then drowns. Next up is Stan, who is waiting in his car in another part in the desert, his chair lit red from behind the seat. The murder of Stan contains more explosions and trails of blood, as Jen hunts him down with a gun; Stan cuts his foot on a piece of glass that he pulls out in a particularly bloody scene. Richard then rides through the night; helmeted on his motorcycle he seems like a fly, an alien, surrounded by red light. In the morning he arrives at the house, and while he knows of his friends' deaths, he orders the helicopter to take him back home as if nothing had happened, and undresses to take a shower. Jen, however, has entered the house and attacks him while he is naked; an orgy of blood follows. Even wounded, Richard continues to hunt Jen, but his leaking body betrays him and he finally falls to the slippery ground.

Jeanne Dielman certainly has a superheroine slasher daughter. Jen has not only beaten the Angel in the House but also the demon of good behaviour and the commercial options that promise happiness on the TV set ('Hi girls, we take you to the mega online shopping mall of Shopclubusa. com'). The house is no longer candy clean but covered in gallons of blood

Figure 1.3 *Revenge* (Coralie Fargeat, 2018).

when Jen walks out, liberated like the laughing women in *A Question of Silence*.

There are other rape-revenge movies directed by women in which women take control after having been assaulted. In *American Mary* directed by the 'Twisted Twins' Jen and Sylvia Sotska (2012), a surgery student named Mary Mason (Katharine Isabelle) becomes involved in the world of body modification to earn extra money.[11] After she is raped by her teacher during a sex party organised by the surgeons at the hospital (who call themselves slashers and who drug the female students they invite), she becomes cold blooded, which earns her the nickname Bloody Mary. She decides to perform some body-modifying operations on her assailant, a revenge story from which she does not walk away alive. *M.F.A.* (dir. Natalia Leite, 2017) features Franscesca Eastwood (Clint Eastwood's daughter) as Noelle, an introvert art school major who is raped, and then discovers that many women on campus have suffered the same fate without any action being taken to punish the perpetrators. The women are diagnosed either as unstable, bipolar or depressed, or depicted as sluts, while the men simply do not acknowledge their actions as being harmful. Noelle's quest for justice, which she takes into her own hands, is parallelled by a creative energy that translates her rage and makes her the best student of her year, before she is arrested for multiple murders. These films present interesting variations on the rape-revenge plot, though not in such a pure and bare bones way as *Revenge*.[12]

Two additional elements deserve more elaboration and study than I can give here, but I would like to mention them because they offer interesting variations on the rape-revenge sub-genre: films that present revenge but no rape, and films that deal with rape but no revenge. In Korean cinema there are often avenging women who are not necessarily victims of sexual assault. Vengeful spirits often appear as ghosts, so called *wontons*, and are usually female (Lee 2013; Ong 2016).[13] While there are few women directors in Korean cinema who have ventured into horror aesthetics, Lee Kyoung-mi's *The Truth Beneath* (2016) is an example of a Korean revenge film where a living woman, a mother named Kim Yeon-hong (So Ye-jin) whose daughter goes missing, embodies the spirit of revenge. While her husband continues his campaign for political office, she sets out on an investigation that leads to the discovery of a terrible truth that involves her husband's secret love affair, blackmail and the murder of his own daughter. Kim Yeon-hong's rage entwines him in a plot that transforms towards the end into a slasher film that is not a response to rape but to deep betrayal.

In her film *Joy* (2018), Iranian-Austrian director Sudabeh Mortezai presents a stinging portrait of Nigerian women without any legal status who are exploited as prostitutes in Austria. While fiction, many of the events and situations are based on real life. Joy (Anwulika Alphonsus) is a young Nigerian woman who sells her body to pay off her debts to Madame (Angela Ekeleme), to support her family in Nigeria and to provide for her small daughter in Vienna who is raised by another Nigerian woman (who probably does have legal status). When a new girl, Precious (Mariam Sanusi), arrives from Nigeria we get a glimpse into the harsh conditions of these women's lives. The horror in the film is hidden in the entire system that keeps the women in the grip of human traffickers, organised by Nigerian women, the Madames who have made it from prostitute to pimp. It is shocking to see how these Madames recruit 'new flesh' and negotiate the price for freshly arrived girls. Besides the humiliation of being sold as an object of use, the physical violence against the women is evident: when Precious does not want to sell her body and asks for another job, Madame's bodyguards/errand boys rape her. Joy is the victim of a violent gang rape organised by one of her clients. As in *Revenge*, Mortezai chooses not to show the violence done to the women directly, which occurs off-screen.

What makes the film so poignant and terrifying is that there is no possibility of revenge; the women are kept in place by an entire network of actors both in Nigeria and Europe, where civil servants at immigration offices, for instance, do nothing that could help the women escape their impossible situation. In Nigeria, mothers send their daughters knowingly into a life of prostitution, asking for ever-more money to be sent home. One of the elements that works most powerfully is a Juju ritual, a sort of voodoo oath taking, which women who want to leave for Europe must undergo before they are allowed on the boat for a large sum of money.

During the ritual, they swear to pay all their debts and never to talk to the police. The Juju priest keeps pieces of the women's bodies (toenails and fingernails, hair, a picture) with him in an amulet, and if the women break their oath, something terrible will happen. The belief in this is so strong that the chicken blood with which this ritual is performed (we see Precious's oath at the beginning of the film) is perhaps the most powerful weapon to keep the women in their impossible situation. But what is also evident from the film is the resilience of these women. When at the end of the film Joy, betrayed by her Madame whose debts she has just settled after ten years, is deported back to Nigeria, we see her arranging another Juju oath for her return. After all, her daughter is still there. She is not broken.

Domestic Violence: Unsafe Mental Spaces

While Fargeat's adaptation of the extreme body-genre rewrites the slasher film on the outside pole of the horror spectrum, Esther Rots addresses the problem of violence to and by women at the other end of the spectrum by moving the camera completely into the mental space of her heroine in *Retrospekt*. Where Fargeat shows implicitly that societal structures that invite certain male and female behaviours are part of the problem of a culture that indulges rape, Rots paints another picture in which women are not purely victims but also play a part in acts of abuse. Contrary to *Revenge*, Rots's film is not a genre film, and hence the horror is not derived from the baroque and carnivalesque exaggerations that in their exorbitant off-reality provoke a freeing laughter and empowerment. *Retrospekt's* horror is more like a constantly humming menace of knowing that something will go terribly wrong, but never knowing exactly what, how and why dread will strike. As reviewers have remarked, we are trapped in the main character's jagged mind, which steeps everything in terror.[14] Rots's previous film, *Can Go Through Skin* (2009), is told entirely from the inner perspective of the traumatised mind of a rape victim who seeks seclusion to recover from the assaults, keeping the camera always close to the protagonist's skin, seeing everything through her eyes. In *Retrospekt* domestic violence lurks underneath every image but is less clearly defined, confusing, with no escape into the phantasmagoric, which creates a tension that makes the film harder to watch than *Revenge*.

Let us look at a few elements of Rots's aesthetics to see how she extends the poetics of horror. The main components of the tension are created by the offbeat and experimental soundtrack combined with jagged editing. Before the opening credits, *Retrospekt* sets the ill-omened tone through a disassociated audio and image track: over the sound of tinny percussion and slightly out-of-tune piano chords to which a jaunty tuba is added, we hear an ostentatious male baritone (Bas Kuijlenburg's voice) singing 'In her white fluffy bath robe/ in her model topped kitchen/ with her power driven juicer/ and her global knives . . . In this neat and tidy little life/ she is a neat and tidy little wife/ in the house made of brick and stone/ she is never alone.' At the same time we are introduced to the main character Mette (Circé Lethem), sitting on the tiny toilet of a camper, her belly indicating the last term of pregnancy, on holiday with husband Simon (Martijn van der Veen), who is driving, and their young daughter Harrie. We see (but do not hear) her laughing and chatting, pressing her hands to her belly while they park the vehicle. It is not clear if the music is a direct commentary on the situation we see. The lyrics do not exactly describe Mette's situation, though they may very well describe the 'feel of her situation', but in any case, they leak into the images disturbing the portrait of a happy family. The music stops when they park the camper and Mette gets out to buy some clothes in a clothing store. Thereafter, a second pre-credit scene follows that will linger in our minds during the rest of the film. While in the fitting room, Mette overhears a man attacking his wife in a fit of anger in the next cubicle. Mette addresses the woman and asks if she should call the police. The husband then turns to her aggressively and tells her to stay out of things that do not concern her. She returns to her fitting room and suffers a panic attack. Back with her husband, she tries to tell him what happened but he does not take her seriously. When she panics, he wraps an arm around her and then leaves her again, while the baritone voice resumes the disjointed commentary. The tone is set, the opening titles appear.

The commentary of the operatic voices (sometimes it is a female voice, soprano Luc Ket) recurs throughout the film at a regular intervals, offering a wry commentary with slightly eerie instrumental music. The film takes us in a fragmented way to different time periods after the birth of Mette's second daughter, Michelle, to moments from a later timeframe where we see Mette recovering from an accident, one side of her hair shaved showing red scar tissue from a serious head wound; at some moments we see wounds on her face healing under a bloody crust; at other moments her hair is slightly longer, her face no longer bruised. This again makes the entire viewing situation quite terrifying, as we know from the beginning that something terrible will indeed happen. From the jigsaw puzzle of Mette's mind, as she tries to remember what happened and why it happened, we know as little as she does. We see her searching for words, sometimes voiceless – underneath the opera

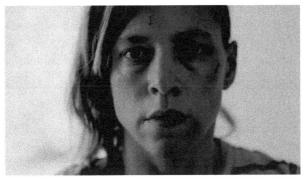

Figure 1.4 *Retrospekt* (Esther Rots, 2018)

voices her silent screams have a Munchian quality (this image seems to be repeated at another eerie moment in the film when Mette, before the accident, visits her demented father who falls silent in the middle of sentences, while his face turns into a spasmodic expression of anxiety, before he then continues talking again).

What we can piece together from the bits of Mette's confusing memories is that she works for an organisation that offers support to victims of domestic violence, and that her husband asked her to extend her maternity leave on an unpaid basis to take care of their daughters at home. She unwillingly accepts, and seems unhappy that her replacement is well liked by her clients and colleagues alike. At one point, she exclaims that she has two children and a great husband, and fights for her family to be happy. We see how, when her husband is on a business trip, she offers (contrary to the regulations of her job) one of her clients, Miller (Lien Wildemeersch), a place in her house. Miller is hiding from her aggressive partner, but she also seems quite obsessed with him and unwilling to completely sever the toxic relationship. The looming danger of him arriving at the house creeps out from under every image, as does the suggestion that Miller somehow depends on his violence.

Equally disturbing is the fact that Mette seems to long for some interruption of her own unease. She provokes fights with her husband and makes his blood boil to the point that he almost wants to hit her. When they reconcile, the love scene is equally spooky because of the music and editing effects. Squeaking, scratching, pulsing sounds accompany Mette and Simon in laughing embrace, soon to be interrupted by flashes of fights, panic attacks and more anxious facial expressions, and a swooshing high-pitched sound that begins to speed up until the next abrupt flash of an incomplete memory sliver. The soprano sings 'The closer you get/ the more you are real/ the more you are real, the more that I feel/ the more that I feel/ the more pieces you find floating around in my mind.' We see Mette arguing with Miller, then with Simon; in recovery being moved from one bed to another; leaving her house in the middle of the night, and taking her oldest daughter Harrie with her, to Miller. Flashes of a car accident appear. Mette panics when her husband wants to bring Harrie to visit her in hospital.

With her experimental aesthetics, Rots brings us into the terrifying reality of a traumatised mind that is still in shock from some event that she cannot clearly recall, but that seems to ask for self-reflection and the rethinking of her life. The 'feel of horror' of this film is in the combination of the experimental soundtrack and the ironic-sounding opera voices that haunt the images, as well as the fragmented and non-chronological editing. We are as confused and frightened as the main character. *Retrospekt* is what I would call a horror-image of the neuro-image, Mette being a 'newly wounded' character who lives in her injured brain and PTSD-suffering mind (Pisters 2012; Malabou 2012). The accident is not the cause of the suffering. The true horror is the fact that neither she nor we as spectators can pinpoint what exactly went wrong, who is to blame; and perhaps also in an existential feeling of vague frustration and irritation, small and ugly feelings (Ngai 2007) that she does not seem able to name very clearly herself, that have led to her even wanting the violent accident to happen, nearly killing her daughter. Does she feel guilty? Is the accident a way of changing her life? The end of the film is as enigmatic as it is ambiguously hopeful: we see our tormented heroine in a new job, smiling and happy as she drives a tram, while the baritone voice encourages in a closing chant 'Go go go Mette/ go go go!'

During the entire film we have been inside her mind, and this puts *Retrospekt* at the opposite side of the contemporary female-directed horror film spectrum, as it is dreadful for every second of the journey.

Contrary to *Revenge* there is not much blood in this film, except for Mette's wounds; the blood hides in the constant threat of ordinary violence. This makes Mette the other daughter of Jeanne Dielman, showing the interior of her mental life directly, revealing just as little, except for a similar drive towards breaking the pattern of an unfulfilled woman's life (perhaps affected by postnatal depression) that at first sight has greatly improved, but that is still in existential crisis about harder to grasp gender dimensions and power relations.

Historic Murderess: Opacity of Her Mind

Glissant's poetics of relation allows for an engagement with the ambiguities in the fabric of fiction and reality in films that give us insights into perspectives not otherwise easily obtained. In the final section of this chapter, I elaborate on the further dimensions of such poetics of relation in a discussion of *Alias Grace* (2017), a Canadian television miniseries about a historical murderess. *Alias Grace* is completely female-authored. Based on the novel of the same title by Margaret Atwood from 1997, the screenplay was adapted by Sarah Polley and Mary Harron, who directed the series.[15] *Alias Grace* is based on the story of Grace Marks, a 'famous murderess' in a notorious criminal case from the nineteenth century that garnered much public attention at the time. Grace Marks and James McDermott, both Irish immigrants to Canada, were put on trial in 1843 for the double homicide of Thomas Kinnear and Nancy Montgomery, a rich Scottish landowner in Richmond Hill, Ontario, and his housekeeper mistress. Grace was 16 at the time of the murders. James McDermott, who was 21, was executed by hanging. Grace's sentence was commuted to life imprisonment. After thirty years in prison, she was pardoned. In her novel, Atwood added fictive characters to the historical ones: the psychiatrist Dr Simon Jordan who questions Grace in an attempt to find reasons to pardon her; Mary Whitney, Grace's best friend and room-mate in one of the households where she worked; and Jeremiah Pontelli, a travelling merchant who also poses as Dr Jerome Dupont, neuro-hypnotist. The story unfolds from Grace's point of view when she, as a free woman at last, writes a long letter to Dr Jordan, recalling the events of her life as she had already told him years earlier when he interviewed her. But now, she also comments on her inner thoughts, those she had at the time but chose not to express.

Like some of the films discussed in the previous sections, *Alias Grace* does not belong to the strict poetics of the horror genre as such. However, I do think the series employs a poetics of horror, not least because there are quite a few scenes literally drenched in blood, and not only related to the violent murder that we see in repeated flashes. The show introduces a contemporary perspective to the historical conditions of Grace Marks's story, which contains enough gruesome elements of solitary confinement and cruel treatments of all sorts, including domestic violence from an abusive father. Moreover, with an all-female creative and production team, the show is another example of strong female authorship, which makes it interesting for the purposes of this book. As Sarah Polley comments: 'The show explores what it meant to be a woman and how much it meant to be a young woman at that time, but also what it means to be a young woman at any time. I think a lot of women can relate to that, right now and at every period in history' (Shannon Miller 2017). And while undeniably much has improved in the situation of women, and taking into account again that for black women there are additional challenges evident from the Black Lives Matter movement in the 2010s, it is no coincidence that Atwood's work seems to speak to us with additional force in the twenty-first century, in a time of #MeToo sexual harassment charges and the simultaneous conservative backlash of removing rights to abortion and self-determination.[16] Moreover, it will allow me to expand the poetics of horror by exploring it 'from the inside', and to consider the poetics of relation and the right for opacity, which permeates contemporary poetics of horror.

The first episode of *Alias Grace* opens with an 1863 quote from Emily Dickinson that brings us immediately into a different universe of horror that I think is typical for female-directed present-day horror: 'One need not be a chamber to be haunted – one need not be a house – the brain has corridors surpassing material place. Ourselves behind ourselves, concealed – should startle most – assassin hid in our apartment be horror's least.' Before even the credit sequence begins, this quotation reminds us of the deepest vaults of our inner places. It is followed by an image of Grace (Sarah Gadon) in front of the mirror, who continually changes her facial expressions ever so slightly, while in voice-over we hear her wondering about the many different ways she is perceived by others, the many different things written about her: an inhuman female demon; an innocent victim forced against her will; too ignorant to know how to act; well and decently dressed; robber of the clothes of a murdered woman; of solemn disposition and a quarrelsome type; a good girl with a pliable nature; cunning and devious; soft in the head and little better than an idiot. While she looks in the mirror, adopting the facial expressions that would match these descriptions of others, this prologue ends with her question: 'And I wonder, how can I be all these different things at once?'

It is significant that we see here 'a lady in a looking glass', who escapes the one perfect and transparent image that would capture her essence. As Woolf in her famous essay 'The Lady in the Looking Glass' suggests, the image of a woman does not tell you who she is. Grace is actually like Woolf's Isabella in front of the mirror, who does not want to be known but cannot escape: 'It was absurd, it was monstrous. If she concealed so much and knew so much one must prise her open with the first tool that came to hand – the imagination' (Woolf 2001: 66). From the director's point of view, Harron also reflects on the many faces of Grace, which makes her a narrator who keeps escaping. Harron gave Sarah Gadon instructions to play the scene with different facial expressions, ranging from Good Grace to Bad Grace – and then in the editing she could mix these versions (Shannon Miller 2017). This directorial and editing choice adds to the ambiguous status of Grace, which is the main topic of the show: is she Grace or her alias?

While all he gets is the outside (Grace's faces, her words), her deepest thoughts and memories are what Dr Jordan (Edward Holcroft) wishes to discover when he is hired to examine Grace and to bring back her memories of the murders, of which she claims to have no recollection, so as to determine whether or not she could be held accountable. Dr Jordan does not measure her skull for any deviations, but experiments with a new method, based on the method of psychoanalysis that was not yet clearly established in the mid-nineteenth century but soon would find in Freud its main architect. For weeks Dr Jordan interviews Grace, writing down every detail of what she tells him about her life, trying to get at the deepest levels of her mind. We perceive her story on three intermingled levels: the times when she is in the house of the governor of the penitentiary where during the day she works as a housekeeper and tells her story to Dr Jordan; the events in visualised flashbacks; and her voice-over commentary from the long letter that she writes to Dr Jordan after she is released from prison.

While she is talking in the house of the prison governor she is sewing a quilt for the daughter of the household, and this is the first thing she tells him, that every woman should have a quilt before she marries. A quilt, spread on a bed as a cover, contains a warning, Grace argues:

> There are many dangerous things that may take place in a bed. It's where we are born, our first peril in life. It's where women give birth, which is often their last. And it's where the act takes place between men and women, sir. Some call it love, others despair, or merely an indignity they must suffer through. (S1E1)

I will return to the quilt in a moment, as it is a recurring image in the series; here the most striking thing to notice is the immediate connection of the bed with danger. Especially when one is a woman.

Implicitly connected to these dangers of the bed is a poetics of blood that returns at regular intervals. The opening credits already show blood-soaked pieces of cloth, as well as a quill pen writing on paper, engravings of a nineteenth-century girl and a boy with an axe (possibly newspaper prints of the real Grace and James), and finally an abstracted image of a quilt. Obviously blood is connected to the murder of Nancy Montgomery (Anna Paquin), which first appears as an involuntary flash when Dr Jordan brings along a beetroot to provoke some associations. Here we learn from the image flash and the voice-over that Grace does not reveal her thoughts but talks about the fact that beetroot stains. Flashes of the murder, as well as the dreamlike image of Nancy in a pink dress picking thick red velvety roses, appear at regular intervals throughout the series; the last time this image appears, Nancy falls to the ground revealing a mark of blood on her forehead.

Most prominently, blood is associated with menstruation and abortion. When Grace discovers blood between her legs and thinks she is going to die, Mary, her room-mate in the house where they are both employed as housemaids, reassures her and lends Grace her red petticoat, which she should wear under her dress on those days of the month. However, most gruesome is the blood loss that Mary suffers after an illegal abortion. Finding herself pregnant by the son of the house, she does not see any other option – with fatal consequences. 'More blood, more blood', Harron allegedly called on set to emphasise the ghastly reality for many women in the Victorian age that *Alias Grace* does not censor away, thus creating what she calls 'the anti-Downton Abbey' view of the darker sides of this period. One can also add here that the long red dresses of the women in *A Handmaid's Tale* (HBO 2017), the other series based on Atwood's work that came out at the same time, appeared all over the world during protests against the scaling back of abortion legislation and other women's rights, 'a wall of women dressed in scarlet cloaks' (Beaumont and Holpuch 2018).

At the end of the series, Grace makes a 'quilt of her own'; it includes a yellowish white piece of cloth from her prison nightgown that she wore for thirty years, a pink one from Nancy's dress that she was wearing when she was murdered, which appeared in Grace's dreams and which she had on during the trial, and a piece of the red petticoat from Mary. Together, these pieces form a female horror story. Nevertheless, it is not a completely transparent story that fits neatly within the confines of classic genre structures and normative subject positions. The quilt can be seen as a powerful metaphor for a poetics of relation that keeps the individual pieces visible. The story of the quilt is an example of what Deleuze and Guattari, in *A Thousand Plateaus*, call a 'smooth space', a non-hierarchical patchwork technique that can go on in an open space (it is not limited, for instance, by the frame of the weaving machine) (Deleuze and Guattari 1988: 475–7). This does not mean there are no limits or that there are no encounters with the 'striation' of norms, rules and measurements; in fact 'the smooth and the striated' always interconnect, but with different variations and intensities (Lysen and Pisters 2012).

There is, however, a greater possibility to open up and create what Glissant called a 'relayed aesthetic' (Glissant 1997: 203) that allows linking and relinking, in this case women's stories across time and place. Through the story of Grace, we also connect to the story of the migration of Irish people to North America, which again connects to other migratory and nomadic trajectories. The story of the indigenous people in *Alias Grace* is not explicitly addressed, even though quilting was an ancient technique of indigenous people before the settlers appropriated it. And the historical Grace Marks can be compared to another 'murderess' from the nineteenth century, Margaret Garner, a black woman who temporarily escaped slavery, fictionalised by Morrison in her novel *Beloved*.[17] The fictionalised versions of these nineteenth-century 'murderesses' that Atwood and Morrison created in their respective novels make clear that the historical situations of white and black women were minority positions full of comparable hardship, but at the same time that the condition of slavery was different from the situation of Irish migrant women entering Canada at the time. In *Alias Grace* there is only one scene in which we see and hear a woman of colour, but it is a telling moment. When Grace is treated with contempt for being a murderess by one of the other servants in the governor's house, a black maid defends her. When Grace remarks that she does not seem to be afraid of her as many others are, she looks at Grace and says, 'Afraid of you? For raising up against your master? Miss Grace, where do you think I come from?' (S1E5). Her following observations about Dr Jordan also indicate her perceptiveness. This is only a very short moment in the series, but it does add a connection with another colour to the quilt of relations.

As Glissant has argued, the condition for such a poetics of relation is based on the non-totalitarian grasp of the other as striated in a fixed place, but leaves open room for not knowing, for uncertainty and ambiguity, for places where the other can be without apparent transparency. Glissant claims this place for ethnic and racial otherness where there is room for the other to move and to be beyond fixed power structures and normative behaviour.

And within the framework of her specific historical conditions, this is also the room that Grace claims for herself. Astutely she remarks to Dr Jordan in her letter: 'You want to go where I can never go, see what I can never see inside me. You want to open up my body and peer inside. In your hand, you want to hold my beating female heart' (S1E2). However, she refuses to tell him everything. Not only because she knows that telling everything would make her even more vulnerable (the demon of good manners and conventional gender behaviour that Woolf has trouble forgetting), but also because there is a kernel of the unknowable that always remains, no matter how deep we dig. Grace describes Jordan's desire to know and report on her as follows:

> When you write it is as if you are drawing on my skin as if thousands of butterflies have settled on my skin and are softly opening and closing their wings. But underneath that there is another feeling, a feeling of being awake and watchful like waking up in the middle of the night with a hand over your face and you wake up in fear but no one is there. And underneath that is another feeling, a feeling of being torn open, not like a body of flesh but like a peach. It is not even torn open but too ripe and splitting of its own accord and inside the peach is a stone. (S1E2)

The hard kernel of the unknown always hides inside the truth and the deepest layers of the mind.

In the last episode, Grace is hypnotised by Dr Dupont (the merchant Jeremiah who presents himself as a hypnotist to the group of people who want to free Grace). Dressed in a black dress, covered with a black veil, she is led into to the depths of her unconscious and asked about the murders. Suddenly Grace speaks with an abnormal voice, uses frank words that she would never allow herself to utter, and confesses to the murders, but as the spirit of Mary, whose soul could not escape at her death because Grace forgot to open the window, and who nestled within Grace. Mary's spirit claims innocence for Grace who was outside in the garden at the time of the murders.

The scene presents the murders as an act of revenge pursuant to Mary's repressed rage. However, in spite of the popularity of mesmerism, spiritualism and hypnotism in the nineteenth century, this revelation does not solve Dr Jordan's problem. He suspects that mesmerism and hypnotism have been invented for women to speak their mind freely, to say what they would have liked to say but never could. It literally drives him insane, unable to reach the kernel of the truth; he refuses to write a report that could lead to clemency. He leaves without a word, and enlists to serve in the Civil War. Grace returns to prison for another ten years. At the end of the series, we arrive at the moment when Grace is writing her long letter with afterthoughts to Dr Jordan, who is actually not able to hear it all: he returned from the war in a catatonic state – perhaps literally made mad because of his inability to cope with the opacity of Grace.

In the final moments, finally a free and pardoned woman, Grace muses: 'It was strange to realize that I would not be a celebrated murderess any more, but an object of pity rather than horror and fear. It took me some days to get used the idea. It calls for a different arrangement of the face' (S1E6). We see her again in front of the mirror, 'a glass darkly'. Another quote by Dickinson – 'I felt a cleaving in my mind, as if my brain had split, I tried to match it – seam by seam – but it would not fit' – emphasises once more a poetics of relation, which allows for places that do not fit, like blood trickling through the interstices of the patchwork quilt.

Blood Seeping Through a Glass Darkly

This chapter has looked at the ways in which women have grabbed the camera in order to speak out about their position in a society that has for long not granted women much agency or room for thoughts of their own. Most of the women we have encountered in the female-directed films discussed on the previous pages are enraged, avenging women who have turned to violence; 'Angels in the House' turned Demonic Furies. In one way or another, they are 'Carrie's murderous sisters' in that they find their empowerment by striking back. While the central reference in this chapter has been the sub-genre of the slasher film, and in particular the rape-revenge film, clearly the borders of the horror genre have been stretched: first of all by rereading feminist and women films of the second generation of filmmakers (*Jeanne Dielman*, *A Question of Silence* and *Welcome II the Terrordome*) through the lens of a poetics of horror; and secondly, by looking at the spectrum of horror from over-the-top splash and splatter gore as a phantasmagorical carnivalesque feast of empowerment (*Revenge*) to the more uncomfortable and unsafe aesthetics of violence of and in the female mind (*Retrospekt*), inviting a whole spectrum of ugly feelings and uneasy emotions that are harder to identify with. Finally, *Alias Grace* presents a contemporary reflection on the historical position of women by diving into the impenetrable mind of a famous murderess, weaving a tapestry of relations between fiction and reality, between inner and outer spaces, all through a glass darkly, red.

CHAPTER 2

Growing Pains:
Breasts, Blood and Fangs

Kiss of the Vampire: Embracing Lust and Loss

One of the oldest revenant figures of the horror genre is the vampire. The vampire as blood-sucking spirit, jinn, incubus, pontianak, succubus and other demonic incarnations belongs to the mythology of many different cultures, each with their own variations on the theme of nocturnal creatures who crave blood (Bane 2010; White 2000). Often the vampire is associated with suicide victims or other unlucky returning dead ones who want revenge or redemption, and frequently the vampire is connected further to monstrous creatures such as werewolves. The best-known modern version of the vampire appears in Bram Stoker's 1897 novel about Count Dracula, which introduced the vampire as a charming seducer, and popularised vampire symbols such as the bat-ridden haunted castle, the coffin in which the vampire sleeps during the day, and his sensitivity to sunlight, garlic and crucifixes. There are countless versions of the vampire myth in film and popular culture that have been described extensively by others, all beyond the scope of this book (Weinstock 2012; Bramesco 2018).

With respect to gender, Count Dracula has been associated with feminine seductive powers, closely associated with the legendarily bloody Countess Elizabeth Bathory (McNally 1985; Penrose 2012) or Carmilla, the lesbian vampire from Sheridan Le Fanu's gothic novel of 1872. In *The Monstrous-Feminine*, Barbara Creed focuses in particular on the lesbian vampire, which became popular in the 1970s with films such as *Vampyros Lesbos* (dir. Jesus Franco, 1971), *Daughters of Darkness* (dir. Harry Kümel, 1971) and *The Hunger* (dir. Tony Scott, 1983). Creed discusses the lesbian vampire as an archaic mother figure, giving and taking life, and living for eternity herself. The lesbian vampire is doubly dangerous:

> as well as transforming her victims into blood-sucking creatures of the night, she
> also threatens to seduce the daughters of patriarchy away from their proper gender

roles. She is abject, not only for this disrespect for proper sexual conduct but also because she crosses the borders between the living and the dead, the human and the animal. (Creed 1993: 61)

Creed argues furthermore that the female vampire can be seen as a 'menstrual monster' (1993: 62). In some cultures the popular belief was that woman became vampires 'in order to replace the blood she lost during menstruation' (1993: 63). Moreover, the vampire myth is sometimes seen as a *rite de passage* when young girls have their first menstruation (the phenomenon of the menarche), and the vampire that can transform into a bat or werewolf is also associated with the full moon and the menstrual cycle (Shuttle and Redgrove 1978; Zimmerman 1984). The vampire is also associated with sexuality and defloration; the blood loss that occurs when a woman engages in coitus for the first time. Therefore, the vampire is also related to coming-of-age stories and the sexual awakening of girls in particular.

Carol Clover contends that vampires, like werewolves, belong to the one-sex era and carry with them 'a premodern sense of sexual difference' (Clover 1992: 15). Furthermore, the intimacy of their weapons – teeth, beaks, fangs and claws – are extensions of vampire bodies 'that bring the attacker and attacked into primitive, animalistic embrace' (Clover 1992: 32). Hence, the vampire is also closely related to transgressive sexuality, gender exchanges and contamination. Both men and women can be penetrated at any place on their body, though usually it is the neck that is preferred for the vampire's bite, which often casts an erotically immobilising spell over its victims. In any case, a 'kiss' from a vampire is certainly bloody. As Jean-Luc Nancy argues in his beautiful text about Claire Denis's take on the vampire myth in *Trouble Every Day* (I will return to this film later), the kiss precipitates the bite and the taste of blood, recalling that 'Eros and Thanatos [are] not in a dialectic of opposites, but in a mutual excitation and exasperation, each asking the other to go further, to go all the way to the end, to get completely lost' (2008: 2). Thick lustful gushes of deep-red blood penetrate the vampire-image on different levels: blood as a symbol of vitality and rejuvenation; blood as a spiritual or religious symbol of sacrifice and redemption that the vampire scorns; blood as a symbol for addiction and contamination; blood as a symbol of sexual intimacy and reproduction; or to begin with, the very materiality of blood as 'splashes, drops, streams, and stains, clots and ribbons that will never again be restored to a form', exposing a kind of 'horrific sublimation' of the tearing apart of sex and death (Nancy 2008: 2).

The vampire figure, in all its gendered monstrosity, has been reincarnated on screen most famously as Dracula (among others, in the films of Tod Browning and Francis Ford Coppola), Nosferatu (put on screen by W. F. Murnau and Werner Herzog) and in female versions as Carmilla or Countess Bathory (as in Jesus Franco, Harry Kumel and Toni Scott's films). So what happens when the lens of a woman director filters the same myth? As early as Stoker's famous book, Florence Marryat wrote *The Blood of the Vampire* (1897). Some of the most popular retakes of the genre are based on novels written by women, notably Anne Rice's *Interview with the Vampire* (1976),[1] *Dead until Dark* (Carlaine Harris, 2001),[2] *The Gilda Stories* (Jewelle Gomez, 1991) and *Fledgling* (Octavia Butler, 2005).

In this chapter, I focus on vampire films made by women. After encountering Virginia Woolf in a vampire tale, I return to one of the first vampire films directed by a woman, Stephanie Rotman's *The Velvet Vampire* (1971), and Kathryn Bigelow's better-known vampire Western *Near Dark* (1987). As the vampire is so closely associated with 'first blood' (menstruation, defloration), the next section is concerned with stories of sexual awakening, coming of age and (family) trauma. I discuss several coming-of-age vampire tales set on screen by women, focusing on Mary Harron's take on the vampire in *The Moth Diaries* (2012). The legend of Countess Bathory is given a feminist twist by Julie Delpy in *The Countess* (2009) and has its own version of the mad quest for beauty and eternal youth in contemporary Japan (and beyond) in Mika Ninagawa's *Helter Skelter* (2012). Claire Denis's *Trouble Every Day* stretches the vampire tale to its limits, to the material limits of the body and the limits of the image, while also allowing a critical postcolonial reading. The final section examines present-day empowering takes on the genre in original and relational ways in Octavia Butler's novel *Fledgling* (2005) and in *A Girl Walks Home Alone at Night* (dir. Ana Lily Amirpour, 2014).

Bury Your Fangs in My Flesh: Blood Transfusions of a Genre Trope

The bloody physicality of the vampire seems to be far removed from Woolf's legacy. Vampires and their undisguised erotic lust do not seem to match with Woolfian sensibility, even if there is an occasional reference to vampires as a metaphor for grief and pain. In *The Waves*, for instance, one of the characters (Neville) exclaims that horror has seized him with its fangs: 'For this moment, this one moment, we are together. I press you to me. Come, pain, feed on me. Bury your fangs in my flesh. Tear me asunder. I sob, I sob' (Woolf 2015b: 89). The vampire's fangs in this passage are erotically charged in connection to the pain of a traumatic loss; the moment occurs when one of the characters, Percival, has just died. And this connection between pain, trauma and loss and the vampire kiss will return in many transformations, as we will see.[3]

While vampire metaphors are rare in Woolf's prose, as a persona Woolf herself is incarnated in a vampire story, Jody Scott's *I, Vampire* (1977). I want to raise this vampire tale briefly before turning to the bloody cinematographic heroines of this chapter. In Scott's eccentric science fiction novel, Sterling O'Blivion is a 700-year-old vampire who has outlived fifty-two lovers and now operates a dance studio in Chicago. One day, while looking through her telescope at the busy streets, O'Blivion sees Woolf, introduced as follows: 'Wait a minute. This was crazy. Were my eyes playing me false? Virginia Woolf, the famous author, died years ago' (Scott 1977: 44). It appears that O'Blivion once met Woolf in 1923, in Paris. 'She hadn't yet written *To the Lighthouse* or her science fiction classic (if I may call it that), *Orlando*', O'Blivion recalls (1977: 45). The two encountered each other in the ladies' room ('of all absurd places') and their eyes met in the mirror, 'locked together, a knife-thrust glance' (1977: 45). Already at that first meeting the vampire fell in love with Woolf because she fired 'her imagination into an almost visionary state' (1977: 47). And imagination is something we certainly need to savour in Scott's sometimes hilarious and biting prose. The new Woolf of 1984 who O'Blivion re-encounters is actually named Benaroya. She is a disguised alien from the planet Rysemus, where she has the form of a sea-pig, a sort of cloned telepathic dolphin. Benaroya Woolf has come to Earth to save the planet, fight the evil Sajorian slave-trading aliens and upgrade the human race. In order to do this, Woolf and O'Blivion must set up a business in telegenesis, selling 'Famous Men's Sperm Kits' to housewives. They go on a promotional tour: ' "And now!" Woolf trumpeted, "I wanna introduce my friend Sterling O'Blivion, longtime vampire and mastermind of sales pitches, who'll tell ya all about it" ' (1977: 111). Scott's wild and witty reimagining of Woolf, in association with the lure of the vampire myth that stabs at society's treatment of women, consumer culture, big business and politics, presents a satiric feminist tale on lesbian love and feminine power that is beyond the scope of this study. However, it does allow me to look for other vampires that took one of Woolf's lessons intended for Sterling O'Blivion to heart: ' "Quit with the self-pity," growled Woolf. "Develop some guts and you can reverse any process" ' (1977: 204). So what are the reversals or slight subversions or transformations of the horrors of the vampire myth in the directorial hands of women 'with guts'?

One of the earliest female-directed vampire films that I have been able to track down is Stephanie Rothman's *The Velvet Vampire* (1971). In 1964 Rothman was the first woman hired by Roger Corman's New World Pictures, having been awarded (again as the first woman) the Directors Guild of America Fellowship for student film directors.[4] In 1966 she was asked to create some additional scenes for the film *Blood Bath*, a vampire tale that had an uneasy production history (and for which she was credited as co-director with Jack Hill). In 1970 Corman invited her to direct *The Student Nurses*, which became a rather successful exploitation film about nurses (in red capes) who are 'learning fast from the men who teach them what it's all about', according to the voice-over in the trailer. And yes, sexual fantasies about uniformed nurses doing wild things with their patients are certainly part of the film's cult status. In an interview with Henry Jenkins in 2007, Rothman explained that she was actually never happy making exploitation films, but that it was the only opportunity for her to work as a director at the time. While the genre required nudity and violence, Rothman insisted that

> My struggle was to try to dramatically justify such scenes and to make them transgressive, but not repulsive. I tried to control this through the style in which I shot scenes. That was one of my greatest pleasures, determining how my style of shooting could enhance the content of a scene. (Jenkins 2007)

She continued that once the debt to the genre was paid, she had the freedom to address other issues such as the question of immigration and the poor situation of Mexican workers, or women's right to have a safe and legal abortion when, at the time, abortion was illegal everywhere.

> I have always wondered why the major studios were not making films about these topics. What kind of constraints were at work on them? My guess is that it was nothing but the over-privileged lives, limited curiosity and narrow minds of the men, and in those days they were always men, who decided which films would be made. (Jenkins 2007)

She stopped working for Corman because he did not pay any wages. Since he was giving young directors a chance to access the industry and obtain visibility, he argued that this would lead to better-paid work. In contrast with the male directors of the 'Corman film school', many of whom indeed became famous and well paid, this was not the case for the female directors.[5] In the same interview, Rothman argues that with the possibilities of today's cheap digital equipment and the potential of online distribution, she might not have chosen the exploitation genre, but at the time she had no other option.

Despite Rothman's reservations about the genre's constrictions, it is nevertheless interesting that she mentions the freedom that the margins of the film industry allowed her to express, both thematically and stylistically, freedoms that otherwise might not have been permitted. So, let us revisit her vampire film and explore its style and themes, its poetics of horror. *The Velvet Vampire* (also known as *Cemetery Girls*) opens with abstract images of a rotating blood-red stone that gradually becomes superimposed by two intersecting black lines above the Los Angeles city skyline, a cross atop a modern concrete church. As day fades into night, we gradually discover a small red figure moving through the image, and in the next shot we see a woman in a bright-red suit and matching go-go boots, walking alongside a red-lit water-filled public fountain. Her footsteps are accompanied by an ominous sound; she stops and looks around at the empty space when suddenly a man appears behind her, drags her to the ground, assaults her with a knife and begins to rape her. She bites his hand and then stabs him with his own blade. Seemingly unmoved, she washes the blood from her hands in the fountain, adding blood to the red-coloured water, and then retrieves a mirror to adjust her make-up. While we are still contemplating the unruffled way in which she handled the situation, we see her eyes in close-up, red-rimmed, and we hear a blues-styled voice in a sound bridge to the next scene. Here, the actual blues singer Johnny Shines is present, performing at the opening of a downtown Los Angeles art exhibition. We meet the woman in red, Diane LeFanu (Celeste Yamall), and the married couple Lee and Susan Ritter (Michael Blodgett and Sherry Miles). Diane invites the couple to come and stay with her at her Mojave desert mansion. Diane LeFanu appears to be a nineteenth-century vampire. Her name is a reference to Sheridan Le Fanu, the gothic novelist who wrote *Carmilla* (1871), the female vampire story that influenced Stoker's *Dracula*, among other things with the idea of the vampire sleeping in a coffin.[6]

I want to comment briefly on this opening scene to highlight a few elements that stand out. First, most strikingly, there is the vivid presence of red elements in the *mise en scène*, all uniquely associated with Diane. Because of the title of the film, we know that she must be a vampire, but the assault at the beginning is remarkable and unusual, since it is almost forgotten during the remainder of the film, which portrays Diane as a lustful vampire who 'swings both ways'. Here at the beginning, however, her violence is motivated by self-defence, and this may be an example of how Rothman introduces some form of justification for the violence of the genre. At the same time, she also seems to comment on

Figure 2.1 *The Velvet Vampire* (Stephanie Rothman, 1970).

the issue of sexual violence by turning the tables and making the woman
the perpetrator instead of the victim. Shines's melancholic blues music
seems initially at odds with the vampire story setting, but the song he
performs is entitled 'Evil Hearted Woman', and when he sings 'when
you and the devil walk side by side', this reflects directly on Diane. On
the other hand, the blues performance might be another instance where
Rothman hints at other issues that she would like to communicate, within
the confines of the genre. Shines's voice and guitar playing transports us
to the African roots of large parts of Afro-American culture. This might
present a subtle reference to forced migration, hinted at later in the film
when Diane refers to her Mexican housekeeper Juan (Jerry Daniels) as
somebody whose family was killed before she took him in and raised
him. These small gestures can easily be overlooked within the overall
style of the exploitation genre. They could also just as well be considered
stereotypical presentations of 'the other', since Shines does not reap-
pear beyond this performance, and especially since Juan soon becomes
another victim. Nevertheless, both the assault on Diane and the presence

of Shines's blues-styled voice remain remarkable in the overall aesthetics of the film's opening.

What follows is a luscious vampire tale set in the desert, with a vampire who can bear sunlight but is attracted to coffins, raw meat, sex and the blood of her victims, shot on Kodak's Eastmancolor film stock (processed under the trade name Metrocolor), with its expressively vivid psychedelic orange reds, blue, yellows and purples. Both in its *mise en scène*, especially the clothing and hairstyles of the protagonists, as well as thematically, the 'summer-of-love' feel of uninhibited sex, the film is highly entertaining and has achieved cult status. Watching her guests in bed through a one-way mirror, Diane induces synchronised erotic dreams into her sleeping victims, where they see themselves on a red-draped bed in the desert, lured away by Diane, also dressed in red. Once Susan falls under Diane's spell, there is another brief moment where Rothman seems to comment on female sexuality, when Diane asks Susan to notice how envious men are about the pleasures of female sexuality that they can never know. Again, this is just a brief remark that gets hidden beneath the abundant aesthetics of this campy desert vampire film, which is worthwhile rediscovering, even if Rothman remains close to the monstrous lesbian vampire stereotype that was in vogue at the time of the film's making.

Kathryn Bigelow's *Near Dark* is perhaps the best-known (early) vampire movie directed by a woman. Bigelow counts as one of the few women who made it to big commercial Hollywood productions, and is the only woman to date to have ever won a Best Director Oscar (for the war film *The Hurt Locker*, 2010). *Near Dark* was her first feature film, and contrary to the sun-dappled psychedelic colours of *The Velvet Vampire*, Bigelow's version of the vampire tale takes place largely in the dark. The rising and falling sun at dawn and dusk gives the film its rhythm, together with its foreboding moody soundtrack by Tangerine Dream. Bigelow's vampires certainly cannot withstand the sun and will burn alive as soon as light hits their skin. The iconography of *Near Dark* is that of a Western; its main character Caleb Colton (Adrian Pasdar) is a farm boy in jeans, boots and a Stetson hat, who rides his horse through tumbleweed rolling across dusty deserted roads. He falls in love with Mae (Jenny Wright), who turns out to be a vampire living with a rowdy tribal vampire family. Turned into an unwilling vampire himself, Caleb follows Mae and her nocturnal clan during their violent journey in search of blood. At the same time, his father and little sister are looking for him. When they find him, Caleb's father (who is a veterinarian) per-forms a blood transfusion so that he can return to his family with new blood. Equally transfused, at the end of the film, Mae can also withstand sunlight.

Sara Jones has analysed how brilliantly and idiosyncratically Bigelow imbues the typical American Western genre with the elements of European gothic horror (Jones 2003). In terms of its ideological framework, the movie has been considered more conservative, relating the vampires both to the 'racial other' and queer sexuality. Comparing *Near Dark*'s plot structure to John Ford's classic Western *The Searchers* (1956), Jones links the vampires with Native American Indians and their 'intrusion' into the idyllic safety of settler life: 'The notion that blood, socio-cultural belonging and lifestyle are inextricably linked has a powerful resonance with concepts of racial identity and the fear of racial mixing that underlies depictions in many westerns' (Jones 2003: 63). The deepest fear that vampires seem to instil is their ability to transform humans into vampires by contagion, 'the viral transmission of vampirism from saliva to blood' (Jones 2003: 69). This also reinforces the metaphoric reading of the vampire not only as 'the racial other' but also as the sexual other, especially in terms of male homosexuality: 'The intense need of the vampire's deadly kiss and feeding blurs together codes of violence and desire. Teeth penetrate yielding flesh, drawing blood, feeding on the juices of human prey, reversing the trajectory of ejaculation' (Jones 2003: 69). In 1987, when *Near Dark* was released, it was difficult not to relate vampire kisses to the AIDS epidemic that was peaking at the time, with no cure yet in sight. Caleb's receiving 'clean blood' from his father is also particularly hard not to see as a return to the normative patriarchal family.

However, as reviewers have remarked, when at the end of the film Mae is released from her vampire status (receiving Caleb's purified blood), her anxious expression and the dark and gloomy mood of the scene make this 'happy ending' rather ambiguous (Jones 2003; Schneider 2003). In fact, Bigelow's vampires continue to undermine the strong patriarchal modes of the Western, which she certainly knows how to deploy. In addition, in her later work, Bigelow has proven that she understands the masculinist language of Hollywood cinema, and this has kept her for a long time as the only female director considered 'one of the boys'. However, things are changing.

Menarche Vampires: Coming of Age, Blood, Sex and Death

The other early female-directed vampire film that should be mentioned here is Fran Rubel Kuzui's largely forgotten version of *Buffy the Vampire Slayer* (1992), brought to screens five years before the popular television series began. Unlike its television adaptation, Buffy the film received a lukewarm reception and its director is seldom mentioned. Even Joss Whedon, the creator of the Buffy story and later showrunner, does not seem to remember Kuzui when he expresses his disappointment at the film: 'I finally sat down and had written it, and somebody had made it into a movie, and I felt like – well, that's not quite her. It's a start, but it's not quite the girl.'[7] And yet Buffy certainly is a formidable action heroine who, alongside other empowering women warriors such as Xena, the Warrior Princess and La Femme Nikita, made their appearance in popular television shows during the 1990s.[8] Early 2001 Buffy has been labelled 'the Third Wave's Final Girl', a more 'girlie' type of feminism, sometimes addressed as 'post-feminism' (and therefore sometimes also not recognised as 'third wave') (Karras 2002; McRobbie 2008). Buffy is no longer the boyish and sexless 'final girl' described by Clover, but her (white, urban, privileged) femininity is a source of strength; she reassures boys and men that she can take care of herself, but she still enjoys men (she is comparable to other post-feminist girl friends of the equally popular television series of the 1990s, *Sex and the City* (1998–2004)).

In Kuzui's film version of Buffy, which admittedly has a high camp feel to it, the heroine (Kirsty Swanson) is a typical late 1980s/early 1990s high school cheerleader who prefers mall shopping with her friends to attending classes. She also happens to have dreams of 'the European dark ages', where she is apparently a vampire killer. It does not take her trainer Merrich (Donald Sutherland) long to convince her to join him in the graveyard, where she discovers her skills and confronts the vampire-king Lothos (Rutger Hauer), who secures a red ribbon around her neck at the place where he wants to bite her and whom she recognises from her dreams. In all its tackiness, this Buffy is certainly perceptive, strong, agile and knows how to fight, but I simply want to emphasise one striking element that seems to recur in vampire tales in relation to women. When a vampire is near, Buffy gets a cramp in her stomach. When she dismisses this as PMS, Merrich tells her to understand precisely these 'female' pains as her vampire alert system. There is no better literal interpretation to make the connection between menarche, menstruation and vampirism as a metaphor for sexual exploration and danger. In many vampiric coming-of-age stories, blood is closely related to the female bodies' reproductive organs and sexual awakening.

In a similar vein, feminist interpretations of the fairy tale of Little Red Riding Hood have made the connection between the red cape, menstruation and sexuality. Elsewhere, I have elaborated on Angela Carter's rewriting of the folk tale and her script for Neil Jordan's 1984 film *The Company of Wolves* (Carter 2015; Pisters 2003: 164–6). In Carter's version of Little Red Riding Hood, the girl (called Rosaleen in the film) chooses the company of wolves, and especially 'the leader of the pack', which allows her to discover the sexuality associated with vampire stories. It is this passion that girls in coming-of-age stories are curious to discover, and this is what Riding Hood's cape stands for, as well as the dangers that this longing implies. Red as the double sign of passion and danger is symbolised in Catherine Hardwicke's fantasy film *Red Riding Hood* (2011).[9] As a sort of *Twilight* series set in a Middle Age forest village haunted by a werewolf, the film plays with all the elements of the Red Riding Hood story, giving it another Carter-like twist. Valerie (Amanda Seyfried) is a girl entering womanhood who is not in love with the man she is supposed to marry. She only wants her long-time childhood friend Peter (Shiloh Fernandez), who has also matured into a man. While she discovers that her mother had an affair and a child with another man, and she suspects her grandmother (Julie Christie) to be affiliated with the werewolf, it is finally her own father of whom she should be most afraid. The story takes place during the three days of a 'blood moon' during which a werewolf's bite becomes like the vampire's kiss, transforming the one who is bitten into another werewolf. The village vampire slayer is a religious man, Father Solomon (Gary Oldman), who does not succeed in subduing the beast. However, Riding Hood seems to be able to talk to the werewolf and clearly, in the end, Valerie also willingly chooses 'the company of wolves'. What I mainly want to emphasise by mentioning Red Riding Hood in relation to coming-of-age stories that involve blood, vampires and werewolves is that the feminist twists on the famous story do not exclude romantic liaisons, and in the feminist versions of Carter and Hardwicke, their choices are made freely. Obviously, in Hardwicke's film, Valerie's red cape in an entirely snow-covered *mise en scène* cannot mean anything else but the loss of sexual innocence.

This is also the point of Lucille Hadžihalilović's much-acclaimed *Innocence* (2004), which takes place in a girls' boarding school secluded in the woods. Much has been written about this adaptation of Franz Wedekind's 1888 novel *Mine-Haha, or the Corporal Education of Young Girls*, discussing the sensual, oneiric and haunting qualities of the *mise en scène*, its intimate portrayal of an all-girls' world, its enchanting soundtrack and its uneasily disturbing viewing experience (Sobchack 2005; Wilson 2007; Quinlivan 2009; Lübecker 2015). I will return in Chapter 4 to Hadžihalilović's equally or perhaps even more haunting later film *Evolution* (2015), which presents an all-boy world (as well as to her short film *Mimi*),

but here I simply want to note *Innocence*'s gesture to the vampire myth
and the coming-of-age narrative with which it is connected. At the beginning of the film a new girl, Iris (Zoé Auclair), arrives in a coffin, like
a 'mini-vampire'. The eldest girl, Bianca (Bérangère Haubruge), opens
the coffin and welcomes the 'new born' into the strange world of girls'
education. They are all dressed in identical white skirts and blouses, only
differentiable by their coloured hair ribbons. The youngest receives a red
ribbon, the oldest purple. The girls are mainly trained in biology (larvae
transforming into butterflies have a special place in this classroom) and
dance. The dance teacher Mademoiselle Eva (Marion Cotillard) does not
seem to be very happy in her role, but she teaches the girls that only obedi-
ence will keep them safe.

The oldest girls leave at night and go to a mysterious and ominous other
house, where they appear to perform for an (unseen) audience of men.
When the day arrives when the purple-ribbon girls experience their first
menstruation, they are educated about how to take care of the blood, and a
little later they leave the woods, prepared for the world. Here, Bianca and
the other girls meet boys for the first time, and the spurting water fountain
that covers them at the end of the film is not easy to dismiss as anything
other than an erotic eruption, which, after the haunting world of the forest
school, leaves us quite uncomfortable about what this education was really
about, other than preparing them for mating. The red ribbon of the 'mini-
vampire' at the beginning of the film finds its real-world destination as her
body begins to bleed. It is a terrifying and rather depressing thought that
constantly looms underneath *Innocence*'s images.

The film I focus on in this section is Mary Harron's under-appreciated
vampire coming-of-age film *The Moth Diaries* (2011).[10] Harron wrote
the film's screenplay after Rachel Klein's novel of the same name. *The
Moth Diaries* is also set in an all-girls' boarding school in the woods, but
rather than a general education for girls, this film focuses on the inner
voyage and transformation of its main character Rebecca (Sarah Bolger),
who returns to the Brangwyn boarding school after the summer. The
film opens with a larva transforming into a moth, the nocturnal insect
that symbolises vulnerable wisdom and secret knowledge; the moth then
transforms into a pen, while we hear Rebecca's voice explaining that she
began to write a diary 'to know exactly what happened to me when I was
sixteen'. We soon meet Rebecca's friend Lucy (Sarah Gordon) and others
in the clique: Charley, Dora, Sofia and Kiki. The arrival of a new girl,
Ernessa (Lily Cole), immediately gives Rebecca the shivers; something
about her pale tallness and piercing blue eyes makes her uncomfortable
and when Ernessa begins to alienate Lucy, Rebecca is not only jealous

but also begins to suspect that Ernessa is a vampire. This idea is encour-
aged by the fact that for her literature class assignment Rebecca reads Le
Fanu's *Carmilla*, which, as in Rothman's *The Velvet Vampire*, is a strong
reference to female vampires. As her teacher indicates, all vampire stories
share three elements: blood, sexuality and death. Let me now consider
how these three elements of the poetics of vampire horror return in *The
Moth Diaries*.

Blood, or references to blood, are slowly built up during the course of
this film. The first time we see a bright-red blood drop, it is actually not
blood at all but nail polish spilled by Lucy. Red nail polish has a special
attraction in terms of violence, liberation and sexuality, which recurs often
in the poetics of red in women's cinema. For instance, in *Morvern Callar*
(dir. Lynn Ramsay, 2003), the main character (Samantha Morton) is constantly painting her nails while she tries to deal with the suicide and corpse
of her boyfriend, quitting her job and leaving on a road trip. In *The Moth
Diaries*, the drop of thick ruby polish foreshadows the vampire lust that
will soon befall Lucy, and the other bloodsoaked scenes. The second
bloody moment is when Rebecca suddenly has a nosebleed. Looking in
the mirror and washing her bloody hands, she sees flashes of some other
blood-covered hands, male hands, presumably those of her father, who,
we have learned in the meantime, committed suicide two years earlier; a
traumatising event that is still imprinted on Rebecca's brain. The third
moment of blood is related to menstruation. At the dinner table, Rebecca,
pale and weak, indicates that she is experiencing a haemorrhagic feeling.
When she wakes up in the middle of the night, her white nightgown
(another of these iconic images of virginal women) and bed linen show
a large bloodstain, an experience any woman will recognise. It is at this
precise moment that Rebecca discovers Lucy and Ernessa in a ferocious
embrace, a point to which I will return in a moment. The last image, which
is literally drenched in blood, is a sequence when Ernessa visits Rebecca in
the library and invites her to 'finally free herself', offering Rebecca a razor
blade; she cuts her own wrist which gushes a sanguineous fountain that
covers her, Rebecca and all the gothic novels she is reading in a torrent
of blood. It appears to be a vivid hallucination, because the next moment
Rebecca is alone and back in the (pristine) library. The horror aesthetics of
the scene put all other references to the vampire tale into the perspective
of the fantastic. However, it does translate the intensity of the feelings of
desperation, the feel of horror experienced from an inner world, the psychological world of Rebecca, a young girl dealing with family trauma and
insecurities about friendship and physical transformations.

Sexuality is quite literally embodied in the girls' curiosity about this

Figure 2.2 *The Moth Diaries* (Mary Harron, 2011).

topic. When they return to boarding school after the summer, one of the first conversations they have in their clique is about losing their virginity – which most of them have not yet experienced. One of the girls, Sofia (Laurence Hammelin), confesses that she has found somebody to give her this experience, and she asks Rebecca and another friend to come along with her to keep watch in the fields near to the place where she will engage in coitus with the boy. While sleeping in the field Rebecca has a dream that shows how Sofia is actually raped, instead of being delicately deflowered with her consent; she wakes up with very unpleasant images in her mind. When the morning comes and Sofia returns from her sexual adventure, her answer to the question 'How was it?' is rather underwhelming. Shrugging her shoulders, she declares that it was 'kind of nothing', adding that she hopes she will get used to it and is glad it is over. The loss of virginity has not often been portrayed in such a sobering way. This is in stark contrast with the usual erotically mesmerising power of the vampire, whose bite literally hooks its victim to its embrace; as cruel and vicious as it may be, it is often also associated with pleasure. And so indeed, after this 'nothingness' of the sexual encounter (the kiss that Rebecca's only male literature teacher gives her may also count as such a voided moment), she watches Lucy and Ernessa in an embrace that resembles Henri Fuseli's 1781 painting *The Nightmare*, of a demon attached to a woman's chest. Rebecca is shocked but also fascinated and jealous, since sex seems to be an overwhelming experience after all. In *The Moth Diaries*, the question of sexuality moves between these two extremes: nothing, or something that at best one can become accustomed to; and complete absorption and annihilation by the other in a vampiric encounter. All of this is hidden by the neat appearance of the school uniforms, which cloak the girls in shrouds of decency.

Like blood and sex, the third element of the vampire myth, death, is everywhere in *The Moth Diaries*. First of all, people are literally dying in the school. Rebecca's friend Dora (Melissa Farman) falls from her window, probably after she goes out on the ledge to peek into Ernessa's room, something that Rebecca did the night before when she discovered that it was filled with moths. In addition, one of the (cruel) teachers is found dead in the woods, another accident. Under Ernessa's spell, Lucy loses so much strength that she succumbs. Was she anorectic or suffering from some other illness after all? Was she perhaps literally suffocating in the possessive friendship of Rebecca, 'pulling her down with her pain' as she exclaims just before she dies? Rebecca blames Ernessa when the red flowers that she brings to Lucy in the hospital fade after Ernessa has visited.

However, the main reference to death is associated with Rebecca's trauma, the suicide of her father. Towards the end of the film, we see another memory flash of her finding her father, who cut both of his wrists in the bathtub. All through the film Rebecca wonders if she suffers from the same disease as her father, playing with the razor blade that she uses as a bookmark in her Carmilla novel, where she reads that 'a person may become a vampire if he dies unseen'. Her father wanted to die unseen. Furthermore, there is always Ernessa to remind her of the question of the death of her father, as Ernessa's father, as will become clear, chose a similar fate in the distant past. While Ernessa retains all the familiar vampire traits (including a coffin in the basement), she also transforms into a ghost from a bygone era when Rebecca finds a diary from 1907, written by Ernessa Bloch, once a guest in the hotel that became their school. This Ernessa chose to kill herself just like her father. And it is her incarnation as vampire that Rebecca has been processing in her mind all through the film, until she discovers how to walk away from death and throws away the razor blade.

So in the end, we understand that this is not an ordinary vampire film but an inner trajectory, a moth's diary indeed, where a maturing girl must to come to terms with a pain that buries its fangs in her flesh, to speak again in Woolf's terms. This pain materialises in Harron's film as a vampire girl, the alter ego and dark side of Rebecca on the road to self-discovery.

Virgin Suicides: Symptoms of a Larger Violence

It is worthwhile noting the particular role of the family with respect to vampire stories. As remarked earlier, vampires are often related to stories about suicide (and this might be another reason why Woolf's ghost resonates in all the vampire films discussed in this chapter). If we combine this with budding breasts, blood, sexual desire and the confusion of transforming bodies, the role of the family seems to be of particular importance. While not subscribing to the aesthetics of the horror genre, Sofia Coppola's first film, *The Virgin Suicides* (1999), should be mentioned in this context. Coppola's film tells the story of five sisters who, stifled by their strict father and especially their suffocating mother, are locked in the house for fear of losing their decency. The beautiful girls all commit suicide and the story is told from the perspective of their bewildered neighbour boys, who grapple to understand 'what it is to be a thirteen year old girl'. Deniz Gamze Ergüven's powerful film *Mustang* (2015), also about five sisters who are kept inside for fear of giving away their virginity before marriage, could be considered the Turkish variation of this story of imprisoning family ties. Rebecca Thomas's *Electric Children* (2013) presents an absolutely astonishing and original take on the same problem by presenting an angel-like main character who has her own way of freeing herself from an oppressive home situation and unacknowledged incest (she thinks that listening to a song on a tape recorder has made her pregnant; and yet she is fierce in her quest to find the guitar player who must be the father of the baby). I mention these films here briefly because they address vampire-like coming-of-age issues that invoke family members or social conventions as symbolic 'coffins' from which the girls can only escape as 'vampires' or 'werewolves' who break their familial ties.

Katharina Wyss's *Sarah Plays a Werewolf* (2017) can be considered a horror film within these parameters.[11] Like *The Moth Diaries*, it brings us entirely into the inner life of its main character, which makes it difficult to distinguish the line between reality and fiction, perception and feeling. Like *Retrospekt* discussed in the first chapter, it is a horror film of the subdued kind. The film is about 17-year-old Sarah (Loane Balthasar), who lives in a small town in Switzerland. She likes to act, feels increasingly lonely and has mixed-up emotions. In an interview, Wyss explained that she wanted to make a more realistic coming-of-age drama for girls that reflected the labyrinth of emotions that teenagers can get mixed up in at that transformative age (Majteles 2018). Moreover, the story was inspired by several suicides and psychiatric disorders that she witnessed closely during her own teenage years growing up in a Swiss town. She decided to film everything in the present tense, even though the beginning of the film is actually the end (we hear helicopters arriving after Sarah has drowned herself): 'It was like taking somebody out of the grave, and letting them live again for a while' (Majteles 2018). So in a way, Sarah is a vampire to begin with. But the realism of the setting subdues this horror element, unlike films that adhere more explicitly to genre tropes.

The film brings us into Sarah's mind space, and therefore, like her, we sometimes lose our grip on the border between fiction and reality. What is clear is that she does not speak for herself (her father is always speaking for her), something that Wyss recognises as typical for female coming-of-age stories. Moreover, we find here another closed family system, where the three children are never allowed to invite friends over, and where Sarah listens to opera with her father in the car – the suggestion of incest is palpable but never explicit. Sarah is weird, clumsy, irritating sometimes, lonely, does not know how to behave, and can only express herself on stage, which she does to the point of losing herself in a way that scares others. She is fascinated by violence and death, the deaths of Romeo and Juliet for instance; she declares her brother dead when he is not. She does not fit in anywhere. She is not a nice pretty girl like Valerie in *Red Riding Hood* or Rebecca in *The Moth Diaries*. As a more unsympathetic heroine, it is difficult to observe her struggle, especially when one is not aided by the typical genre conventions and poetics of blood and seduction that would add splashes of the fantastic to make it more bearable. We realise that her 'werewolf' might be nearby, within the family, within the structures of everyday life. As Wyss contends, this small story of horror can become a metaphor on a greater scale, a story that should warn us not to blame suicide (and perhaps by extension depression and other mental health disorders) simply on the 'crazy individual' but to look at the bigger picture. As she expresses it:

> That's something interesting about these suicides of my youth: it was always about a girl, and how she has a strange character, or she has too much imagination, or she's too much of a perfectionist, so that's why she killed herself. And this was always the thing, in all the stories I heard. To not see a young person as some kind of victim of something. That's a really dangerous mechanism, in a society, when we stop having solidarity with the people who break, because they are the ones who are symptoms of a larger violence. (Majteles 2018)

Like *The Moth Diaries*, *Sarah Plays a Werewolf* brings the confusion of the vampire and werewolf into the inner life of its main character, expressing the pain and sorrow of disillusionment and jealousy, insecurity in friendship and love relations, and especially, in the confinements and oppression of family trauma, including social isolation and incest. Beyond the lures of seductive and dangerous sexuality that so many vampire myths stand for, the vampire and werewolf, and the empowerment that they might offer (especially for women as vampires or as heroic vampire slayers), ultimately represent the lure of death that can end all the pain. This is a dangerous lure indeed, that demands a questioning of the poetics of blood and horror beyond its aesthetics and into the real world, to which it relates in many different ways, a point to which I return in the last section.

For now, it is important to read the poetics of horror that we have seen so far on an affective level, as a translation of real feelings: erotic attraction as well as pain and all the ugly feelings that are connected with coming of age. There is the reality of the sensation of becoming-animal that is entrapped in the poetics of horror. Elsewhere, I have explored becoming-animal and horror cinema, but let me here briefly recall a quote from Deleuze and Guattari, where they elaborate on this concept in *A Thousand Plateaus*. It should be noted that becoming-animal takes place on the level of affects that allow connection to another being at the level of molecules, speeds and slowness, where the 'I' dissolves:

> Man does not become wolf, or vampire, as if he changed molar species; the vampire and werewolf are becomings of man, in other words, proximities between molecules in composition, relations of movement and rest, speed and slowness between emitted particles. Of course there are werewolves and vampires, we say this with all our heart; but do not look for a resemblance or analogy to the animal, for this is becoming-animal in action, the production of molecular animal . . . (Deleuze and Guattari 1988: 275)

I think it is important to keep in mind that the poetics of horror embodies this reality of the feel of horror on an affective level, something of the animal's (the bat, the moth, the wolf), movements, gestures and sensual perceptions that enters into intense and intimate proximity with humans. While we feel the attraction, the pain, the fear and confusion raised by the images and sounds of the films, we understand that they may actually stand for psychological and social traumas.[12]

Forever Young: Sucking the Life out of Others

Besides sexual transgression, sexual awakening and the pains and sorrow of coming of age, the vampire is imbued with all kinds of magical powers.[13] Most famously (or notoriously) vampires, like zombies and werewolves, do not die; they can live for eternity, unless they are killed via a special ritual (with a silver bullet, a cross, or some other ritualistic gesture). All these monstrous creatures feed on blood (or raw flesh), but the special benefit of the vampire is the promise of eternal youth. A few female directors have picked up this theme in their revisions of the vampire myth. With the period costume drama *The Countess* (2009), Delpy presents her take on the myth of the historical figure Elizabeth Bathory, the cruel countess who lived from 1560 to 1614 and allegedly killed over 400 virgins so as to bathe in their blood to remain youthful. Delpy, who wrote the story, directed the film, composed the music and played the leading role, certainly provides a feminist interpretation of the bloody countess. Her version of Bathory is a sharp-tongued rich woman who is feared by the king and to whom he is indebted. Even during a banquet with noblemen (who speak aloud their doubt about the female intellect, 'always clouded by emotions') she remains unmoved. When the bishop (dressed in full regalia) asks her what her weakness is, she replies, 'I'm a woman, I like beautiful dresses and jewellery, just like you Bishop.' The bishop is not amused, and during the film there are multiple references to the witch-hunts conducted by the Church and state.

When her husband dies, the countess is courted by Gyorgy Thurzo (William Hurt), who seeks to steal her money and land. But instead of accepting his marriage proposal, she falls in love with his son Istvan (Daniel Brühl); she also occasionally sleeps with one of her female servants, Darvulia (Annamaria Marinca), who is accused of witchcraft. The affair with Istvan, of course, goes against the pride and plan of his father, who blocks their liaison by sending his son to Denmark to marry the daughter of a rich merchant. The countess wonders whether the age difference between her and her much younger lover was a possible cause for his departure. Consequently, she begins to look for ways to turn back time, to stay young, which is how her blood thirst comes about.

By framing the Bathory story as a failed love story (all the events are told after the fact by Istvan, who still loves her, and casts doubt on the ways in which her story has been taken up by history; 'the story that is told by those who win', he says at the beginning and end of the film), Delpy makes this famous 'mother of vampires' more humane, powerful and seductive, though in any event doomed. Because of her nobility she is not burned at the stake or beheaded, but instead is walled-up alive in her castle. 'I wish I was born a man, I would have killed thousands of men, taken over countries, burned witches, I would have been a hero', exclaims Delpy's Bathory, just before she bites herself and dies in a pool of her own blood.

A more modernised version of the vampire myth of beauty is Mika Ninagawa's exuberant and extravagant *Helter Skelter* (2012), based on the manga of the same name by Kyoko Okazaki from the 1990s, brought to contemporary Tokyo.[14] In *Helter Skelter*, there are no references to the gothic and Eastern European roots of the vampire, and there are no fangs, coffins or sensitivities to light. There is, however, the myth and promise of eternal youth and beauty, soul eaters, and lots of extreme, vermilion-coloured elements in the *mise en scène*, blood and horror. Hence, I suggest it is justifiable to view the film as a Bathory-story in contemporary Japanese style. The main character in the film is Liliko, played by the controversial 'bad girl' of Japanese cinema, Erika Sawajiri. Liliko is a fashion model and idol in Japan, 'pretty on the outside, but like fruit that bugs have eaten from within', as she is referred to in the film. Ninagawa is also a well-known fashion photographer who has directed several music videos, and this can be seen in the vivid colours and intense visual style with which the film was shot.

The film opens with a warning: 'Laughing sounds a lot like screaming'. Then, to the characteristic voice of Nina Hagen's 'Natürträne', a rapid fire of images of contemporary Tokyo girls buying beauty products (eyelashes, fake nails in bright colours, hair dye, lipstick, beauty magazines, everything shared via social media) is alternated with even more rapid-fire images of Tokyo's speeding traffic by night, and the slow and stylish unwrapping of a model (Liliko) from bandages on a set that looks like a huge sugary lollipop. Hagen's 'natural tears' immediately comments ironically on the images. Towards the end of the opening sequence, we see the model posing for her magazine covers, in an ever greater frenzy of flashing camera lights, while Hagen reaches her highest pitch. Liliko confesses in a voice-over: 'There is a sound inside me. Tic Toc it says, telling me to hurry. The sound inside me says that something will be over soon.' We return to the lollipop set, where Liliko is now unwrapped. The music suddenly stops and a thick red gush of blood spills on to a completely white floor. The title *Helter Skelter* appears over a liquid red surface. The link between the super-glamorous fashion model and the beauty pressure on girls in Tokyo is something quite recognisable for many women today, all over the world. Hagen's punk opera voice and the violence of the red splashes at the end of the prologue indicate that we are dealing with contemporary horror story.

During the rest of the film, we see how Liliko embodies another gothic figure who does not want to age, Dorian Gray. She is dressed most of the time in fury red (except in the photo shoots, where she wears all colours), in a bedroom or bathroom coloured entirely red, and all her apartment walls are covered with images of herself. Her cold-hearted manager is Hiroko Taala (Kaori Momoi), whom she calls 'Mom' following the tradition of the geisha, who were also pushed to perfection by geisha house proprietors (Kotzathanasis 2015). Mom is not unlike the Nigerian Madames that we encountered in *Joy* in the previous chapter, and is another archetype of female empowerment within the confines of patriarchy, but an empowerment that keeps the system of exploitation firmly in place. Mom pushes Liliko continually to undergo plastic surgery ('she has none of her original parts except for her eyeballs, ears and vagina', she tells a reporter), not to eat (or to throw up if she has eaten something) and to completely sell her soul for her image. The horror that was announced at the beginning arrives soon enough when Liliko discovers a black spot on her forehead. The rotting has begun, and will require more (illegal) operations, which will nevertheless not retard the process of decay.

When a new model arrives, her desperation grows. Liliko is monstrous, not because of the black spots that appear on her body, but because her body has become an empty shell. 'Whenever they click the shutter my head empties out', we hear her say. In response to the thousands and thousands of clicking shutters and flashing lights, the 'uglier' she believes she becomes. In this sense, Ninagawa's film is a biting commentary on the moral corruption and total objectification of the (female) body in con-temporary commercial media culture. Liliko abuses her assistant Michiko (Shinobu Terajima), who adores her to the point that it becomes creepy. Liliko is obsessed with perfection and remaining forever young. While the plastic surgery and the beauty products are not exactly the same as Bathory's virgin's blood, they serve the same purpose, and lead to the same self-destructive end. Towards the end of the film, Liliko, with a high sense of drama, dressed in pristine white, in front of hundreds of cameras, stabs herself in the eye; the gush of blood on the white floor that we saw in the beginning returns. Liliko falls to the floor, covered in a storm of red feathers, when presumably she dies. In any case, that is what the people around her, who throughout the film comment on her life and speak of her in the past tense, suggest. However, at the end when we see her again, bathed in red light, wearing a highly theatrical red garment and coordinat-ing eyepatch. She might be a vampire after all.

Figure 2.3 *Helter Skelter* (Mika Ninagawa, 2012).

Ferocious Bodies and Wounds in the Fabric of History

In speaking of transfusions of the vampire genre in the hands of female directors, Denis's *Trouble Every Day* (2001) is a contemporary classic that cannot be ignored.[15] The film has inspired many interesting reflections that confirm the richness of this ungraspable and idiosyncratic take on blood, lust, love and death (Nancy 2008; Beugnet 2004, 2007, 2011; Morrey 2004; Taylor 2007). I will recollect a few of the commentaries on this film to bring them into focus within the frame of 'new blood' in contemporary horror cinema. First, a return to Nancy's passionate tribute to what he calls Denis's 'icon of fury'. Nancy's reading takes place entirely on the formal material level of the film, beginning with the kiss–image at the beginning, the kiss that wants blood, the kiss that is the beginning of the fury. Lips touching skin is not only touching but 'takes touch to its most extreme point: where touching becomes searching, touching under the skin, tearing out what it covers up, what it protects and announces, what it signals as the layer and the stream that it encloses' (Nancy 2008: 3). The kiss, according to Nancy, also mingles souls as 'the bloody bite explodes the soul: blood, life, spirit, desire, irrigation giving way to irritation in the impossibility of coming to an end, of getting to the end of the soul without becoming lost, gorged with blood' (Nancy 2008: 3). The film, Nancy observes, is one of pure passion, pure rage, pure fury where the body cannot but disintegrate, at the limits of pleasure. Nancy zooms in on the images of blood, beginning with the kiss of a just-married American couple, June and Shane Brown (Tricia Vessey and Vincent Gallo), in an aeroplane on their way to Paris, and the mysterious and haunting moment later when the husband retreats to the toilet and has visions of his bride completely drenched in blood, erotically bathing in a red fluid. We immediately understand that something dangerous looms in his mind, underneath the images of the couple on honeymoon. Nancy remarks that the bride has a bite mark on her skin that keeps her intact, but marked. Throughout the film, June will remain somehow like a counterpoint to the vampire, a reference to the endangered purity of virginity with which the vampire is traditionally so obsessed. I will return to this point shortly, but for now I want to dwell a little longer with Nancy's formal take on the blood-image of fury.

The epitome of fury is another character in the film, Coré (Béatrice Dalle), who is afflicted by the same mysterious virus as Shane, which makes her uncontrollably blood lusty, only in a more advanced state (Shane is still looking for deliverance but Coré has long passed this stage). We see her escaping into the streets (indeed, her black coat recalls bat wings), hunting down her next prey. Her husband, Léo (Alex Descas), always finds her, cleans up the mess, and locks her up in their house to prevent further trouble. Until one day Coré, exhausted after another cruel bloody seduction, descends the staircase, soaked in blood, and sets fire to the house.

The narrative, however, is not important. Nancy emphasises the ways in which this element of bloody fury, which touches the body, the soul and the image in Denis's film, has reached the substance of vision itself: 'a vision like livid, exposed flesh. Eyes full of blood, eyes injected with blood, plunged into a scene where the only thing to see is unbearable, invisible excess, where screams and groans disgorge the saturated color, the screen like a sponge' (Nancy 2008: 4). The screen is torn into a wound streaming with blood, Nancy continues: 'the image becomes a torn image: no longer an image, or a figure, but an icon of access to the invisible' (2008: 6). Shane and Coré, the man and the woman, move between vampiric-erotic symbols and the savage act of rape, including biting to death, Nancy writes. They are the mad woman and the maniac, between mythology and sickness, the hyperbole of monstrosity, and 'the film takes the risk of slipping between them' (2008: 8). The blood-image is an icon of impossible access to the invisible realms of our physical and mental realities. Taking a more theoretical approach in referring to genre theories and psychological explanations of horror, David Morrey also emphasises the material levels on which *Trouble Every Day* rewrites the horror genre to highlight 'the interpenetration of mind and matter that constitutes our experience of the world' (Morrey 2004: 5–6).

Of course, it is possible to add a more semantic and metaphoric reading to the poetics of blood in Denis's film. This is what Kate Taylor proposes in her analysis of the monstrous abject bodies of Shane and Coré from a postcolonial critical perspective. She discusses how we learn about the nature of the infection that Coré and Shane are suffering from, and that it is related to the 'experimentation and the genetic modification of various African natural plant extracts' (Taylor 2007: 26). The plants have invaded their brains (suggested by brain-tissue samples in the lab that Shane visits) and turned them both monstrous. We also learn that they became infected because they stole Léo's work and misused it. As Taylor argues, rather than a Frankenstein gone mad, Léo tries to repair and control the damage done. Metaphorically speaking, there is another message hidden, as 'the figure of Léo [is] infused with the legacy of the French colonial past'. Linked frequently with Africa,

> in his attempts to protect Coré, the postcolonial body (Léo) is still having to collude with the white (wo)man. In terms of Foucauldian relations of power, Coré as a white, French, ex-colonial body has great power over Léo, the black postcolonial body; however, Léo's attempts to control Coré, although they fail, can be seen as an attempt to invert the old colonial power relationships. (Taylor 2007: 26)

Stealing and misusing the plants and the research also point to the greed of Western capitalism (Shane works for a pharmaceutical company), and brings in another layer of neo-colonial capitalism. Taylor thus frames Denis's non-normative use of the horror genre, which defies the traditional oppositions between genders and races (as analysed, for instance, by Creed and Clover in the modern horror films of the 1970s and 1980s), and opens up the discourse on monstrosity: 'Denis's film explodes this mythology, thus critiquing the structures that offer up the "other" as monstrous and highlighting how the infection that Coré and Shane suffer from is an extreme outcome of normative narratives, or in other words, capitalism at its most beastly' (Taylor 2007: 28).

Martine Beugnet brings materialism and postcolonial critique and historicity together in her article 'The Wounded Screen', where she makes a compelling comparison between the French political historical backgrounds of Agnès Varda's *Cléo from 5 to 7* (1962) and *Trouble Every Day*. She reads Cléo's (fear of) cancer allegorically as the colonial, as a cancer within the national body (Beugnet 2011: 35), and the gothic city that Paris has turned into in *Trouble Every Day* as a reference to monstrous colonial legacies. Weaving the images of blood and wounds into the tapestry of history, and arguing that 'history is reality in the flesh', Beugnet concludes that ' "to speak of history's horrors, or historical trauma, is to recognize

events as wounds . . . wounds in the fabric of culture and history that bleed
through conventional confines of time and space"' (Lowenstein quoted in
Beugnet 2011: 39). With all the ontological force of the materiality of the
body and the screen that Nancy addresses, the wounds of colonial history
and the postcolonial present bleed through the screen as well.

By means of these references to some of the profound reflections that
Denis's film provokes, I would like to emphasise that the intertwined
material and metaphoric poetics of horror and blood are exactly what
makes the new blood of contemporary horror cinema innovative as a
creative and critical practice. I now want to introduce one more character who I have not yet discussed, that of the innocent bride figure who
Shane wants to keep untouched, uncontaminated. June indeed looks like
Audrey Hepburn, in anachronistic suits that could have been worn by
Tippi Hedren, and she has been referred to as a girl entering womanhood,
like many of the heroines in the coming-of-age vampire stories discussed
earlier in this chapter. And with respect to her character, too, we can see
how Denis plays with the material elements in the *mise en scène* to perhaps
uncover another message (one that is never self-evident). Nancy remarked
that at the beginning of the film she has a bite mark that places her on
the threshold of the danger zone. When they arrive at the hotel, while
embracing, Shane tells June that he will never hurt her. Considering the
bloody visions on his mind-screen that we have already seen, this sounds
ominous. Shortly thereafter, they are on top of Notre Dame cathedral,
where Shane embodies the gestures of a classical Nosferatu, a joking reference of course to what is going on in his body and mind. June appears
ravishing in a black coat and bright-green scarf, which she removes and
which then flies away over the Parisian skyline. Morrey mentions this
remarkably beautiful scene as another example of the materialism of
Denis's approach. I think we can also add here the symbolism of colour.
Her scarf is green, and although green can have many different connotations depending on the context (I will return to the colour green again in
the last chapter), here it is clear that green signifies safety, a safety that
is lost with the green scarf flying over Paris. In the final moments of the
film, June returns to their hotel room, wearing bright-red gloves. On her
upper lip we can observe a tiny, blood-encrusted wound. Shane is in the
shower and when she enters the bathroom, he has barely washed away all
the blood from his body (the blood of one of the hotel's cleaning women,
whom he has literally devoured moments before). They embrace; we
see one watery-red stream still running down the shower curtain. The
film ends with June looking, the redness of her gloves just visible at the
edge of the frame. Everything suggests that her virginity and innocence

are over, just as white innocence is over with respect to the postcolonial situation (Wekker 2016).

Mixing Blood: New Ethics of Vampirism

Except for *Helter Skelter*, the female-directed vampires that I have discussed so far in this chapter are in one way or another all descendants of white European gothic horror, even if they are subverted to a greater or lesser extent. Obviously, there are vampires that are more diverse. In her 1897 novel *The Blood of the Vampire*, the British writer Florence Marryat presented Harriet Brandt, a Creole succubus-vampire of mixed blood.[16] As Brenda Mann Hammack asserts, Marryat's vampire is completely framed within the Victorian fear of the 'mixing and confounding of species that Nature would not allow' (Hammack 2008: 888). Harriet is frequently associated with large cats, puma, panthers, lynxes and tigers, and 'embodies or replicates the social and scientific conventions of its day rather than critiquing or at least illuminating them' (Hammack 2008: 893). Considering the transnational variants of vampire stories in many cultures of the world, the dominance of its pale white gothic versions remains striking.[17] Nevertheless, new and racially diverse variants of the vampire continue to gain influence (Löffler and Bast 2011; Höglund and Khair 2013). Jewelle Gomez, for instance, in 1991 presented Gilda, a black lesbian vampire, in her collection *The Gilda Stories* (Gomez 2016), who is much less fear-inducing than other vampire ancestors. As Virginia Fusco argues, Gomez's black feminism challenges gothic literary traditions as 'she promotes bloodletting as a means to survival and a "queer sexuality" as a "symbolic" vehicle of care and affection' (Fusco 2014: 245). In several stories, each moving through different episodes of American history, Gilda takes us from slavery to its abolition, the emergence of an educated black middle class and into the near future, presenting an alternative black historiography. Like the figure of Léo in Denis's film, Gomez's black lesbian vampire is far removed from the violent and scary stereotypes of 'otherness' so often encountered in monstrous figures in dominant (white, patriarchal) narratives and images, even if in the end Gilda does not escape discrimination.

In *Fledgling* (2005), her last book before her untimely death in 2006, Butler also presented a very different and refreshing type of vampire – perhaps, indeed, the kind of vampire this age needs, as Ali Brox argues in her evaluation of Butler's vampire vision. *Fledgling*'s vampire is named Shori, a black female who is actually 53 years old but appears as a young girl who 'blurs the lines among race and species through conflicting instances of acceptance and rejection of hybridity' (Brox 2008: 393). Due to an attempt on her life, which she survived but which wiped out her entire family, she has lost her memory. The narrative takes us, together with Shori, on a journey to discover her powers, her history and the manner in which she lives. Like Gomez's vampire, Shori is not a dangerous monster. While she certainly needs blood to regain strength (and raw meat to heal her wounds), Shori belongs to the Ina-vampire race that lives alongside humans. Each Ina has a group of (male and female) human 'symbionts' to whom they are connected both affectionately and sexually. Since she lost all her symbionts in the attack, Shori assembles a new community of loved ones around her. While the Ina feed on their symbionts, their blood is rejuvenated; consequently, the humans can grow older and stronger as well. Moreover, the bonds are mutually addictive. There is a level of intense and intimate proximity between species that can only be described in terms of becomings, the contact zone of molecular movements and sense perception. Shori's animal-like qualities are mostly distinguishable by the different ways she can engage her olfactory sense in an intensely territorial, animal-like way (symbionts and Ina connect through smell), and the way she can propel herself at great speeds (Ferreira 2010). Hence, both Ina-vampires and symbiont-humans are locked into a hybrid relationship of blood exchange and becoming.

And yet Shori herself is even more hybrid, since it becomes clear that she is the result of a DNA experiment that infused her vampire DNA with human DNA, which makes her skin darker and more resilient against sunlight. Shori is the only Ina that can remain awake during daylight hours and does not burn from exposure to the sun (provided she is well protected by clothing and dark glasses). Not all Ina families appreciate this miscegenation, which ensures that Shori and her (new) family face murderous attacks that during the course of the novel are managed according to age-old Ina law. There is racism among certain Ina groups in Butler's speculative fictional world, which otherwise presents an extremely non-normative conception of sexual and family practices as well as power structures of alliances, rather than of domination (Lacey 2008). Susana Morris argues that Butler's vampires not only transgress conventional tropes of monstrous entities because they create communities of love and care, but also because they experience and succumb to 'hierarchical division, such as those of racism, mirroring the violent systems of oppression that are the foundation of much of the human world' (Morris 2012: 161). In this way, Butler demonstrates that the true problem lies not in the vampire (or any other type of monstrous construction), but in our own world:

Butler's Afrofuturist feminist vision in *Fledgling*, then, illuminates the futurist potential in radically restructuring our conceptions of intimacy and family while also providing a cautionary tale about the ways in which culturally sanctioned practices of violence and discrimination can threaten even the most promising futures. (Morris 2012: 161; see also Nayar 2012)

Butler's work has been and continues to be an inspiration for many. Donna Haraway found inspiration in her work when she developed her cyborg theory in the late 1980s (Haraway 1991) and Butler's speculative fiction continues to be an influence in her later work, which is equally full of symbionts and speculative fiction (Haraway 2016). The artists of the Otolith Group, Kodwo Eshun and Anjalika Sagar, present their films and video installations with explicit reference to Butler's *Xenogenesis* trilogy (*Dawn*, 1987; *Adulthood Rites*, 1988; *Imago*, 1989), in opening their over-view show *Xenogenesis* with a huge portrait of Butler at the entrance.[18] However, they never refer directly to her work. According to the Otolith Group, the translation of Butler's work into popular culture is taking a long time because the world is not yet ready for the 'white fragility' and 'black complexity' that her writings present (Bodegom 2019: 54). Ava Duvernay, however, is reported to be working on a screen adaptation of Butler's *Dawn*. And Nikyatu Jusu's short film *Suicide by Sunlight* (2018) is motivated by (among others) Butler's *Fledgling* and West African and Caribbean vampire myths.[19] Like Shori, Valentina (Natalie Paul) in *Suicide by Sunlight* is a black female vampire who is protected from the sunlight by her melanin. *Suicide by Sunlight* is intended to be the pilot for a series of films about the near future in which African–American vampires walk the streets of New York. Their only sign of vampirism is an occasional illumination of their eyes that radiate like small suns, and a vague light that seems to shine through their black skins but does not kill them. Working in a hospital, Valentina is struggling to see her daughters Faith and Hope, and must juggle different urges ranging from protection and care to lust for blood and aggression. Visually stunning, this short film is another indication that, very soon, the world will be ready for Butler's complex trans-human figures on screen.

For now, I want to raise Butler's vampire story as a way of imagining the poetics of horror as a poetics of relation. In this way, Butler's fiction is close to Glissant's emphasis on a poetics of relation that acknowledges how, on a deep historical level, we are all related. Valéria Loichot has analysed how Butler's novel *Kindred* provides what Glissant has called 'prophetic visions of the past' (Loichot 2009: 40), addressing the violence of slavery by 'inserting into the past a medial technique from the future'; this allows *Kindred*'s heroine, Dana, to succeed not only in 'giving birth to her ancestor, and by the same token in securing her own future birth, but also in escaping, albeit for a short time, her immediate violent categorization and settling in the established structure of slavery' (Loichot 2009: 44). I will return to *Kindred* in Chapter 5. Here, I want to turn to another vampire film directed by a woman that equally presents a very different kind of vampire girl, and that transfuses the poetics of horror with a poetics of relation.

Ana Lily Amirpour's *A Girl Walks Home Alone at Night* can only be described in relational terms: a black-and-white Iranian-American spaghetti Western vampire film that presents a lonely chador-wearing girlish vampire roaming the deserted streets of Bad City. The film opens with a James Dean-like young man, in white T-shirt and jeans, smoking a cigarette and leaning against a wooden shed. He throws away the cigarette, steps into the shed, comes out with a cat and begins walking the empty roads of a desolate town. Meanwhile on the soundtrack a gravelly voice (Arash Sobhani from the Iranian rock band Kiosk) starts singing 'Charkesh e Pooch'. We see a close-up of a transwoman (Reza Sixo Safai), her eyes following the young man passing her by. The landscape is now industrial. With the next shot, the singing voice warps when the young man and his cat cross a bridge that bisects a glen strewn with bodies. It seems nothing special to the young man as he casually continues his walk. The voice on the soundtrack, however, distorts further and seems to lose its life force, like a radio with an almost-empty battery. With a loud bang and in spaghetti-Western letter type the title of the film appears: 'A Girl Walks Home Alone at Night'. The white letters gradually change to black.

It will take a while, though, before we will meet the titular girl. First, we discover the forsaken town, Bad City, and its industrial surroundings that are chockful of pumping hydraulic jacks. These so-called nodding donkeys extracting oil not only resonate with the iconography of James Dean's vehicle *Giant* (dir. George Stevens, 1957), but also indicate the intricate oil connection between the United States and Iran, a reminder perhaps also of the great dependence of America on oil from the Middle East. The isolation of the municipality recalls typical deserted Western towns, but it is mixed with industrial elements and eccentric characters who inhabit the place. The young man from the opening, Arash (Arash Marandi), takes care of his father Hossein (Marshall Manesh), who has become addicted to heroin after the death of his wife. We also encounter a nameless young boy, a street urchin and silent witness (Milad Ekhbali), and the self-assured Saeed (Dominic Rains), who seems like the devil incarnate, with the words 'sex' and 'pimp' (in Farsi) tattooed on his neck. He maltreats Atti (Mozhan Marnó), a prostitute who he throws out of a car (a convertible 1957 Ford Thunderbird that he brutally confiscates from Arash as payment for his father's drugs). The characters speak little, but when they do speak, they speak Farsi. It is only after fifteen minutes, when Saeed is busy abusing Atti in the car, that we see the first glimpse of the 'Girl' (Sheila Vand). She looks at the car from a distance; the camera shoots her black shadowy chador/cape from the back while in a diagonal line we see the car at a short distance, looking along her line of sight. Inside the car, Saeed notices the shadow. I will return later to this diagonal image composition.

First a few remarks about the *mise en scène* and the characters. In interviews, Amirpour, born in the United Kingdom to Iranian parents, who immigrated to the United States when she was young, declares that Bad City, the Iranian ghost town, shot in Bakersfield, California, was 'the Iranian environment in my brain' (Juzwiak 2014). Together with Sheila Vand, she affirms that 'we kind of made our own place that was as Iranian as we are, which is a mash-up of so many things' (Ito 2014). On every level of the film, the 'mash-up aesthetics' creates a unique poetics of relations via its style elements. Bad City as Iranian town has a touch of David Lynch's *Twin Peaks* and Antonioni's *Red Desert* about it. The iconography further combines James Dean's coolness with 1980s pop culture, drag and costume parties and the Iranian chador; Gothic European fiction with Sergio Leone's Italian versions of the Western. This spaghetti-Western feel is mainly evoked through Federale's soundtrack 'which is like the musical spine of the film' (Amirpour quoted in Edelstein 2014). The soundtrack itself is completely hybrid; it combines the music of Iranian rock groups Kiosk and Radio Teheran ('like the Iranian The Cure'), American Armenian composer Bei Ru, the British band White Lies and German techno from Daniel Brandt. Amirpour found many of her crew and cast among the large group of Iranian film professionals in Los Angeles when she won an award in 2007 for a script she had written about teenagers living in Iran. 'All these people came into my orbit, because they want to do stuff that is not like "Terrorist 1" and "Terrorist 2" on *24*' (Ito 2014). For all the familiar elements that the film plays with, nothing is stereotypical in *A Girl Walks Home Alone at Night*. With its unique aesthetics, it weaves a tapestry of pop cultural relations that makes visible the complexity of transnational and diasporic identities that is the reality for so many people in the contemporary world, and that does not often find its translation to the big screen.

In their analysis of Amirpour's film, Shadde Abdi and Bernadete Calafell call the Girl the reimagining of a superhero as a 'monstrous feminist' (Abdi and Calafell 2017). It is an interesting twist on the monstrous feminine, because it immediately gives agency to the heroine. As a vampire feminist, she embraces the chador, a black scarf. While the chador and the veil are contested symbols in both Western and Islamic feminism, clearly here

> the chador, which covers her entire body, allows the vampire to be simultane-ously visible and hidden, therefore enabling possibilities for transgression. By re-imagining the chador as a superhero's cape and a source of strength, Amirpour's vision embraces the complexities and contradictions that many (queer) Iranian and Iranian-American women must live with. (Abdi and Calafell 2017: 363)

The Girl's monstrous feminism is also expressed in her ethics. Like Shori in Butler's *Fledgling* and Gomez's Gilda, she has a protective side, choos-ing her victims in some sort of 'poetic justice' kind of way. While we can assume that the bodies under the bridge might be victims of the Girl, they might metaphorically translate into the victims of so many oppressive systems that are embodied in certain scenes and characters.

Obviously, the abusive Saeed is her first victim, whom she symbolically castrates by biting his finger. She only warns the street urchin to 'be a good boy' and tells him that she will always be watching him. Most notable is that she protects Atti, the prostitute, not only from Saeed, but later also from Hossein, who drugs her against her will. 'The Girl is a protector of women, and, by virtue, humankind in general', Abdi and Calafell argue (2017: 364). Thus, the Girl and Atti are connected, but not in the usual way of the predatory lesbian vampire in many of the queer vampire films we know. Arash meets the Girl after a costume party where he shows up as Dracula: 'I'm Dracula, I won't hurt you', he introduces himself (sound-ing much less menacing than Shane in *Trouble Every Day*). When he feels her cold hands, he wraps his cape around her; shocked by this unexpected gesture, she invites Arash to her home where she hesitates but chooses not to bite him, 'instead relishing in the possibility of humanity denied to her' (Abdi and Calafell 2017: 365). The vampire Girl is poor, lonely, a woman, perhaps queer and ethnically other (she is the only one wearing a chador in the film). The violence of patriarchy, class, gender and race she is fighting is embodied in the film not only in the character of Saeed, but also in the wealthy people for whom Arash works; in a television advertisement in which a man addresses an imagined woman, declaring that she will prob-ably one day lose her husband to a younger woman; and in the connections to the 'underdog' characters in the film, the drag queen, the prostitute and Arash, who lives in poverty with his father even if he does have a job.

However, rather than just the narrative elements, it is the film's aes-thetics that create this oneiric quality that makes it a place of the mind, an inner kind of dream world that begins to operate on its own. The graphic qualities of the completely constructed set, the black-and-white photography, the soundtrack and the cinematography create their own poetics. Most strikingly in the cinematography, there are vertical and diagonal lines between the Girl and her potential victims. She watches them always from a distance at first, and then follows them. An exemplary scene occurs when the Girl in her chador follows Hossein on the street at night. They are on opposite sides of the street, and in a reversal of the expected situation (the man following the woman); she follows him until he becomes frightened. Another beautiful vertical moment in the *mise en scène* is when the Girl brings Arash to her residence. She puts on 'Death' by the White Lies; Arash (still in his Dracula cape) is high on drugs from the party and stares at the mesmerising illuminations in the Girl's room. Then a close-up reveals just the Girl listening to the music, bathed in twinkling light reflected by the disco ball. After a while, from the left side of the image, Arash moves onto the screen, looking at her neck; he moves slowly towards her. When their silhouettes meet, she very slowly turns around, looks him in the eyes, bends his head backwards to expose his throat, and, after a moment of hesitation, rests her head on his heart. As Abdi and Calafell observe, this scene is immediately followed by a more abstract scene of the transwoman dancing with a balloon, marking a 'queer doubling of the vampire: we see the joy of the transwoman capturing and dancing with the balloon mirroring the joy the Girl feels in finding intimacy with Arash' (Abdi and Calafell 2017: 365). The juxtaposition of these scenes is a powerful instance of a poetics of relation, full of enigmatic opacity and connection.

The choice to shoot in black and white ensures that blood in this film appears black. Red appears on the posters but is absent from the *mise en scène* of the film. However, as Richard Misek has pointed out, in black-and-white film, blood is an example of an 'absent colour, that trace of colour reality that underlies black-and-white-images' (2010: 83). In a similar vein, the black blood in *A Girl Walks Home Alone at Night* signifies the traces of reality that underlie the dream logic of the film.

A final note on Amirpour's vampire Western needs to address a comparison with Bigelow's early vampire Western, discussed at the beginning of this chapter. Contrary to Bigelow's romantic vampire-human protagonist couple, the Girl does not revert to having clean blood. On the contrary, Arash, fully aware of the 'bad/bat girl' that he has fallen in love with, does not try to turn her. Like Atti, he understands where she is coming from, what her blood thirst stands for; they decide to leave Bad City together in his Thunderbird. Again, this is a scene marked by a slowness of mutual recognition when in the car we see them (almost in slow motion) look at each other. The cat that Arash picked up at the beginning of the film (another transformed symbol from horrific monstrous femininity to a figure of relation) is sitting in the middle of the car between them, staring directly at the spectator, inviting further connections and extending the poiesis of the film.

Dark Blood of the Body of Mythology and History

The 'dark blood' of the vampire in this chapter has traced a trail from the fantasy of transgressive (lesbian) sexuality to the confusions of bodily transformation and awaking sexuality in coming-of-age stories, as well as the ugly feelings and deep traumatic (family) traumas that the vampire and its kindred spirit the werewolf can unleash. The vampire's promise of eternal youth has its roots in the Bathory myth that finds its terrifying incarnation in contemporary culture's insistence on the normativity of

Figure 2.4 *A Girl Walks Home Alone at Night* (Ana Lily Amirpour, 2014).

perfection. The vampire also relates to contemporary global capitalism in a way that transmits its blood to the legacies of colonialism. Finally, the vampire is also an empowering figure when the poetics of horror transmutes into a poetics of relation that transgresses dominant relations. All through the work of the female directors discussed in this chapter, we see that the vampire increasingly translates inner worlds, landscapes of the imaginary that transfuse the poetics of horror into the feel of horror by connecting inner and outer worlds. Most importantly, the poetics of the blood-images discussed in this chapter demonstrate that the material and the metaphoric are bound by contagious affiliations that cannot be disentangled.

CHAPTER 3

Longing and Lust, 'Red Light' on a 'Dark Continent'

The Horror of Female Sexuality

'I'm fed up with the way women's sexuality is portrayed on screen', director Julia Ducournau exclaims in an interview about her film *Raw* (Thomas 2017). She adds that female sexuality in cinema is often presented as a victim story about fear, doubts and anxiety about reputation. Alternatively, we may add, female desire and sexuality are conceived as Sigmund Freud's infamous 'dark continent'. In *The Question of Lay Analysis* Freud wrote, 'We know less about the sexual life of little girls than of boys. But we need not feel ashamed of this distinction; after all, the sexual life of adult women is a "dark continent" for psychology' (Freud 1959: 212). And so women in cinema are often portrayed stereotypically as either innocent victim or *femme fatale*, virgin or whore. In line with this unknowable and hostile conception of female sexuality, the horror genre has connected this sexuality to danger: the danger of being assaulted by a castrating woman with occult powers or of girls becoming possessed when the age of mature sexuality and menstruation arrives. Regan in *The Exorcist* (dir. William Friedkin, 1974) and Carrie are cases in point. Moreover, the sexual pleasure of women is usually punished, not only in horror cinema where, as a basic rule, only the final girl who does not have sex survives, but also in other genres such as melodrama. Think of *Mildred Pierce* (dir. Michael Curtiz, 1945; dir. Todd Haynes, 2011), in which Mildred loses her youngest daughter the moment she takes a lover and becomes sexually transgressive. So what happens when women address the sexuality of their own lived experiences? How and when does sexuality become entangled with a poetics of horror in a female address of the camera?

While this chapter shares some of the coming-of-age elements of sexual awakening with the previous chapter's vampire kisses, we will dive more deeply into the 'impenetrable darkness' of female sexuality as explored and expressed by women. As in the other chapters there will be blood, of differing types: menstrual blood, once more, but as a sign of sexual maturity; animal blood; ritual blood; and the blood of victims. There will also be a lot of red: the infamous 'red lights' of prostitution are transformed into ruby filters, scarlet spots and specks that express female sexuality on their own terms. Virginia Woolf's daughters have come a long way from her more covert and metaphorical ways of addressing sexuality. The heroines we encounter in the following pages could be described as vulgar, perverse, lacking shame, or as witches, cannibals or final girls, but they do not exactly behave according to conventional dictates. Interwoven with accounts of some chief theoretical positions regarding female sexuality, this chapter will first return to some early female perspectives on sexuality in the work of Carolee Schneemann and other 'bloody' avant-garde artists who have dared to be outspoken about desire, hetero- and homosexuality. The middle part of this chapter is devoted to 'hard core' horror which brings us to, among others, Ducournau's *Raw* and other intense and unsettling visualisations of longing and lust in female experience. Finally, I return to the more poetic erotic horror of *In the Cut* (dir. Jane Campion, 2003), *Body and Soul* (dir. Ildikó Enyedi, 2017) and *Longing for the Rain* (dir. Lina Yang, 2013).

From 'A Match Burning in a Crocus' to a Slithering 'Interior Scroll'

As indicated in Chapter 1, Woolf was very conscious of the fact that she did not dare to speak frankly and freely about her bodily self, which does not mean that she was a purely intellectual writer. Erotic desire, especially of and for women, is present everywhere in her work, often disguised in metaphorical language, and has been commented upon frequently. As Patricia Morgne Cramer explains, the covert way of addressing female sexuality, apart from personal character and class background, is quite understandable, since in the Victorian context in which Woolf was writing public exposure of female desire, let alone homosexual desire, was dangerous.

> Because Woolf protected her privacy, cared not to hurt [her husband] Leonard, and justifiably feared public exposure, we cannot expect to find such overt self-definition in diaries or letters. Besides, 'coming out' with a public declaration of gay identity is a recent gay and lesbian tradition, so it is anachronistic to impose such criteria on Woolf or others of her generation. (Morgne Cramer 2013: 130)

Hence, 'I cannot say what I feel. But I feel it! . . . I can see it. I can touch it, I cannot say it', from the drafts of her novel *The Years* (quoted in

Morgne Cramer 2010: 180), are exemplary moments when Woolf explicitly hits the stumbling block of the demons of public opinion and normative gender decency that she mentioned in 'Professions for Women' and
that I raised in Chapter 1.

Nevertheless, Woolf often 'mocks chastity ideals by exposing men's
adoration of idealized women as masks for their domestic abuse, narcis-
sism or repressed homosexuality' (Morgne Cramer 2010: 181). Her novels
present many female characters who desire other women, as expressed
in Lily's paintings and her love for Mrs Ramsay in *To the Lighthouse*,
Clarissa's lifelong regret about the loss of Sally in *Mrs Dalloway* (as well
as Septimus's repeated cry for Evans in the same novel), Rhoda's longing
for Alice in *The Waves* and Kitty and Eleanor's kiss and feeling queer in
The Years; and of course Woolf's autobiographical 'declaration of love'
to Vita Sackville West in *Orlando*. Morgne Cramer points out that Woolf
constructed new languages for such feelings that were adequate for the
tabooed emotions and desires of the time. Love memories and vulva imag-
inaries written in metaphorical terms are part of that language: 'a little
ball kept bubbling up and down on the spray of a fountain' (Woolf 1999:
369) or 'a match burning in a crocus' or a 'diamond . . . infinitely precious,
wrapped up' (Woolf 1992: 35) are some of the noteworthy and famous
examples. This reticence was particularly necessary considering the fact
that at the time men equated female sexual knowledge with pathology and
deviance: 'The belief in inborn female sexual passivity was so extensive
that some physicians considered a woman who expressed even heterosexual desire pathological' (Morgne Cramer 2010: 189). Therefore, it remains
remarkable even today to see how Woolf invented a new type of language
to describe experiences of female sexuality for which there were no words
before.

It took until the 1960s for women to break these taboos of sexual passivity and chastity and bring explicit female sexuality to the screen. It was
only then that several women artists began to address taboos about the
female body, menstruation, leaky bodies and the vagina that for centuries
had been (and still are in many ways and in different parts of the world)
surrounded by religious and patriarchal rules of concealment and restric-
tion. One of the most remarkable artists who I want to recall here for her
taboo-breaking artworks and films is Schneemann.[1] Schneemann's moti-
vation for her artwork is worth quoting at length because it encompasses
many issues and problems that return in the poetics of horror of contemporary women directors that feature in this book. In 'The Obscene Body/
Politic', Schneemann argues:

Political and personal violence against women is twined behind/within this stunting defeminization of history. For many of us, the layers of implicit and explicit censorship constructing our social history combine with contemporary contradictions to force our radicalization. Even though we live in the best of times – as our reading, writing, research, and creative preeminence attest – one out of four of us will be subjected to rape; but we will not have been torn from our childhood sleep for a brutal clitoral excision (still practiced in some Islamic cultures in Africa, parts of Egypt and the Sudan, and most recently introduced into France by workers from these places). We will not have endured the probable fifteen pregnancies of our fertile years (forbidden contraception or abortion); so we are less likely to have died giving birth; we will not be burned as witches or sold into slavery, and even the most transgressive among us may evade being locked up in an asylum. The burgeoning recent work of women in the arts is fueled by three thousand years of fracture – the masculist [*sic*] enforcement of self-righteous institutionalizations that have dogged our heels. My anger, when I first discovered this subtle and pervasive censorship, this excision, paralleled my later rage and confusion at being denied a feminine pronoun (The artist, *he* . . .) and upon discovering that my culture denies females an honorable genital. My sexuality was idealized, fetishized, but the organic experience of my own body was referred to as defiling, stinking, contaminating. (1991: 28)[2]

Schneemann's autobiographical trilogy (*Eye-Body*, *Meat Joy* and *Fuses*) from her early work is remarkable as avant-garde poetics of horror cinema. *Eye-Body* (1963) presents frontal nude photography of Schneemann with snakes crawling on her body, alluding to an archaic eroticism that was not well received. Schneemann explains that the reactions to her work made her understand that there were only two roles for her to fulfil: 'either that of "pornographer" or that of emissary of Aphrodite. But elude political and social effect insofar as these roles both function as dumping grounds that cloud constructed differences between the erotic and the obscene' (Schneemann 1991: 29). In her performances of *Meat Joy* (1964) she wanted to invigorate the culture of guilt and censorship described in the quote above. *Meat Joy* was a dance performance for nine dancers, men and women, dressed in scanty red-feather and fur coverings. They touch each other flesh to flesh, and then a woman dressed as a servant throws raw fish, chickens and sausages on them, which touches their skin and their genitals in erotic pleasure. The performances stirred up many vehement emotions and protests. In London the police stormed in and ended the piece, and in Paris a man from the audience was so enraged that he went on stage and tried to strangle Schneemann, who was rescued by three bourgeois-looking women from the audience.

Her erotic film *Fuses* (1967), featuring herself and her boyfriend James Tenney engaging in sexual intimacy (and Kitch the cat, who appears as a sort of silent witness), was greeted as much with prizes and praise as with booing and censorship (MacDonald 2016). Schneemann began filming

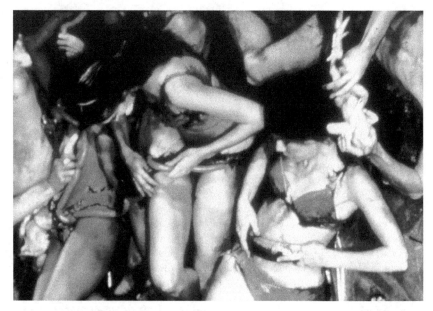

Figure 3.1 *Meat Joy* (Carolee Schneemann, 1964).

Fuses in 1964 on borrowed wind-up Super 8 Bolex cameras that allowed thirty seconds of film time for each lovemaking scene. The film material was reworked (scratched, coloured, filtered) and the result is an abstract and poetic film of an erotic encounter that displays the male genitals as much as the female genitals (both explicitly and abstractly), capturing and expressing the 'fusing' quality of lived sexuality. The equality between the partners, and the erotic quality of the images of the bodies as well as their haptic and tactile quality (Marks 1999; Barker 2009), still stands out today. However, the film was often met with strident protests, most remark-ably during its premiere at Cannes, when 'a group of forty men went berserk and tore up all the seats in the theater, slashed them with razors, shredded them, and threw all the padding around. It was terrifying, and peculiar' (MacDonald 2016: 10). On many other occasions the film stirred up intense emotions, but it is perhaps one of the first films to present a non-fetishised image of the female body in a sexual encounter.

I will return to this point in the next section when I move to the horror genre and the reactions to this 1960s and 1970s feminism. Here, I just want to mention one other work by Schneemann that is remarkable for its audacity, her performance *Interior Scroll* (1975). Schneemann comments: 'I didn't want to pull a scroll out of my vagina and read it in public, but the culture's terror of my making overt what it wished to suppress fueled the image; it was essential to demonstrate this lived action about "vulvic space" against the abstraction of the female body and its loss of meanings' (Schneemann 1991: 33). The words that are legible on the scroll (some of the performances were recorded)[3] include 'you are a monster', 'have slithered out' and 'excess' – all terms that fit the poetics of horror of contemporary filmmakers.

Schneemann's work was part of the re-evaluation of female sexuality and female genitals, which was a larger issue discussed in second wave feminism. Luce Irigaray's famous *This Sex Which is Not One* was a strong case in point for theorising sexual difference in new ways. Irigaray was considered just as rebellious as Schneemann, as an 'unruly daughter' of Jacques Lacan, thrown out of the psychoanalytic societies for her explicit rejection of Freud's penis-envy theory, which was supposed to haunt his dark continent of female sexuality. Irigaray proposes a different form of sexuality, where there is not just one phallic sexual organ, but where the female genitals have their own specific (autoerotic) qualities that go beyond simply being a passive receptacle waiting for an active male counterpart to fill up 'the lack'. In independent cinema Sarah Jacobson's low-budget *Mary Jane is not a Virgin Anymore* (1996) could be considered as an Irigarayan film, in which a young woman who works in a cinema goes on a quest for female sexuality. After the disappointing experience of losing her virginity, she asks her colleagues and friends about their first time. One of her friends advises her to take a mirror and get to know her own vagina (advice that she takes). The gritty and sleazy quality of the images combined with the frankness of addressing these intimate issues make it a still remarkable film.

Black and White Sapphic Attraction

Besides equal heterosexual relations and the autoeroticism of female sexuality, lesbian eroticism and interracial sexuality also found their way to the screen in the wake of the second wave of feminism. *She Must Be Seeing Things* (dir. Sheila Mclaughlin, 1987) and *The Watermelon Woman* (dir. Cheryl Dunye, 1996) are two remarkable films to mention among the landmark films of lesbian filmmaking.[4] While neither displays sexuality as a 'poetics of horror', it is useful to note that both films use a *mise en abyme* structure to talk about 'Sapphic sisters' (as Cheryl Dunye in *The Watermelon Woman* refers to lesbians), and thus address the importance of the female gaze and female agency via the construction of the self-reflexivity of the medium itself. Therefore, I want to briefly mention these films in this section about early voices of female sexuality. In *She Must*

Be Seeing Things filmmaker Jo (Lois Weaver) is making a film about the historical figure of the seventeenth-century nun Catalina de Erausu, who travelled under her male identity (as Alonso Diaz) through Spain. Her girlfriend Agatha (Sheila Dabney) is a lawyer who discovers Jo's old diary, which recounts all her adventures with men (including graphic Polaroids of their sexual organs), and she becomes suspicious of Jo. She begins 'seeing things' and the film takes us into the growing paranoia in her mind as she follows Jo; we see her hallucinating Jo being stabbed or in bed with men. In one scene Agatha enters a sex shop, investigating dildos and wondering if she should buy one to match some of the pictures that she found in Jo's diary. The lovers reconcile at the end of the film without giving any certainty about the illusionary or real status of the images we have seen before. While Agatha is a black woman and Jo is white, questions of race and ethnicity are never made explicit in this film; this may be telling of the white authorship of the film, in not addressing race or ethnicity as a 'white privilege', which cannot as easily be dismissed for black filmmakers.

In Cheryl Dunye's *The Watermelon Woman* Dunye herself plays the part of a black lesbian filmmaker who wants to make a film about an unnamed and uncredited black actress from the 1930s who plays the stereotypical role of a black mammie.[5] Like a vlogger *avant la lettre*, Dunye, as Cheryl who works at a video store, talks into the camera to discuss her film project. She shows us a clip from the video *Plantation Memories*, directed by Martha Page in 1937, which features an actress who is referred to as 'the watermelon woman' (without any further name). She discovers that the watermelon woman was named Faye Richards, and that she appeared to have had a relationship with the white filmmaker Page. So in Dunye's film there seems to be a sort of doubling going on between the film-in-the-film and Cheryl's story, as she also enters into a sexual relationship with a white woman, Diana (Guinevere Turner). Contrary to *She Must Be Seeing Things*, race and skin colour turn out to be issues that cannot simply be skipped over, at least not before they have also been addressed and acknowledged, as Cheryl's friend Tamara (Valarie Walker) as well as Faye's later lover and companion June (Cheryl Clarke) remind her. The relationship with Diana (who seems to be wanting to claim black history as her own) does not hold, but Cheryl discovers and retrieves much about the identity and life of Richards.

The Watermelon Woman also features Dunye's own mother, as well as the theorist Camille Paglia and people on the streets of Philadelphia who offer their 'memories' of the watermelon woman, who comes to stand for the invisibility of black lesbian women from the screen whose 'stories have never been told'. The footage from the 1930s films and the photographs of

Faye were created by Zoe Lennard, and seamlessly inserted into the film. 'Sometimes you have to create your own history. *The Watermelon Woman* is fiction', Dunye writes at the end of the film. Through this exploration of lesbian sexuality and racial identity, Dunye's film pays homage to all those hidden stories and overlooked figures in film history and history at large.

Dee Rees's sensitive and powerful debut film *Pariah* (2011) appeared fifteen years after Dunye's film.[6] *Pariah* is the coming-of-age story of Alika/Lee (Adepero Oduye), who struggles with her coming out, especially in relation to her mother. Rees's film also does not employ a direct poetics of horror. Rather it could be seen as a 'poetics of power' – even if many of the scenes where Alika/Lee feels at home, such as in an all-women's club, are colour-coded by red light and settings. As Frances White argues in her book *Dark Continents of our Bodies*, black feminism needs these stories that break with what she calls 'the politics of respectability'. As she puts it:

> In the arena of sexuality, we have allowed our history under racism to dictate what we tell ourselves. It is true that racists have equated blackness with perversity and out-of-control libidos. But the silence around queer lives will not counter that racist narrative. Most important to me, it is in this context of 'willful oblivion', as Morrison might term it, that queer youth are forced into homelessness and an increasing number are murdered for breaking with the politics of respectability. (White 2001: 24)

It is exactly this problem of rejection by the community that *Pariah* brings to the fore, the politics of respectability embodied by the mothers of Lee and her friend Laura (Pernell Walker). Alika's poetry at the end of the film when she decides to leave for a writer's bootcamp in Berkeley (waved off by her father, sister and Laura) allows her to join the legacy of female writers who have opened the path to finding their own voice. Rather than being a daughter of Woolf, Alika and Rees herself could be considered Audre Lorde's 'Nachwuchs'. Lorde's 'intensely erotic' lesbian writings in the 1980s, such as her novel *Zami*, 'urged strenuously for the importance of the erotic and open sexuality in women's lives' (White 2001: 186). *Pariah* opens with a quote from Lorde ('Wherever the bird with no feet flew, she found trees with no limbs') that signals her legacy. Alika's heart-breaking but empowering 'I'm broken/ I'm broken open/ . . . My spirit takes journey / My spirit takes flight/ . . . I am not running/ I am choosing . . . Breaking if freeing/ Broken is freedom/ I'm not broken/ I'm free', the poem she writes and reads aloud at the end of the film, shows how important it is to find a voice and ways of expressing, breaking with the silences of the hushed stories of black female sexuality and desire.

Vagina Dentata, Witches and Other Man-Eaters

Returning now to a full-fledged poetics of horror, I first want to recall
some of the classics of the modern horror genre and the view of female
sexuality, gender and race as pointed out by Creed and Clover in their
seminal studies of the 1990s. All the famous horror films discussed in *The
Monstrous-Feminine* and *Men, Women and Chain Saws* were directed by
men, and much of their aesthetics and thematic issues were in one way or
another a reaction to the sexual freedom and power that women gained
during the second wave of feminism. The reaction of men cutting up their
cinema seats with razor blades after seeing *Fuses* could be seen in parallel
to many of the monstrous females who appeared on screens in the 1970s
and 1980s. While the avenging women of the slasher genre in Chapter
1, and many of the lesbian vampires in 1970s vampire films that were
mentioned in the previous chapter, clearly translate a fascination with and
fear of female sexuality, I here want to focus on some of the other ways in
which this fear is translated into horror aesthetics in cinema.

In *The Monstrous-Feminine* Creed does not discuss race but focuses
implicitly on femininity taken as an undifferentiated category, which turns
out to be largely white femininity. She quotes Stephen King's answer to
the question of his greatest sexual fear: 'The vagina dentata, the vagina
with teeth. A story where you were making love to a woman and it just
slammed shut and cut your penis off. That'd do it' (King quoted in Creed
1993: 105). In all the mythologies of the world, myths regarding the
dangers of vaginas with teeth are prevalent. Often considered the 'mouth
of hell' and 'the devil's gateway', it turns women into man-eaters; this idea
of woman as Medusa-like, castrating, malicious vixen has found many
translations in the horror genre. Besides the previously mentioned bloody
lips of the lesbian vampire, there is the trope of the dangerous passage-
way: blood-filled, inward-sucking, full of snapping alien teeth or riddled
with snakes, spiders and other creepy animals (as in Stanley Kubrick's
The Shining [1980], Tobe Hooper's *Poltergeist* [1982] and Ridley Scott's
Alien [1979]). Creed rereads Freud and Lacan's conception of women as
castrat*ed* (it is the father who will inspire castration anxiety as punishment
for the son's desire for the mother) into women as castrat*ing*. Menstrual
blood could be seen as a sign of the dangers of sexual intercourse; a
bloody sheet is the sign of the fantasy that 'the man who inserts his fragile
penis into the mother's vagina is taking great risk' (Creed 1993: 112). She
further argues that Freud's conception of fetishism (a replacement image
that can make men forget the reality of castrated female genitals) is valuable, but it should be acccompanied by the more active image of woman

as castrating. The 'phallic woman is the fetishized woman – an image designed to deny the existence of both these figures (woman as castrated/ castrating)' (Creed 1993: 116). Typical of the horror genre is that the images are censored by fetishistic cover-ups for anxiety: and so we see women with knifes in *Sisters* (dir. Brian De Palma, 1972) and *Next of Kin* (dir. Tony Williams, 1982), women with electronic mouths in *Videodrome* (dir. David Cronenberg, 1985), or as sharp-toothed sharks in *Jaws* (dir. Steven Spielberg, 1975). I will return to the trope of the castrating mother that Creed discusses in the next chapter. Here I have pointed out some of the classic translations of the power of female sexuality in the horror genre to see how female directors raise these tropes. Slightly further on in this chapter I elaborate this point in relation to Ducournau's *Raw*. However, I want to begin with two appropriations of the vagina dentata trope that remain closer to the traditional conventions of the genre, albeit with some twists.

In *The Love Witch* (2016), Anna Biller (who wrote, produced, directed, styled, edited and scored the film) presents a luscious colourful pastiche of the idea of female sexuality as a dangerous form of witchcraft. The film was shot on 35mm gauge film and its colours and *mise en scène* are reminiscent of 1960s Technicolor and the bright Eastmancolor stock which Rothman used for *The Velvet Vampire* discussed in the previous chapter. Elaine (Samantha Robinson) is a fabulously good-looking witch who drives to a new house after her husband dies. The opening images present her driving, rear projections keeping her splendidly made-up face in full glamorous focus.[7] Hints of Hitchcock's *Marnie* (1964) are present when Elaine grabs her handbag and empties it with perfectly manicured hands, filmed in fetishistic close-up.[8] However, contrary to Hitchcock's heroines who tend to dress in pastel tints and 'decent' colours, Elaine is colour-coded red: she drives a red convertible, wears a red dress, has red lips and red fingernails, her handbag is red, the cigarette case that falls out is red, as well as a tarot card with a big red heart transfixed by three knives. While driving she muses (*à la* Marion Crane in *Psycho*) about how she will begin a new life, and about how devastated she was after her husband decided to leave her. We see flashbacks of her husband, bathed in red light, drinking from a red chalice, spitting blood and dropping dead. When she arrives at her new apartment in a Victorian mansion, she gets out of the car wearing her red shoes and retrieves her red suitcases.

Throughout the film the colour red, together with all kinds of other bright psychedelic colours, is prevalent and heightens the sense of danger, comedy and pastiche. Yet Biller's film also offers interesting feminist self-reflexive twists that are noteworthy. As a love witch, Elaine certainly seduces her men with her eroticism and sexuality, usually after having offered them a love potion that they willingly drink. They begin to experience her in hallucinatory rainbow spectra and become overwhelmed by emotion. 'I'm not used to feeling so many emotions, I can't take it', one of the men cries out. The next morning he is dead. Elaine buries him together with a bottle that contains her urine, two bloody tampons and a twig of rosemary. Urine and tampons are abject images of horror *par excellence*. However, in Biller's version these become a sexy magic brew that is attractive, rather than the abject bodily fluids so characteristic of the abject monstrous-feminine in male-directed horror films. Under the spell of the love witch, all men become emotionally unstable. And while the villagers in the nightclub that is frequented by Elaine's circle of witches and wizards harass her at the end of the film, she escapes and does not end up being burnt at the stake. In a playful and entertaining way, Biller's love witch comments on the stereotypes of the power of female sexuality through a woman who uses her body to critique the conventional social organisation of men, who are not supposed to exhibit emotions.

Karen Kusama's *Jennifer's Body* (2009), written by Diablo Cody, is another female-authored film that works with the fantasy of the terrible vagina dentata of female sexuality. The film is about a high-school girl, Jennifer (Megan Fox), who is demonically possessed and kills her male schoolmates using her sex appeal. She needs to feed on the blood of a boy once a month to retain her good looks. The film is told from the perspective of her best friend Anita 'Needy' (Amanda Seyfried), who tells the story as a flashback while incarcerated in a psychiatric prison. On the surface, the film seems to follow many conventions of the modern horror film. Cody and Kusama were partly inspired by 1970s and 1980s horror films. *Carrie* was one of the films they often discussed (Nichols 2019). Jennifer and Needy can certainly be seen as Carrie's younger sisters in the way they struggle to fight injustice and find their power. And when Jennifer transforms from being irresistibly sexy into a man-eating succubus, the film certainly shares some of its dentate-iconography with Amanda Bearse's 'vaginal nightmare' in *Fright Night* (dir. Tom Holland, 1985), one of the examples in Creed's *Monstrous-Feminine*. *Jennifer's Body*, while not well received on its release, has turned out to be more substantial than its initial bad reviews indicated. Because of Megan Fox's sexiness, the film was mismarketed to boys, while the makers intended it to be a film for girls, or in any case also for girls, as the story is told from a female perspective. In an interview, Cody explains that the film was focus-grouped among boys and they hated it:

I still have one of the cards. I'll keep it forever. They screened this movie for young men, of course, and the question was 'what would you improve about this movie?' and the guy wrote 'needs moar bewbs' [*sic*]. That's what we were up against. It makes me sad in retrospect. (Nichols 2019)

In a way, the initial lukewarm reception of *Jennifer's Body* is comparable to that of *The Moth Diaries* discussed in the previous chapter. Both films use elements of the horror genre, but with a twist that does not follow all the rules, and hence rejection follows.

Like *The Moth Diaries,* Kusama and Cody's film addresses the complex intimacy and intensity of female bonds and teenage friendships (Kwan 2009). There is an obsessiveness in this relationship that the film expresses in Needy's 'need' indeed to be close to Jennifer; she admires her in everything she does and obeys her every wish (not unlike Rebecca and Lucy in *The Moth Diaries*). The intimacy of their relationship also leads to a 'slumber-party' kiss, and hints at same-sex desire, which is also part of the complexity of teenage friendships where admiration and dependency translate into erotic attraction. However, Needy is not the typical 'final girl' who refrains from sex as opposed to her sexy friend, as convention would have it. She has a boyfriend, a goody, but in quite a funny scene (which involves a condom, which of course never occurs in Jennifer's seduction scenes) they engage in pleasurable intercourse.

Another feminine/feminist issue that the film addresses is that it is clear that Jennifer is a product of a culture where women continue to be coerced into creating an image. Cody recalls:

There is the scene where Jennifer is sitting alone smearing makeup on her face. I always thought that was such a sad image. She's so vulnerable. I don't know any woman who hasn't had a moment sitting in front of the mirror and thinking 'Help me, I want to be somebody else.' (Kwan 2009)

What is also evident, and has been picked up upon more since the #MeToo movement, is that Jennifer's body is not possessed purely by virtue of being a female body. Her body transforms after a group of men, the rock band Low Shoulder, perform an occult ritual on her, offering her to the devil in return for fame and success. However, the ritual goes wrong (because Jennifer is not a pure virgin as demanded by the sacrifice), and the scene is actually more a rape than anything else. In the end, Needy turns out to be a kind of final girl after all, when she escapes from the asylum and exacts revenge on the band by killing them all.

What we see in these female-directed horror films which couple female sexuality with myths about the vagina dentata is that they become less about male anxiety and more about female desire that speaks on its own account, without being relegated to passive heterosexual normativity.

Turning the Witchboard: Opening Up, Breaking Free

The other sub-genre of the modern horror film that is charged with female sexuality is what Clover has called the possession film. While the possession story can take different shapes, in *Men, Women and Chain Saws* Clover demonstrates that there are general tendencies such as the female story of possession that covers up for the male story of a man in crisis, and that the possession usually involves a split between two systems of explanation: 'White Science and Black Magic, to use the terminology of *The Serpent and the Rainbow*' (Clover 1992: 66). The lesson of the modern occult film, Clover argues, is that 'White Science has its limits, and that if it does not yield, in the extremity, to the wisdom of the Black Magic, all is lost. If a woman is possessed by the devil, neurosurgery is not the answer; an exorcism is' (1992: 66). Besides films such as Wes Craven's *The Serpent and the Rainbow* (1988), *Poltergeist* (dir. Tobe Hooper, 1982) and *Don't Look Now* (dir. Nicolas Roeg, 1973), Clover focuses her analysis on *The Exorcist* (dir. William Friedkin, 1973) and *Witchboard* (dir. Kevin Tenney, 1986). In both of these films, it is the women who physically 'open up' to spiritual possession, while the actual story is about the men in psychological crisis.

Clover observes how in the female story of these films, a whole range of 'female portals' are connoted as portals to the devil, voodoo, witchcraft and other demonic spirits, especially female sexual organs: 'The word *vulva* itself is related to *valve* – gate or entry to the body – and so it regularly serves for all manner of spirits, but the unclean one above all, in occult horror' (1992: 76). Again, menstruation is the most vulnerable moment of the month when these spirits can easily enter, and Clover recalls how Carrie's schoolmates shout 'plug it up, plug it up!' while throwing tampons at her when at the beginning of the film Carrie discovers blood between her legs. Contrary to the vagina dentata myth that Creed emphasised in her analysis of the monstrous feminine, in the occult film menstruation seems to 'red flag' that something potent is going on behind this orifice, in the dark interior mysteries of the body. Regan in *The Exorcist* becomes possessed at the age of her first menstruation, and Linda in *Witchboard* is impregnated by the devil (developing a phantom pregnancy).

On the male side of the story the men are in emotional or psychological crisis: Father Damien Karras in *The Exorcist* goes through a crisis of

faith and an existential crisis with hints of 'queerness', and in *Witchboard*
Jim, who is 'closed up' in his emotions, reconciles with his childhood
friend Brandon, a relationship that also includes homosexual feelings. In
this sub-genre, the characteristics of which Clover describes so aptly, the
occult film presents female heroines much in the way pornography speaks
of the female body to make it 'speak' its experience: 'Through moaning,
vomiting, fevers, hypnotic revelations, swearing, swaggering, swelling,
and the sudden appearances of rashes, bruises, and scars (sometimes
spelling out a message), the woman is made to bring forth her occulted
self' (1992: 109–10). All this is to make room for men to move emotionally towards more 'openness'. And while women are connoted by 'black
magic', men are typically equated with 'white science'.

The typical occult film of the 1970s and 1980s has the women return to
their initial state (being put back in their place), while the men somehow
transform:

> Whereas the female story traces a circle (she becomes again what she was when the
> film began), the excesses of its middle disappearing without a physical or psychic
> trace (Regan is explicitly amnesiac, Linda implicitly so), the male story is linear (he
> is at the end radically different from what he was at the beginning), public (he and
> the world know that he has changed) and apparently permanent. (Clover 1992: 98)

Again my question here is: what happens when women take up the theme
of possession and other occult powers? While Biller and Kusama flirt with
the occult in *The Love Witch* and *Jennifer's Body* to tell a story of female
sexuality, empowerment, anger and revenge, black female directors have
taken the occult in very different directions, with storylines and images
that go beyond the tropes and patterns of the possession films recalled
above. *Eve's Bayou* (dir. Kasi Lemmons, 1997) and *I'm Not a Witch* (dir.
Rungano Nyoni, 2017) are two noteworthy films that offer completely new
perspectives on these typical horror tropes.

Although it deals with voodoo and other occult powers, *Eve's Bayou* is
not a horror film as such. This is, of course, the first remarkable thing, as
in predominantly white film history the occult as 'black magic' is by and
large relegated to such genres as the possession film, at the margins of the
cinematographic landscape. But in the hands of Lemmons, *Eve's Bayou*
brings together different and multiple storylines that centre on the lives of
a group of women living in smalltown Louisiana during the early 1960s.
They are descendants of an African-American slave woman named Eve
and the French plantation owner Jean-Paul Batiste who freed her and gave
her a parcel of land near the bayou after she cured him of a deadly illness
(they had sixteen children together). The story is told by the child Eve

Batiste (Jurnee Smollett). She has an older sister Cisely (Meagan Good) and a younger brother Poe (Jake Smollett). They live with their mother Roz (Lynn Whitfield) and father Louis (Samuel L. Jackson), the community's doctor. Their father's sister, Aunt Mozelle (Debbi Morgan) is also a close family member.

The story begins with Eve's voice-over over black-and-white images that evoke her ancestor's past, recalling: 'Memory is a selection of images, some elusive, others printed indelibly on the brain. The summer I killed my father I was 10 years old, my brother Poe was 9 and my sister Cisely was 14.' And so we meet (in full-colour cinematography) the well-to-do Batiste family during the summer when Eve discovers that her father has had affairs with his patients to boost his ego, even though he also clearly loves his family. Eve, who has inherited the power of second sight that runs along the female family line, often spends time with her Aunt Mozelle, who is a psychic counsellor who helps her patients with their visions (these are rendered in black and white, like the images at the beginning of the film). After the discovery of her father's affairs, Eve visits another woman, a fortune-teller and possible witch, and asks her to cast a voodoo spell on her father. Expecting voodoo dolls and needles, nothing happens, undermining stereotypical expectations. Meanwhile Cisely begins to behave strangely after her first menstruation: she withdraws from the family and seems depressed. She confesses to Eve that their father tried to assault her one evening. This enrages Eve and leads her to make the husband of one of her father's lovers suspicious and jealous. This does not end well for her father, as we could surmise from the beginning. The voodoo spell might have worked after all, but in less obvious and more intricate ways.

The film does not, however, simply condemn the father, as evidenced in the letter to his sister where he explains what happened in a different way. Even when Eve uses her emerging clairvoyant powers to help her sister find the truth, the flashback images are confusing: we do not find out who 'the victim' or 'the perpetrator' were in the general confusion of the highly emotionally charged memories. This ensures that the story does not close with an all-knowing and reconciliatory ending, but in a conclusion in which the sisters hold hands and accept that not everything is knowable. In the final shot, the camera zooms out, revealing the two sisters illuminated by pinkish evening light at the edge of the bayou, each flanked by a tree that stretches its branches to the sky as well as being reflected in the water. We then return to the first voice-over phrase: 'Memory is a selection of images, some elusive, others printed indelibly on the brain. Each image is like a thread, each thread woven together to make a tapestry of intricate texture and the tapestry tells a story, and the story is our past.'

This film deserves repeated viewing and more analysis. Here I just want to point out that while elements of the possession film are present (fortune telling, voodoo practices, and menstruation as an important moment of change in a female body), all these elements are used in a very different way: not in the service of male psychic transformation but as elements in a female story. The elements of voodoo are released from their purely evil connotations (Mozelle uses them for good causes), and while she is accused of being a black widow (her husbands have all died), she is not an evil person but someone searching for happiness. The transformation of a girl's body entering womanhood does bring along confusion about sexuality, but it does not mean opening up to the devil. Strange things do happen, but they might have a much more complicated and perhaps ultimately unknowable cause. And so *Eve's Bayou* integrates occultism with the power of memory and telling stories in a new way, from a black female perspective, addressing a poetics of relation.

Another remarkable film that puts 'occult things' in a totally different perspective is *I'm Not a Witch*. Rungano Nyoni wrote and directed this film in Zambia after she had visited modern-day witch camps there and in Ghana. 'There is nothing extraordinary about witch camps. They are like normal villages but populated by older women. They have the women working on the land and doing everyday activities', says Nyoni in an interview (Aftab 2017). Trying to 'get the point of the absurdity of something that is so misogynistic', she made the film from a place of anger, adding that the best way to vent this anger was by using 'cruel humour'. Indeed, the film is funny to the point of absurdity while being harsh at the same time. The main character is a nine-year-old girl named Shula (Maggie Mulabwa). When she appears out of nowhere in a rural African village, she is accused of being a witch. In her book on race, gender and sexuality in British cinema, *Fear of the Dark*, Lola Young opens with a memory that when she was a little girl attending primary school, she was always asked to play the witch (Young 1996: 1); she wrote her book both to understand and break away from these stereotypes. Approximately twenty years later, Nyoni's film about a little girl being put in a witch's situation was listed on the British submission for nomination for the Academy Award for Best Foreign Language Film. Nyoni's portrayal of 'witchcraft' is far beyond the typical horror scenario.

After police officer Josephine (Nellie Munamonga) has interrogated the villagers (one man talks about the horror that the little girl, who is silent most of the time, inspires: 'She hit me with an axe, all blood spilled over the ground as I lost my arms', and then argues that this *dream* made him afraid), she hands over the girl to a government official, Mr Banda (Henry

B. J. Phiri). As a state-appointed guardian from 'the Ministry of Tourism and Traditional Beliefs', he thinks he can make a profit from the little girl as a witch. He takes her to court cases to point out the perpetrators of thefts, being rewarded with offerings of gin and other consumables. He places her under the auspices of a community of witches, a group of old women who have all been accused of being a witch at some point. The women work the land, and are exhibited as tourist attractions. Shula and the old women, attached to enormous white ribbons on huge bobbins, are transported on a big truck when they travel from place to place. The white ribbons, perhaps an homage to Michael Haneke, as one reviewer suggests (Kermode 2017), give the *mise en scène* a surreal quality that underscores the absurdity of the situation, namely that people still engage in this prac- tice against women. While the entire film is fiction, the ribbons and huge bobbins can be seen as the weight of rules and traditions that people find it hard to break away from.

While the visual poetry, humour and cruelty of the images, and Shula's deadpan face throughout all that is imposed on her, never cease to amaze, there are a few scenes that I would like to highlight. First, there is the encounter with Mr Banda's wife, Charity (Nancy Murilo), who shows Shula her own bobbin with ribbons in a corner of her house. She tells Shula that she sometimes dares to take off the ribbon because she has earned 'respectability' through marriage. 'I did everything they asked, and if you do the same you can be like me', she tells Shula. It is pain- fully evident, however, that Charity is not respected at all when she is attacked in a parking lot, and when her husband makes her crawl on the floor to encourage Shula to conduct a rain dance for a white official (Shula refuses). Another painful scene occurs when Shula is a guest on a televi- sion talk show with her 'state guardian'. When the show's host wonders 'What if she actually is just but a child?', even the chattily arrogant Mr Banda is at a loss for words.

Then there is the ending of the film, when the old women mourn the death of Shula after she has cut her ribbon and we have seen her dance, gesturing with her hands and arms as if she is becoming a bird, growing wings and spreading them in preparation for flying away. All the women, dressed now in bright red, encircle Shula's body, which is covered by a white cloth. It begins to rain; the red clothes of the women seem to liquefy. At no point do we see the captured and accused women being capable of the monstrous acts that they are often accused of, such as 'cannibalism, murder, castration of male victims, and the advent of natural disasters such as storms, fires and the plague' (Creed 1993: 2). There is no sex in the version of witchcraft that is assigned to this pre-pubescent girl and the old

Figure 3.2 *I'm Not a Witch* (Rungano Nyoni, 2017).

women. If anything, they provoke a much-needed rain shower to fertilise the arid land. In the last image we see all the ribbons billowing in the wind, cut loose – the truck is left with flying ribbons on empty bobbins. The 'witches' have escaped cultural traditions. Furthermore, Nyoni's film has advanced the trope of the possessed woman beyond the conventions of the horror genre.

Hunger for Flesh and Blood

While Nyoni presents witches in an unfamiliar way, stripping away the horror from monstrous femininity and the association of witchcraft with female sexuality, Ducournau moves in another direction and focuses on female sexuality in all its horrific and dangerous intensities. The exploration of sexuality from the point of view of a woman has been the topic of several notable female-directed films that give new insights into the emotional turmoil, physical cravings and dangerous situations that girls and women can solicit. Thinking of the films of Andrea Arnold, especially *Red Road* (2008), *Fish Tank* (2010), *Wuthering Heights* (2012) and *American Honey* (2016), there is always an unsafe situation surrounding the sexual encounters, but her heroines are certainly no victims. Eliza Hittman's *It Felt Like Love* (2013) presents her main character on a search for sexual experiences, equally in situations that no mother would encourage any daughter to put herself into, and yet her vulnerability can absorb it. Sarah Polley's *Take this Waltz* (2012) is an intense and layered journey into feminine desire and sexuality. Maja Milos's *Clip* (2012) shows a teenage girl becoming lost in a desperate, self-destructive spree of sex, drugs and partying while filming her search for love on her phone, and resonates at some points with Asia Argento's similar explorations in *Scarlet Diva* (2000). *Take Me Somewhere Nice* (dir. Ena Sendijarevic, 2019) is a female road-movie about a Dutch-Bosnian girl who travels back to her parents' country, which freely deals with sexuality. In *Jezebel* (dir. Numa Perrier, 2019) a young black woman begins working as a webcam model, introduced to the online sex world by her sister. And in *Queen of Hearts*, director May el-Thouky takes us on a gradual descent into the consequences of a sexual relationship between an older lawyer and her stepson that continues to disturb one's mind with confusion and nausea for days. Lisa Brühlmann's *Blue My Mind* (2017) presents the bodily transformations and sexual awakening of its heroine in an aesthetics of horror that at some points resonates with Ducournau's *Raw*. As a film that could be seen to be in line with Schneemann's *Meat Joy*, I will elaborate here on Ducournau's film.

Raw is set during rookie initiation week at a veterinary school out in the provinces of France. Seventeen-year-old Justine (Garance Marillier) is dropped off by her parents (who met at the same school twenty years earlier) in the campus parking lot, left alone with her red suitcase in the grey surroundings. Her sister Alexia (Ella Rumpf) is supposed to pick her up; however, she finds Justine later that evening at a wild party. By then Justine has met her room-mate Adrien (Rabah Naït Oufella), and seen him having sex with a man, and has been chased from her room along with all the other rookies to participate in one of the hazing rituals that the older students impose. The *mise en scène* is packed with sweaty bodies in sleazy cellars, dark corridors and raunchy rooms oozing sexuality, people canoodling on the dance floor. A girl licks a guy's eyeball; they are enveloped by red light as the camera zooms in. The initiation rituals add to the general feeling of sexual excitement and transgression: the first-year students in their white lab coats are covered in gallons of thick red fluid for their annual class photograph, after which they continue their day dressed in this bloody outfit and with sticky hair. They are forced to eat a raw rabbit kidney, something that makes Justine, a life-long vegetarian, nauseous and vomit. At another party, she is covered in blue paint upon entry and locked in a room with a yellow-painted boy, with the instruction not to come out before they are both green.

The entire setting is wild, exciting and, from the beginning, also unsettling as we feel that for all the erratic behaviour around her, Justine has something hidden within herself which will soon emerge. Then there are the animals that the future veterinarians are confronted with: in the cellar, all the annual photographs of previous 'bloody' year groups are displayed in a room that contains countless dead animals in formaldehyde-filled preservation vessels; a cow in a lecture hall has an ultrasound of its uterus on display; all the students receive a dead dog on their workbench that they must dissect; and most strikingly confrontational, at the beginning of the film a horse receives a ketamine injection, collapses and is carried away (presumably for an operation). Of course, there is a realistic context to these actions (the horse's sedation actually took place at a veterinary school at which Ducournau received permission to film). Nevertheless, the animals also signal something else. While veterinarians are trained to cure or help the animals, we cannot help but be reminded of the slaughter and butchering of animals, the meat we eat, and the hunger and violence it implies. Justine develops a hunger for meat, for flesh, only after she has had her first taste. She begins to experience cravings for meat, bites into a raw chicken breast from the refrigerator, and secretes a hamburger in the pocket of her lab coat.[9] At the same time her sexual desire awakens; she feels the closeness of the flesh of Adrien's neck when she helps him fasten his apron; we feel her confusion and desire to bring her mouth to his flesh.

The camera work in *Raw* is always close and never leaves the spectator room to look away. There are many images of abjection in the film in the way Creed describes the *Monstrous-Feminine*. Let me indicate a few such horror images and question how these differ or not from the modern body horror films of the 1970s and 1980s. Directly after Justine has had her first (force-fed) taste of meat, she is woken up in the middle of the night by a severe itch and roughly scratches her skin. When she switches on the light she discovers with a shock (that we can easily share, as anyone who has ever been woken up by an allergy or disease will recognise) a terrible rash all over her body, an allergic reaction to the kidney. Ducournau's camera lingers on the rawness and redness of the skin, blisters and scratching motions, until itch gives way to ache. We can feel it all, we become this erupted skin. In the next scene she is in the doctor's office. We receive another spine shiver when the doctor begins peeling long white flakes from her enflamed skin. Again, without flinching, the camera remains focused on this image of abjection, feeling the horror of it. In the horror genre, a rash is often a sign of possession by a demonic power, and images of abjection can be rejected as the monstrous other; here such rejection is not possible. It is too realistic, too close: we receive the feel of horror without the option to other it. No sign of the devil is spelled out by the rash, it is just what it is: a terribly uncomfortable skin irritation.

While there are many other scenes of abjection that creep and crawl under the skin because the camera loiters beyond the moment of shock, the next scene that I want to mention here is a transitory moment. Alexia has taken up a plan to give her sister a Brazilian-style depilation, which leads in itself to other painfully close moments, especially when the wax does not come off properly and we see it stuck in clumps of pubic hair; we feel the pain with Justine. Then Alexia cuts herself; her entire middle finger falls to the floor and she faints. In panic, Justine calls an ambulance, but while waiting on the floor next to her sister, she becomes obsessed by the severed digit, licks its blood, begins to nibble, and then devours it like a ketchup-covered sausage. When Alexia comes round, we see that she recognises the behaviour of her younger sister (Alexia, it appears, is in a more advanced and gruesome stage of her desire for meat, perhaps comparable to Coré in *Trouble Every Day* discussed in the previous chapter).

Again, this is a trope from the horror genre: cannibalism. However, in contrast with, for instance, the evil, appalling, monstrous cannibalistic family in *Texas Chainsaw Massacre* (dir. Tobe Hooper, 1974), Ducournau confronts us with our own monstrous interior. Not that we would like to nibble on a finger or cheek for breakfast, obviously, but the way the desire for meat is connected with sexual desire is recognisable. Ducournau herself comments:

Figure 3.3 *Raw* (Julia Ducournau, 2016).

Cannibalism is part of humanity. Some tribes do it ritually and have no shame doing it. You have this feeling when you bite someone's arm for fun, that you want to go a bit further, but you don't because you have a moral canvas [*sic*]. This thing is in us, we just don't want to see it. So I thought, since my characters always feel like monsters deep inside, I want the audience to feel like a monster as well, and to understand what she's doing. Because we are all monsters, really. (Godfrey 2017)

Elsewhere, Ducournau explains further that she wanted to create something of a positive monstrosity:

This character who wants to fit in but realizes she can't fit this particular box, no matter what . . . well, what do we do with her? Should she stop existing? I believe that monstrosities are what make us unique. If she realizes she could kill someone but she won't, then she can be her own wild animal. That's a positive thing – to pinpoint who you are once you've been confronted by your first real moral choice in your life. Most people never get to that stage. She's maybe more human than any of us at the end of the movie. (Grierson 2017)

There is much more to say about the film, for instance about the ways in which it addresses the opposite reaction of the body, not hunger and eating but anorexia and vomiting. There are several moments in the film where the problem of anorexia is addressed explicitly (after a long scene where Justine is retching up her hair, a girl in the toilet tells her she should use two fingers to make it easier; after a conversation about AIDS, monkeys and rape, Adrien comments that monkeys do not develop anorexia after being raped; and Alexia tells her sister that anorexia is not cool). Furthermore, there is certainly something to say about familial relations in *Raw* that becomes especially marked at the end of the film, when Justine is back home and has a conversation with her father which reveals that there is a family secret involved in their behaviour. Here, I want to end my observations on *Raw* by looking at the moment where Justine finally does engage in sex.

Knowing her room-mate Adrien is gay, she develops a physical attraction to him. This becomes most evident in a long sequence when he is playing football, bare chested, and she is looking on. And 'when the woman looks', to cite Linda William's famous essay on the female gaze, she takes on an active role. Still, the moment when they engage in sex is unexpected. After the party where she is locked up only to be released when green (a rather erotic scene in itself, though they actually escape because the yellow guy's lips are red, as she has bitten him), Justine takes a shower and curls up next to Adrien in bed. He asks her what is wrong, and she leaves the room without answering; after which he picks up his computer to watch gay pornography. A moment later, she re-enters his

room and they jump on each other. 'Is it that bad?', he asks as they commence having sex. She loses her virginity ferociously, animal-like, biting
her own arm until it bleeds. Perhaps in itself, to have sex with your gay
best friend is a fantasy that many women have (Adrien is rather confused
about his sudden bisexual inclination), but what is more important is that
Ducournau here presents an image of female sexuality that is uncommon.

> The first thing I tried to do is to give another portrayal of female sexuality. That
> was important to me because I'm fed up with the way young women and their dis-
> covery of sexuality is portrayed on screens. I feel it's always a victim's story that's
> being told. It's always about the fear, or the doubt afterwards. 'Am I gonna get the
> reputation?' 'Is he gonna call me?' 'Is it the right guy?' This has nothing to do with
> sexuality. Sexuality is not a victim. That's more about social mores – a voice in the
> head not in the body. For me sexuality is in the body. And you should certainly not
> be a victim. It's not something you go through, it's something that you are active in,
> and it's perfectly okay. (Thomas 2017)

Ducournau and her heroine are rebellious, unruly, 'loud ladies' who can
be placed in the tradition of the Riot Girls, Pussy Riot and FEMEN
(Morris 2018). With *Raw*, Ducournau has certainly twisted the language
of the horror film to present a completely different and explicit portrayal
of female sexuality, lust and desire.

Before advancing to the last sections of this chapter, I want first to
mention one more film that uses a more implicit and subdued form of
horror aesthetics to convey an experience of female sexuality. In *On Body
and Soul* (2017), Ildikó Enyedi portrays the slowly developing love affair
between two people who are surrounded by many animals. The film is
structured with images of a male and female deer in a snow-covered forest:
free, searching (for food under the snow, for water, for each other), pristine, serene, magic, they are alternated and contrasted at regular intervals
with close-ups of cows in a slaughterhouse: enclosed, dirty, raw and realistic. Other structuring elements are changes from day to night, lunches
in the workplace cafeteria, people enjoying glimpses of sunshine, and
nightfall when the two main characters are each in their own home.

The film is about Endre (Géza Morcsányi), the financial director of
an abattoir, and Maria (Alexandra Borbély), the newly appointed quality
controller. Both live alone and are actually outsiders, Endre because he has
a disabled arm (it is never explained why) and feels old (he has an adult
daughter whom he rarely sees), and Maria because she is autistic, which
ensures that she adheres strictly to rules and habits (she keeps her house
meticulously clean, rejects the meat when the cows are two millimetres
too fat, and can remember the exact date of her first menstruation when

asked by the psychologist: 5 November 1998). The company's psychologist discovers that both have the same dreams about the deer. And this is the beginning of a uncommon love affair.

All I want to emphasise here in relation to this film is that in comparison to *Raw*, most of the violence is the real violence of the process of slaughtering cows: Enyedi's camera provides no escape from seeing how the cows are slain, flayed and drained; we see the dirt on their hooves, the rough floors on which they tremble to their death, the paunchy flabby bodies, decapitated heads, the sounds of crushing and cracking bones; the gushing blood sluiced daily into the gutter – all in graphic detail (the employees prefer vegetables for their lunch . . .). This stands in stark contrast with the green-brown-white palette of the dreams. There are other red details in the *mise en scène*, mainly the red overalls of the butchers. Maria is dressed mainly in pastel colours, except for a few moments: when Endre gives her his phone number, she wears a bright-red cardigan. And since she has no phone, she buys one: it is red. Maria clearly wants to enter into a sexual relationship but has no clue about how to accomplish it. She watches pornography with an unmoved face. On the advice of her childhood psychologist, she begins to learn how to touch things (her hand squashes mashed potatoes, she observes people kissing in the park, she touches the cows waiting for slaughter) and to listen to music. When she feels ready, she tells Endre, who has already given up hope.

While during most of the film, the cows indicate nothing but the realities of the slaughterhouse (while the deer clearly stand for Maria and Endre, and they meet every night), at the end of the film Maria enters into a certain becoming-cow when she 'slaughters' herself and almost bleeds to death. The red blood is gushing from her arm when her red phone rings and Endre tells her 'I feel I die so much I love you.' Stopping the bleeding just in time, and after a hospital visit, she then finds Endre. She finally discovers what sex means, but we only see her wondering face. Then we see them at breakfast the following morning. When they try to recall their dream neither of them can. The forest is now empty.

Enyedi's film displays female sexuality combined with cruelty and poetry, which is something that both Lina Yang and Campion, each in their own unique way, also do in the last films I discuss in this chapter.

A Poetic and Lustful Final Girl

Jane Campion's film *In the Cut* (2003) offers an interesting case study with which to reconsider the feminine perspective and agency more ambiguously.[10] Usually described as an erotic thriller, I think it is defensible to consider Campion's female lead character as an atypical slasher or rape-revenge heroine. The film is about Frannie Avery (Meg Ryan), a high school literature teacher who becomes involved with a detective who investigates a series of brutal murders of women in her Manhattan neighbourhood. I will highlight a few salient elements that indicate a different take on gendered violence through horror aesthetics.[11] Let me begin with a scene towards the end of the film where we see Frannie in a red dress, smeared with blood, walking barefoot on the roadside. She has just killed the man who raped and dismembered her sister Pauline (Jennifer Jason Leigh); a fate of several other girls in her neighbourhood, all 'disarticulated' in particularly violent ways. We see bloody body parts being pulled out of a bathtub, a washing machine, and on graphic evidential photographs – all images we are familiar with from the slasher genre (and that unfortunately also still resonate with socially gendered violence). This gruesome fate was almost Frannie's as well. In escaping from the murderer, she has become a 'final girl', and in killing her sister's assailant, she could also classify as a 'castrating woman' of the rape-revenge plot (though she uses a gun rather than a knife). In some respects, the typical gender roles of the slasher plot are reversed. Where in De Palma's *Sisters*, for instance, the twin sisters Danielle and Dominique (both played by Margot Kidder) symbolise the docile 'good girl' and the terrifying 'bad girl', Campion presents us with a perverse version of a 'good cop/bad cop', embodied by detective Giovanni Malloy (Marc Ruffalo) and his partner Richard Rodriguez (Nick Damici). Frannie becomes sexually involved with Malloy, and throughout the film there is a constant ambiguity regarding whether or not he is an '*homme fatale*'. In the final scenes, she discovers that it was Rodriguez who murdered her sister and the other women; the film concludes when she returns to Malloy, whom she has tied to the apartment's radiator pipe so he could not follow.

Even if the film's role-reversal could be considered as a feminist perspective, Campion does not just reverse plot roles. To understand why Campion's heroine becomes involved in this potentially dangerous situation, it is important to take into consideration how the aesthetics of the film creates a fusion between inner spaces and the outside world. From the beginning the film sets up a whole range of ambiguities. Over the opening credit sequence, for instance, we hear a sweet-sounding woman's voice singing 'Que sera sera' while the accompanying piano produces threatening disharmonious tones. Images of a dodgy New York neighbourhood reveal garbage on the streets, filtered through soft morning sunlight; a red flower painted on the pavement vaguely resembles the body contour of a crime scene; a courtyard garden is full of lush plants, some scarlet-red

flowers breaking the harmony and at the same time adding a lively dimension. Pauline, wearing a vermilion-red dress, is in the garden, drinking
coffee, observing the plants, the sky; suddenly white petals fall from the
sky, dotting the summer scenery like a snowstorm. An interior shot shows
the 'snowstorm' through the window, while a red Chinese wind chime in
front of the window reveals a diminutive cosy apartment. Frannie, still in
bed half-awake, sees the white dots and dozes off again; the petals merging
with snowflakes of dreamy sepia, black and white images of a winter landscape, a woman pirouetting on ice, a man's hand forming a fist in close-up
as if he is about to collide, but he then skates away from the camera. When
he returns, his skate carves a deep black groove in the white ice. The cut
ice slowly turns red, the title of the film appears and the letters seem to
start bleeding.

Dream and reality merge in the *mise en scène* of this opening sequence,
bringing us closely into Frannie's private space and mental world. Frannie
and Pauline (who has stayed the night with her sister) leave the apartment,
talking about slang words and their meanings, slang words that are 'either
sexual or violent, or both', as they comment in their dialogue. Frannie has
sticky notes with expressions and poetic phrases hung everywhere in her
apartment. Soon it becomes clear that she is writing a book on slang, loves
poetry, and teaches literature at a high school. Throughout the film we see
her looking, jotting down poetic lines displayed in public spaces, savour-
ing words and expressions, enjoying language and talking with her sister
about lovers and sexuality. Back to the beginning of the film, by the time
the sisters walk outside, the fluid frames of the camerawork and frames
within frames in the *mise en scène* have rendered all spaces small and intimate. The warm yellow-brown colour palette is populated in almost every
scene with flecks of bright red (a dress, a chime, a curtain, a cap, a cup, a
couch, a notebook, a flower, flecks of red light, bloodstains) and the soft
summer light combined with hints of violence in the music, the icy snow,
the title design and the words have established a familiar world that feels
safe, and that at the same time has a threatening undercurrent. The colour
red that pops up consistently as flecks, dots, specks and spots in the *mise en
scène* indicates this ambiguity, perhaps even creating the double affective
quality of violence and sexuality that runs throughout the entire film.

As Creed and Clover demonstrate, the combination of sex and violence
is characteristic of the horror genre, but the differences in Campion's
aesthetics are striking. Instead of a lonely girl in a dreadfully deserted
house, there is confidentiality in an urban setting, an intimate bond
between two sisters who talk about relationships, sex, work and daily
life; Campion presents us with Frannie's private world, where dreams,

memories, poetry, imagination, daily life and the harsh reality of gendered violence all blend together. *In the Cut* explores the female psyche through eroticism and sexual desire, but also through language and poetry, and through the female look. As Justine in *Raw* caught her flatmate in a sexual pose, Frannie secretly observes a man receiving fellatio in the basement of a café, which is one of the most salient acts of looking in Campion's film. All this creates a deeply warped appropriation of the genre conventions of the horror film.

Campion's film addresses something beyond the expression of male anxiety regarding the monstrous-feminine and the thrilling disgust that is usually the affect for which the genre calls (see Williams 1991). Rather, *In the Cut* stylistically constructs affective relations that open up the range of affects that the horror genre can produce, thereby creating space for new perspectives. Here it is useful to make reference again to Brinkema, who argues for a more formal approach to the horror genre, emphasising that horror is a question of design and componentry that 'opens up fields of possibility for thinking horror in unexpected places, within unexpected juxtapositions . . . horror as a problematics of aesthetics, form, design, element, and composition . . . insisting that textual structures and components are not incidental to affective charge but are indeed responsible for it' (Brinkema 2015: 265; see also Brinkema 2014).

As indicated earlier in this study, while I am not sure that form is responsible for affect and meaning (as I think all formal innovations are always connected to content and resonate with wider social developments), I do think that paying attention to the formal aspects of horror aesthetics, and especially thinking about horror beyond genre conventions, is helpful in rethinking its affective meaning beyond gender conventions as well. I will highlight one more element of *In the Cut* that speaks to this point. A central image in the film is the lighthouse. The lighthouse is where the murderer takes his victims, and where Frannie is taken at the end of the film as well. It is here that she realises the truth, and where she kills her assailant the moment he asks to marry her, perversely offering her a blood-covered ring that all his victims wore when they were raped and killed. Obviously, the lighthouse also refers to Woolf's famous novel *To the Lighthouse*. Frannie teaches the novel to her students, and in a scene at the beginning of the film we see her in class, a bright-red lighthouse drawn on the blackboard, while she refers to Woolf's stream-of-consciousness writing style. One of her students complains that nothing happens in the novel, 'just an old lady who dies'. When Frannie asks how many ladies must die to make it good, the student replies 'at least three'. One cannot help seeing this as a self-referential wink to the plot of the film, in which three women are indeed brutally killed, perhaps as a formal reference to popular genre conventions, while at the same time the entire film is much closer to a subjective and meandering consciousness.

Woolf herself had a purely formal conception of the image of the light-house, as she stated: 'I mean nothing by the lighthouse, one has to have a central line down the middle of the book to hold the design together' (Woolf 2004: xiii). I would like to suggest that the colour red in *In the Cut* functions in a similar compositional way as the lighthouse in Woolf's novel. The lighthouse functions as a beacon in the subjective worlds of Woolf's characters, such as Mrs Ramsay:

> She saw the light again. With some irony in her interrogation, for when one woke at all, one's relation changes, she looked at the steady light, the pitiless, the remorse-less, which was so much her, so little her . . . but for all that, she thought, watching it with fascination, hypnotized, as if it were stroking with its silver fingers some sealed vessel in the brain whose bursting would flood her with delight. (Woolf 2004: xiv)

Similarly, the composition of the images, sounds and words in *In the Cut* creates a stream of consciousness, a subjective sphere of intimate relation-ships, of female sexuality as personal experience rather than display, of poetry, vulnerability and sexual pleasure, of trust and fear – and above all of creative agency.

Maud Ellmann argues in her introduction to *To the Lighthouse* that 'if the lighthouse is the "central line" it stands for all dividing lines that hold design together, for division as a principle of creativity . . . *To the Lighthouse* intimates that art is necessarily ambivalent, destructive and reparative by turns' (Woolf 2004: xxii). As an element of composition, the redness of her lighthouse (and of all the other red splashes in the settings) stands for the poetry and erotic love that Frannie is quietly looking for, writing down lines of poetry in the metro, sticking them on the walls of her apartment. 'I want to do with you what spring does with the cherry trees', Malloy reads on one of her notes when he visits her apartment for the first time. The metaphor is strong; it connects to the summery petal storm at the beginning of the film and begins to do its creative subconscious work in the aesthetics of the film, where the destructive physical violence inflicted on women's bodies is countered with reparative happiness from intimate pleasure; where the love for a potentially dangerous man has nothing to do with masochistic thrill-seeking but with a balance between trust and distrust; and where reality merges with subjective perceptions, ambiguous feelings and thoughts in the composition of images and sounds. In short, if we can consider *In the Cut* as a feminine take on the horror film, it renders the notion of the monstrous-feminine itself ambiguous, presenting us with a 'dreamy final girl'. The abject as an ambiguous notion or border, cut and extended into creative abjection, reaches beyond the typical horror emotions of fear, disgust and other negative emotions, infusing it with notions of poetry and feminine desire.

Longing for a Ghost

Documentary maker Yang's first feature film, *Longing for the Rain* (2013), takes us into the most intimate spaces of the mind of a woman longing for sex, in the form of a ghost story. The original Chinese title, 'Chunmeng', has a double meaning of 'dreams of spring' and 'erotic reveries'. The word combines the metaphoric poetry of nature and the body in a beautiful way that reminds one of Frannie's cherry tree sticky note in *In the Cut*. Yang's style combines realistic handheld camerawork and ethnographic portrayals with visual poetry and spectral abstraction to present the story of Fang Lei (Zhao Siyuan), a woman in her early thirties who lives with her husband (Fu Jia) and their small daughter Yifan (Yifan Xing) in a nice high-rise apartment in Beijing. They represent the growing well-to-do middle class of China today. Fang is a sort of Angel in the House. Her husband compliments her on the wontons she makes him for breakfast before he leaves for work; she is a dedicated mother, and an ideal daughter-in-law who takes care of her husband's demented grandmother by simply adjusting to her needs; when the grandmother does not want to shower she simply takes a shower with her and they have fun, even if the grandmother has no idea who she is, calling her 'Goddess of Mercury' and other fantastic names. At one point the grandmother appears in Fang's dreams and talks to her. When she wakes up, she tells her husband that his grandmother has died; after which the phone rings and the old woman's housekeeper tells them that she found her dead in her chair. We also see Fang touring her aunt around the countryside outside Beijing when she arrives with some friends, and spending time in the shopping mall with her best friend (Xue Hong).

However, Fang is at the same time full of unfulfilled desires. Obsessively drawn into his online games, her husband touches his tablet rather than his wife. And so while she is alone in her apartment, staring out the window, the immense city around and below reflected in her face expresses her loneliness and longing. Her silhouette in front of the large window, together with the pink curtains and red flowers, blur together and become ethereal and ghostlike. Desire creeps into the images, in a dreamlike way, constantly interchanged with realistic images. She begins to have vivid dreams of sexual encounters with an unknown man whom she cannot see or touch but can feel. These encounters are filmed in fragmented close-ups, bringing the spectator completely into her 'erotic reveries', which seem to commingle her body parts with those of the unknown man. In these erotic scenes *Longing for the Rain*'s aesthetics resonates with Schneemann's *Fuses*. When Fang wakes up, her husband is lying with his back turned towards her.

Fang begins to become absent-minded. Her husband complains that he has to eat bread for breakfast and wants her wontons back; they do not come back. In a quite hilarious scene in her car parked at a shopping mall, her best friend gives her a present: a pink dildo with pearls that glows in the dark. Giggling, she tells Fang that she has been suppressing her urges for too long. Fang's friend has a new lover, but when they break up, they go out drinking with some young boys, where (in a kind of inversion of Freud's complaint about women), Fang's friend cries on one of the boys' shoulders about the fact that she really does not know what men want and that they certainly do not know the price women pay for love. When Fang mentions the reality of her ghost-lover who seems to visit her increasingly often, and takes possession of her, they go on a quest for an explanation and a solution.

The tour through all kinds of religious and spiritual persons is in documentary style (there are no professional actors in the rest of the film, except for Fang and her best friend). They first visit a Taoist priest who tells Fang that her ghost-lover is a spirit who has come to

Figure 3.4 *Longing for the Rain* (Lina Yang, 2013).

take her soul: 'between 100 days and three years from now he'll have taken your soul away', the priest declares. After this he performs some rituals and gives her a talisman for protection. Of course, his explanation is quite speculative, and yet it sends shivers along our spines. Fang is devastated and tries to stop dreaming, which obviously is not so easy. Then they visit a fortune-teller who declares that the ghost is a husband from a previous life who wishes to reconnect and that he does not necessarily mean her harm. We are relieved with her, but still worried when she throws away the talisman of the priest, who had a different vision.

Sure enough, her spectral lover takes over during one afternoon when she is with her daughter out in the woods. They are both taking a nap in the car, but when, after an extremely realistic erotic encounter, Fang wakes up, her daughter is gone. This leads to an existential crisis and the disintegration of her marriage. Her mother yells at her on the phone, insisting that she see a psychiatrist, or that she should have taken a normal lover, not a ghost. Her aunt takes her to a Buddhist retreat, where monks give consultation to desperate women (another beautiful ethnographic moment) and where she battles her ghost with the 'om mani padme hum' mantra which the women sing and to which they dance all night.[12] While offering the enigmatic Buddhist wisdom, 'We seek six realms of existence in dreams, but only wake up to one boundless universe', the film remains with Fang's desires when, in the final images, she seems to have fallen in love with one of the young Buddhist monks whom she sees through the window, from afar, in a blurry orange haze, like another ghost perhaps.

In its frank portrayal of female sexuality, which includes nudity, masturbation and sex toys, Yang's film seems to be unique in Chinese cinema. Asked about this, the director replied that women's sexuality has always been there but never discussed in the open, even if in terms of sexuality China has become quite liberated:

> What I want is to express women's contradictory emotions and depressed sexuality. It is not like once the society becomes open in terms of sex, everybody enjoys sex without concerns accordingly. Such freedom is a delusion. A rather ungrounded freedom. For example, it seems now in China people can talk about homosexuality, unlike what was in the old days. It has become a trendy topic but in terms of legalizing equal marriage, people are no longer that enthusiastic or allowed to argue. (Xu and Lee 2013)

Produced in Hong Kong, *Longing for the Rain* has not yet been shown in mainland China, which seems to prove Yang's point. Nevertheless, with its combination of spirituality, spectrality, sexuality and social realism,

Yang has made a film that extends the spectrum of the horror genre in an intimate, ghostly, poetic way, giving the possession film a new twist; just as *In the Cut* presents a different type of final girl who battles ambiguous inner demons while exploring longing and lust, and the dangers with which they are associated.

'Pink Like the Inside of You, Baby'

It is perhaps interesting to briefly mention here how much has changed since the 1960s and the violent reactions to Schneemann's *Fuses*, not least because all the female filmmakers discussed in this chapter (and many others) who have begun to speak for themselves, claim spaces for self-expression instead of being spoken about. Also, this is partly a result of the influence of social media platforms that have redistributed power structures in terms of access to a global audiences and introduced a more playful attitude towards gender and sexuality on Instagram and other platforms. This does not mean that all inequalities have now been erased and everything is good for everyone, but that there have been changes cannot be denied.

In 2018 Janelle Monáe presented her third studio album *Dirty Computer* alongside a narrative science fiction film which includes video clips from the album. The entire album is a celebration of diversity and gender fluidity, in particular black female gender queerness, which is most unambiguously expressed in 'Pynk'. The lyrics of the song explicitly address the female sex organ, symbolised by the colour pink (no red in this video). While Monáe snaps her fingers to establish the rhythm of the song, she revels in: 'Pink like the inside of you, baby / Pink behind all of the doors, crazy / Pink like the tongue that goes down, maybe / Pink like the paradise found.' In the video for 'Pynk' (directed by Emma Westenberg), Monáe and her black female dancers perform in a pink-filtered desert setting, wearing pink vagina trousers that leave no doubt about the meaning of the song.[13] Tessa Thompson appears in the video as Monáe's lover and, at one point, with her head between Monáe's legs, suggests an image in which her head is a clitoris and her hair, pubic hair. While the video might easily have turned into another vehicle to sell female sex, in all its pink and brightly coloured glossiness, it does not allow this (in some scenes the dancers wear underwear proclaiming 'I Grab Back' and 'Great Cosmic Mother'). There are no bikini lines, the women are totally in control and they are obviously having fun, celebrating self-love and 'pussy power', and adding that 'deep inside we are all just pink'. As Angelika Floria remarks, the video will make you (black women, women of colour, white women, hopefully also all colours of men) 'feel like a goddess' (Florio 2018). From the 'dark continent' and invisibility, female sexuality, and black gender-queer sexuality, are out in the bright pink sunlight, empowering all with creativity, humour and respect.

CHAPTER 4

Growing Bellies, Failing Mothers, Scary Offspring

Mother of All Horror

Of all the monstrous-feminine tropes in horror cinema, woman's reproductive powers are perhaps the most frightening. Creed evokes the ancient connection between woman, womb and the monstrous as well as the image of the abject inside the maternal body as frequent tropes in horror cinema. Ridley Scott's *Alien* (1979) contains not only a reworking of Freud's primal scene (where the child sees the parents have intercourse and fantasises about the question: 'where do babies come from?') as a scene of birth, but also the idea of the archaic parthenogenetic mother, the mother who can give birth without the help of a male counterpart. Creed analyses several birth scene variations inside the mother-ship of *Alien*, all staged by the invisible alien mother. *Alien* is also an example of a horror film that contains 'monstrous wombs . . . intra-uterine settings that consist of dark, narrow, winding passages leading to a central room, cellar or other symbolic place of birth' (Creed 1993: 53). Other horror films refer to the monstrosity of the womb belonging to a woman who gives birth to some kind of terrifying creature. Some of the most famous male-directed horror films address the archaic or parthenogenetic mother who has the power of reproduction beyond male control, such as the animalistic mother in David Cronenberg's *The Brood* (1979), who incubates offspring in a repugnant sac outside her belly that she bites open to release the atrocious creatures that she grows there. Other horror fantasies pertaining to pregnancy explore the idea of impregnation by the devil or other demon entities (such as evil computers), most famously rendered in *Rosemary's Baby* (dir. Roman Polanski, 1968) and *Demon Seed* (dir. Donald Cammell, 1977).[1] The scary power of the mother is further epitomised in Hitchcock's seminal slasher film *Psycho* (1960), as well as in *Carrie* (dir. Brian De Palma, 1979) and *Mommie Dearest* (dir. Frank Perry, 1981). On the other hand, offspring can also induce fear in the mother, as does the evil daughter in Mervyn Leroy's *The Bad Seed* (1956) or the malicious son in Richard Donner's *The Omen* (1976).

While issues of pregnancy, childbearing and motherhood are so intensely related to the female body, it is astonishing that so few of these themes have been taken up by female directors, at least until recently. This chapter is about films that explicitly address the (sometimes terrifying) experience of pregnancy, desire and the refusal of reproduction, as well as mother–child relations seen through the eyes and camera lenses of women themselves.

When discussing horror related to reproduction and the creation of new life, it is useful to recall that it was a woman who gave birth to one of the best-known fictional monsters of the horror genre. In 1816, at the age of 18, Mary Shelley, then still Mary Wollstonecraft Godwin, had a dream that would lead to her famous novel *Frankenstein, or the Modern Prometheus*. This was during a rainy summer in Switzerland that she spent with her step-sister Claire Clairmont, Percy Shelley, John Polidori (who would soon write the early vampire story *Vampyre*) and Lord Byron. *Frankenstein* first appeared anonymously in 1818, as no publisher wanted to put the name of a woman on such a horrific story. The second edition in 1823 did carry her name as the author. But the subsequent popularity of her book, and the dozens of filmic versions that it inspired, more or less eclipsed her as author once more. Victor Frankenstein, the mad scientist who creates a hideous creature composed of bits of corpses brought back to life by galvanism and other unorthodox experimental methods, took over. His fear of the fiend he created has occupied the popular imagination of monstrosity ever since. Shelley's novel, however, demonstrates compassion for the monster of Frankenstein, who has a voice of his own (the middle part of the novel is his story) and who is actually quite intelligent but rejected and abandoned for being different.

In her film *Mary Shelley* (2018), Haifaa al-Mansour, the first Saudi-Arabian female filmmaker, brings Mary Shelley as the creator of *Frankenstein* back to life. Embodied by Elle Fanning, al-Mansour describes the biographical circumstances that led to Shelley's creation. Her mother, Mary Wollstonecraft, published *A Vindication of the Rights of Women* in 1792, a text that is often considered one of the first feminist writings. She died in childbirth in 1797 and Mary always felt guilty of 'killing' her mother, whom she only knew through her written words. Her father, William Godwin, was a philosopher, famous for his ideas and publications about anarchism. In the summer of 1816, Mary was not yet Percy Shelley's wife but she had already borne him two children: a girl, Clara, who died a few weeks after her birth, and a boy William, who would also die at a very young age. Al-Mansour only shows us the traumatic death of the first child in the film. This experience of losing a child was part of *Frankenstein*'s origins. In her introduction to the novel Wendy Lesser indicates that a few weeks after her first child died, when Mary was only 17, she wrote in her diary: 'Dreamt that my little baby came to life again; that it had only been cold, and that we rubbed it before the fire, and it lived. Awake to find no baby. I think about the little thing all day' (Shelley 1992: xvii). It is fair to say that *Frankenstein*, at least in part, is the translation of that dream of bringing a deceased baby back to life; a dream that turns into a nightmare. While it is commonly acknowledged that Shelley was influenced by scientific demonstrations of galvanism and experiments with electricity that were popular at the time, a fact that is undeniably true, the particular female experience that is behind the Frankenstein story is worth recalling, and lingers behind many of the female-authored films that will be discussed in this chapter.[2]

Virginia Woolf has often been considered as purely intellectual, frigid and barren. She was childless, but she struggled with this all her life, and in her writings, motherhood is often treated with ambivalence (Anderson 2004; Savino 2008; Kanai 2013). For a long time she fought a mental battle with her own mother, Julia Duckworth Stephen, a typical Victorian mother of eight, an 'Angel in the House', who died suddenly when Woolf was 13. Her ghostly spirit never left Woolf until she wrote *To the Lighthouse*, where she reappears as Mrs Ramsay (who equally dies suddenly mid-way through the novel). As Woolf writes:

I wrote *To the Lighthouse* very quickly; and when it was written, I ceased to be obsessed by mother. I no longer hear her voice; I do not see her. I suppose that I did for myself what psycho-analysts do for their patients. I expressed some very long and deeply felt emotion. And in expressing it I explained it and then laid it to rest. (Woolf quoted in Kanai 2013: 145)

From Woolf's diaries it is known that she suffered from her childlessness, an emotion that was harder to come to terms with than the ghost of her mother. When she married Leonard Woolf in 1912, she still expected to have children in the future. However, considering Woolf's fear of physical interaction during sexual intercourse (perhaps caused by a traumatic assault by her half-brother in her youth) and her unstable mental health and occasional breakdowns, the couple decided not to have any children. It was Leonard, however, who was most scared of what childbearing would do to his wife. Woolf would regret the decision profoundly, even though she had no idealist ideas about motherhood (Kanai 2013). Throughout her books motherhood is described in non-romanticised ways, presenting imperfect mothers who fail (Savino 2008), or who struggle with the combination of motherhood and being an artist (Anderson 2004).[3] What Woolf demonstrates is that, especially in the Victorian times in which she lived, childbearing and pregnancy seemed to epitomise womanhood; and (the decision to) not have children leaves its mark. This struggle with motherhood and the ambiguous feelings about desiring (or not desiring) to be a mother, together with societal expectations about motherhood, have been topics for feminists that, as we shall see, are re-encountered and reimagined in female-authored poetics of horror today.

Feminism, Pregnancy and Motherhood

Following Woolf and the first wave of feminists, the feminists of the second wave had even more explicit points of view and mixed feelings about childbearing and motherhood. Many followed in the footsteps of Simone de Beauvoir, whose book *The Second Sex*, which came out in 1949, marked the beginning of the second wave of feminism. De Beauvoir explicitly chose not to have any children, and although she was in an open relationship with Jean-Paul Sartre all her life, she also never married. Marriage and motherhood she considered forms of vassalage and subordination that she wished to break away from. In a chapter on motherhood in *The Second Sex*, de Beauvoir addresses several issues that, as we will see later in this chapter, would return in the language of horror aesthetics in the work of contemporary female directors. Addressing issues of birth control and abortion, themes that would become an important focus of feminists in the 1970s, de Beauvoir argues:

> Forced motherhood results in bringing miserable children into the world, children whose parents cannot feed them, who become victims of public assistance or 'martyr children.' It must be pointed out that the same society so determined to defend the rights of the fetus shows no interest in children after they are born; instead of trying to reform this scandalous institution called public assistance, society prosecutes abortionists; those responsible for delivering orphans to torturers are left free; society closes its eyes to the horrible tyranny practiced in 'reform schools' or in the private homes of child abusers; and while it refuses to accept that the fetus belongs to the mother carrying it, it nevertheless agrees that the child is his parents' thing. (de Beauvoir 2010: 525)

In her seminal book *Women, Race and Class* from 1981, Angela Davis criticises in her chapter on racism, birth control and reproductive rights the failure of the abortion rights campaign to critically evaluate the issue of birth control from a black historical perspective. The history of birth control is related to involuntary sterilisation, and this racist form of abuse of reproductive rights should have been taken into account in the abortion debates that emerged during the 1970s, when involuntary sterilisation was still current (Davis provides the example of sterilisation programmes in Puerto Rico and some US states). Furthermore, Davis points out that among black women kept in slavery, self-imposed abortions and infanticide were often carried out because of the desperate conditions that newborn children would encounter (growing up in slavery, perhaps being sold to other slave holders at a young age, without any rights of parenthood). Toni Morrison's *Beloved* dramatises the same problem. Davis asserts that 'the campaign often failed to provide a voice for women who wanted the right to legal abortion while deploring the social conditions that prohibited them from bearing more children' (1983: 119). Davis equally fights for 'voluntary motherhood' for all women, but she points out that besides a racial dimension there is also a class difference to be taken into account, as working-class women had often fewer means to opt for 'voluntary motherhood'.

Another aspect of the female reproductive body that came into focus during the feminist struggles in the 1970s was the idea that pregnancy and motherhood as such should be valued more positively. Hélène Cixous, for instance, vehemently rejected the taboo of the pregnant body, inviting women to choose this experience if they wished. She does not address issues of class and race, but her *écriture féminine* invites women to write, as it invites them to appreciate womanhood:

> Woman must write herself: must write about women and bring women to writing, from which they have been driven away as violently as from their bodies – for the same reasons, by the same law, with the same fatal goal. Woman must put herself into the text – as into the world and into history – by her own movement. (Cixous 1976: 875)

Both her fiction and academic writing are saturated with maternal metaphors, referring to mother's milk as 'white ink' and talking about overflowing 'breasts with an urge to come to language' (Cixous 1976: 882; Pisters 2007: 72). As indicated in the introduction, writing has always been the privileged means for women to come to self-expression, and it is thematised more than once in female-directed films. Al-Mansour's *Mary Shelley* begins with the sound of a quill pen on paper, before we hear Mary Shelley's voice-over; before we see anything she is writing.[4]

In cinematographic writing it is time to evoke 'the mother of the *nouvelle vague*', Agnès Varda, who in one of her first films opens up film language to the female experience. In her experimental film *L'Opera Mouffe* (1958), whose title in English is *Diary of a Pregnant Woman*, Varda films in an associative way her experiences of pregnancy. It is perhaps one of the first films (outside medical contexts) to show a naked pregnant woman's body in full glory, breathing, the movements of the baby visible underneath the skin. This image is followed by an associative image of a huge pumpkin that is cut open and cleaned of its interior seeds, leaving the round shape of the pumpkin's skin and flesh with a sort of uterine shelter in the middle. Images of the busy market and people in the Rue Mouffetard where Varda lived at the time of filming are intercut with a man and a woman making love in a rather shabby apartment, alternating with faces in the crowd, a chick emerging from its egg, and intertitles. 'Cravings', one of the intertitles says, followed by shots of raw (yes, very raw) fish and meat in close-up, and a pregnant women leaving a flower shop, eating the flowers she holds in her hands. Playful and subversive, Varda's free way of addressing these issues of feminine experience in a personal style has been a source of inspiration to many women directors who followed.[5]

Varda's films in the 1970s take up more explicitly feminist themes such as abortion, birth control (and the feminist slogan 'our bellies belong to us'), as well as the joys of pregnancy and alternative lifestyles beyond marriage, most notably in *One Sings, the Other Doesn't* (1977). Birgit Hein's partially found-footage film *Uncanny Women* (1991) shows (among other 'monstrous' images of women as soldiers, criminals, drunk and sexual beings) images of a woman's body giving birth, and it is still striking for its graphic details, which makes it understandable why birthing inspires so much awe and fear, especially when it is only *seen* and not experienced.

Figure 4.1 *One Sings, the Other Doesn't* (Agnès Varda, 1977).

Yet after the second wave of feminist films, relatively few films directed by woman have addressed the experience of pregnancy and the refusal or desire of reproduction very explicitly. Before considering some recent pregnancy themes picked up by the horror genre, I want to briefly mention one notable exception that has taken up these issues. Referring to an earlier article on the refusal of reproduction in the work of Moroccan filmmakers (Pisters 2007), I want to highlight in particular *The Sleeping Child* (2004), Yasmine Kassari's portrait of women in an Amazigh village in the north of Morocco, which articulates the ritual that pregnant women perform when they want to postpone the birth of a child. Local tradition has it that women can decide to have their unborn child put to sleep in the womb, for instance, in order to wait until its father returns from Europe, where they go to find work, as is the case for the protagonist Zeineb (Mounia Osfour). A traditional magician puts a spell on the foetus and prescribes a special ritual to wake it up. The film shows the harsh conditions of the women in the village who have nothing much to do but wait, and the ways in which their lives remain completely dictated by the men, even in their absence. In the end, Zeineb takes the decision to break the spell and refuses the proper ritual to wake up the child, which implies that the child will not be born at all. It is an active refusal of reproduction of her own restricted life, in light of the absence of any possibility of change.

Kassari's film also demonstrates in a beautiful way that the issue of birth control has many diverse ways of being addressed. Even though everybody knows that biologically it is not possible to put an unborn child to sleep, the belief that women have this power is shared by everyone, and so it offers its own ways of managing tradition (for instance, putting a child to sleep when there is a pregnancy outside wedlock) and resistance (Zeineb's decision to 'abort' the spell). This type of abortion-by-magic in *The Sleeping Child* is also a form of resistance against patriarchy. Here I want to mention Kasari's film in relation to the spectrum of women's own voices about these issues that we also encounter in the language of horror.

The Experience of Pregnancy in Gynaehorror

In her book *Women, Monstrosity and Horror Film*, Erin Harrington focuses on gynaehorror, 'horror that deals with all aspects of female reproductive horror, from the reproductive and sexual organs, to virginity and first sex, through to pregnancy, birth and motherhood, and finally to menopause and post-menopause' (2018: 3). Equally indebted to Creed and Clover's seminal studies as I am, Harrington offers a critical feminist interrogation of gynaehorror, but also proposes alternative readings that reveal other modes of observing this genre. The films that Harrington discusses are (with a few exceptions) largely made by male directors, but the concept of authorship is not important for her, given the fact that none of the films are discussed under the director's name. Harrington focuses on the representations themselves and puts them in a discursive context of popular cultural and sociocultural ideas about girls, women and mothers, thus offering many interesting readings that complement Creed's psychoanalytic approach, the narrative analyses of Clover, and the work of other feminists such as Sarah Arnold on the maternal horror film (2013), and more cognitive analyses of the genre as proposed by Rikke Schubart's *Mastering Fear* (2018), to which I will return shortly.

Harrington's chapter on pregnancy, abortion and foetal subjectivity is aptly titled 'The Lady Vanishes', by which she means that in many horror films that take up pregnancy, the body and subjectivity of the woman carrying the baby vanishes in favour of the unborn child. Given the fact that historically the pregnant body was 'deemed excessive, taboo, and unsightly' (Harrington 2018: 88), the excessiveness of the horror genre is a useful place to consider such a 'monstrous' topic. Harrington's main references in this chapter are Polanski's classic *Rosemary's Baby* (1968) and Julian Maury and Alexandre Bustillo's *Inside* (2007). What is typical in both films is that the body of the mother becomes secondary to that of the foetus she is carrying. Frequently, in these pregnancy horror films the woman is equated with the house she is confined to, and often she is a vessel for some kind of religious or demonic force.[6] In *Rosemary's Baby*, Rosemary's (Mia Farrow) husband Guy (John Cassevetes) seals a pact with the devil in exchange for a successful acting career: unbeknown to her, Rosemary will be impregnated by Satan and conceive the anti-Christ. As Harrington observes, 'the result is that the woman's body becomes abstracted: she is a fleshy stand-in for an incorporeal, spiritual battle that is greater than her' (2018: 107). And for that, she must 'sacrifice her physical and psychological sense of self in the knowledge that she must also bear the child for the good (or ill) of all humanity' (2018: 108).

The French horror film *Inside* has a particular way of explicitly and quite literally disposing of the female body. Here the pregnant woman Sarah (Alison Paradis) has her body literally ripped open by a 'mad woman' named La Femme (Beatrice Dalle), who inserts scissors into Sarah's belly and cuts out the baby. La Femme appears to be a grieving mother herself who lost her own child during the car accident in which both pregnant women are involved at the beginning of the film. Harrington observes that at key moments the child, like a dimly lit Lennart Nilsson image of a foetus, appears in the iconography of the scenes. The primacy of the foetal subject is apparent from the beginning of the film when the almost-ready-to-be-born child floats 'peacefully within the depersonalized maternal environment (that is the uterus)' (Harrington 2018: 118). *Inside* is also elaborately analysed by Schubart. Contrary to Harrington, Schubart argues that while *Inside* is barely watchable because of the fact that the film does not present us with an alien or fantasmatic pregnancy but a 'real' pregnant body (Schubart also refers to real-life 'womb raider' horror stories), the emphasis of this film is actually on 'female terrain with female interests' (Schubart 2018: 187). Both female protagonists are having a sort of super catfight over a baby: 'The attack is carried out with unflinching aggression and while it is revulsive, we understand the motive: La Femme lost her baby' (2018: 187) – and she wants it back. In Creed's psychoanalytic observations, the monstrous pregnant body in the modern horror film is abject in itself and a product of male anxiety. Schubart argues that with *Inside* 'the pregnant body is no longer male territory with male fears. It has become a woman's battlefield' (2018: 187). Nevertheless Harrington's point remains valid – because Sarah literally gets squashed to mush and does not survive, we can wonder if it would make a difference if female directors were to pick up this hyperfeminine theme.[7] Would it change anything in the poetics of horror? Let us look at a few examples that could be considered as reactions to the two seminal films just discussed.

In her micro-budget film *Lyle* (2014), Stewart Thorndike reimagines *Rosemary's Baby*.[8] In her film, the lesbian couple Leah (Gaby Hoffmann) and June (Ingrid Jungermann) come to live with their toddler daughter Lyle (Eleanor Hopkins) in a black brownstone apartment in Brooklyn. The fact that they are lesbian is only part of the story and not the focus of the plot, which is a sign of a changed world in the twenty-first century as opposed to the heterosexual normativity in the 1960s. They are expecting their second child and while June is mostly away at work (she is a record producer), Leah takes care of Lyle, unpacks the moving boxes, prepares the new baby room, and meets the neighbours: an intrusive model living upstairs; and an older, baby-obsessed woman who pretends to be pregnant, living downstairs. Over the course of the months during which her belly grows, Leah feels increasingly uneasy in the apartment. When in an unexpected moment of inattention, no more than a split second, Lyle falls and dies, Leah becomes depressed and paranoid about the house itself, where apparently several babies before Lyle have also died. In a very realistic setting, the film brings one into the mind of a pregnant woman under the pressures of a changing body, homely confinement and the guilt of not being a good enough mother. In spite of the contextual changes that have made same-sex marriages normal, the pressures of motherhood remain unchanged. Moreover, the film brings us completely into the confused mind of the pregnant woman without giving us the certainty of a final truth. Contrary to *Rosemary's Baby*, Thorndike's film never gives us the satanic explanation, but remains ambiguous about Leah's perceptions: is it just her mind, verging on paranoia and madness, or is something else really at work here? What the film in any case does is remain with Leah's subjectivity, and it does not replace it in favour of the baby's subjectivity (despite the title of the film).

In a way, Alice Lowe's *Prevenge* (2016) could be considered a response to *Inside*. Lowe, a British actress, wrote the story and directed herself while she was heavily pregnant. In an interview she indicated that she was reacting to friends advising her not to tell anyone she was pregnant when applying for acting jobs:

> Just keep it quiet, because if you tell people you won't get work. And it won't just be like three months or six months, it will be like five years, because people just assume that you are busy or that you've changed beyond recognition or that you have gone into a different casting bracket or something. People just write you off. (Miller 2017)

Instead of going home and waiting for another role, she wrote the script of a dark horror comedy about a pregnant serial killer, Ruth (Lowe herself) who receives instructions from her unborn baby. It is only gradually that viewers discover the reasons behind the killing spree, but from the beginning there is also the gloomy sadness and pre-partum depression that Lowe puts in her performance.

Let us first follow the blood-red trail in the film. The killings follow the rules of the slasher genre: they are bloody, all performed with a kitchen knife (or heavy handheld object), and as in the rape-revenge plot, the woman uses all the tricks of seduction and feminine vulnerability, especially in the first two murders of rather perverse and misogynistic men. The condescending DJ (Tom Davis), who likes 'fat birds', is shocked when he feels movement in her round belly (he thought she was just heavy); a few moments later he is literally castrated, which is displayed in all its gory detail. But there are also women on Ruth's hit list, one of whom is a lonely but cold and ruthless businesswoman (Kate Dickie) who advises the pregnant job applicant to 'get the motherhood thing out of her system' or she will never find a job. Her remark that the demanding job asks her to make difficult 'cutthroat decisions' is met with a literal confirmation by Ruth who stands up, walks to the far side of the glass table to say goodbye, kisses her and at the same time slams her head down against the glass, and on the upswing, slashes her throat. All this is performed with a speed and

Figure 4.2 *Prevenge* (Alice Lowe, 2017).

force one would not expect from a pregnant woman. There is a lot of blood left on the table when she departs.

We find out that all the people on Ruth's list (she keeps track of them in a 'Baby's first steps' book) were on a mountain-climbing hike with her husband. After an accident, they decide to cut the red rope; it is literally his lifeline (not coincidentally resonating with an umbilical cord), and this kills him, leaving the baby without a father. The final confrontation is with the hiking instructor on Halloween night when Ruth dresses up in a bright-red gown with a death mask painted on her face. However, her waters break and she ends up in hospital with complications. The last blood-drenched images are of a real caesarean section showing a doctor's hand slipping inside the incision and retrieving a blood-covered baby from her womb. The direct link between the gory generic horror and an actual childbirth through the 'poetics of blood' is salient and telling.

There are also two other elements worthy of investigation. First of all, the status of the foetus, as Harrington analysed in *Inside* and many other pregnancy horror films, is remarkable. Contrary to the foetal images in *Inside*, we never *see* the baby in *Prevenge* (at least not before it is born), we only hear her. Ruth even skips a scheduled scan because she does 'not want to know what's inside her'. The baby certainly seems to have autonomy, as she often speaks to her mother in a high-pitched voice to encourage the avenging of her father. She does not, however, obscure the mother. While Ruth hears her unborn child talking and seems to take its advice, she also gets into a moral argument with it when she has to kill a witness who is actually very nice, or when she finds out that the hiking instructor is about to become a father himself. I think it is important that there is no image of the baby, as ultrasound and computer-generated foetuses have much more power to assume control from the intimate internal connection than a mother has talking regularly to her unborn child. They have a dialogical relationship that frightens her, but she retains her own agency. It also reflects the experience of women talking silently to their unborn child.

This relates to the second layer of observations on pregnancy that Lowe conveys. During her scheduled check-ups, Ruth confesses to the midwife that she is frightened of the baby, that she would rather swap her for the return of her husband, and that she feels she is in the grip of a hostile takeover. The midwife on the one hand confirms that Ruth will no longer have control over her body (milk can simply be expelled by her breasts unexpectedly) or mind (unexpected emotions or thoughts can be over-whelming). On the other hand, she reassures the mother-to-be that it is all quite normal. Obviously, she does not know about the killings. When the baby is born at the end of the film, we see a lovely cute little baby girl (Lowe's own daughter Della Moon Synnott); she does not talk to her mother but simply gurgles: 'She is perfectly normal', Ruth says to the midwife, realising that the voice she heard via the baby was actually her own voice speaking to herself. 'I did terrible things, I got it all wrong', she exclaims. To which the midwife replies: 'Look we all get it wrong, always. It's fine.' While the midwife speaks from a different level of experience than Ruth and the spectator, these hospital check-up and post-delivery scenes do indeed 'bleed into' the horror scenes that give them the meta-phoric force to express the strains of childbearing and all the physical and emotional pressures that go along with it.

On the more subdued end of the spectrum of the poetics of horror, *Olmo and the Seagull* (2014) is an emotionally moving film about preg-nancy from a female point of view that actually takes up similar issues as *Prevenge*, expressing the same fears and anxieties about pregnancy, without the gory poetics but with the same intensity. Petra Costa and Lea Glob's docu-fiction translates female anxieties about changes both in the body and in the practical organisation of life caused by pregnancy. The film shows that the bodily changes and inner experiences involved in this life-changing event are both powerful and terrifying. Costa and Glob follow and film actors Olivia Corsini and Serge Nicolai during Olivia's pregnancy. Originally, they intended to make a film about the blend-ing of real life and stage acting during the rehearsals and production of Chekhov's *The Seagull*, in which they are both performing. But when Olivia discovers that she is pregnant, and because of some pregnancy complications that force her to remain homebound, the emphasis shifts: 'I just want to see if there is a way we can see a bit more of what's hap-pening in your mind and in your body', we hear one of the directors in voice-over say to Olivia. They provide Olivia with a handheld camera to create a video diary which she uses to film the confined space of her home, her growing belly, and to speak her mind, which is full of insecurity and doubt. The film seamlessly blends these video diaries with older home movies, documentary scenes with Serge and friends at home and stage performances, in a mix that blends reality with fiction. Olivia also coincides with the two main figures in Chekhov's play, Arkadina, the ageing actress, and Nina, the actress who falls into madness, thus troubling the borders between reality and imagination, life and acting, madness and sanity. The film's opening is characteristic of these slippages: we see the actors performing on stage, Olivia first as Arkadina, then as Nina, following the cues of one of the film directors whom we hear out of view telling her to move closer to centre stage (it might be a voice in Olivia's head); a moment later another off-stage voice (Olivia's) confesses, while performing Chekhov's mad heroine: 'Sometimes I think I could slip into insanity just by accident. The thought terrifies me.'

There is one scene in particular that I want to highlight here, which is the moment when Oliva undergoes an ultrasound scan and the couple receive the news that something is wrong. On-screen, the monitor with the baby *in utero* is clearly visible, and the doctor's voice is heard saying that the baby is all right but that there is a rather large haematoma in the lower uterus that creates the risk of a miscarriage. Olivia must immediately stop working, remain home, rest and avoid stairs. Olivia wipes away a tear; we feel her panic, a mixture of the fear of something happening to the baby and what the consequences of staying home will be. Since she has always worked and performed, it feels like 'a rug pulled from under her feet and she has nowhere to grab'. However, we stay with her, she does not vanish to make room for the baby. We remain focused on her and her 'domestic entrapment' in the diminutive top-floor apartment, with far too many stairs to climb safely, and most of the time in solitude, as Serge continues to work and perform. We witness how she confronts her inner demons and insecurities about the alien inside which is feeding on her, 'imposing the rules of the game' already before birth, and how she tackles her anxieties about being excluded from the world and her new mother-to-be role. Towards the end of her pregnancy she actually goes out, buying flowers for a party that she intends to throw for her friends, like Mrs Dalloway arranging the flowers at home and then receiving guests. The entire tone of the film, the intimacy of the cameras, both Olivia's diary reflections and Costa and Glob's observant camera, the confiding voice of Olivia and the scenes of confrontation and love with Serge, all bring us into an unprecedented proximity with the experience of pregnancy. The last sequence provides glimpses of baby Olmo just after birth, sharing some overwhelming moments of bliss and confusion.

Possessed by a Ghost Child

Pregnancy involves many physical and emotional risks, and the devastating experience of a miscarriage is another female experience that is not often discussed (on film), even though it is an experience that is quite common. As an exception to the rule, Aliona van der Horst's documentary *Water Children* (2011) is a beautiful and sad journey into fertility, miscarriage and stillborn babies, life and death, based on a Japanese mourning ritual to commemorate unborn children ('water children'). In her first film *Blood Child* (2017), Jennifer Phillips presents this topic in the language of horror via the South Asian myth of Toyol, ghost children who are raised by black magic and destroy everyone connected with them.[9] Phillips, who was born in Singapore and is of Malay and Indonesian descent, based the film on a true story involving a ghost child that occurred during the 1940s (Meehan 2018). In the film, she has translated the story to our contemporary age with an American couple living in Singapore, where the woman, Ashley (Alyx Melone), has a miscarriage. Their Indonesian housekeeper Siti (Cynthia Lee MacQuarrie) finds her in great pain and in a pool of blood on the bathroom floor and calls for help. However, before we get to know this backstory, we see Ashley playing with a red ball with a pale, greenish-looking child in a flaming-red dress. They are in a garden; Siti is standing at the side, smiling but with a slightly worried look. They now live in Minnesota and Siti has moved with them to the United States. In a series of flashbacks and flash-forwards, the film unfolds its narrative.

Three interrelated themes propel the story forward with spine-shivering effects. First, there is Ashley, whom we see suffering from depression after the loss of her unborn child. Then there is Siti, and the rather denigrating ways in which the husband Bill (Biden Hall) and others such as Ashley's mother (Lisa Kovack) and her best friend Naomi (Charlotte Cartel) treat her. Finally, there is the spooky presence of the ghost child who turns out to possess dark forces. Ashley's devastation over the miscarriage and depression is clear not only from flashbacks to Singapore, where we see how she does not want to eat or leave the house, but also in the attempts that her best friend Naomi and her mother make to cheer her up when they are back in the United States. She only revives when she finds herself pregnant again.

As a loyal and self-effacing housekeeper, Siti embodies the reality of many lower-class South-East Asian women in service to wealthy

Westerners. The way she is disregarded and spoken of is telling of the neocolonial power relations which show that between the 1940s of the original story and the contemporary setting, not much has changed. In a particularly telling scene Ashley uncovers these relations. Siti finds the ultrasound of the new foetus, which opens a flashback to a similar scan of her previous pregnancy that went wrong, which was kept by Ashley while still in mourning. Siti brings her some food, urging her in broken English to eat. Ashley asks her if she knows at all what it feels like when your world suddenly goes dark and all your hopes are taken away. When Siti answers 'Yes Ma'am', Ashley retorts in disbelief: 'What on earth does a woman of some remote village in Indonesia know about a world going dark? You barely understand me when I ask you to boil some water.' To which Siti replies that her husband died on a motorcycle when it collided with a bus. Ashley realises how condescending she has been and apologises. It is a small scene but it contains many of the misunderstandings and blindnesses of a Western-centrism that thinks according to its own knowledge systems while disregarding 'the Other'.

Immediately after her apology, Ashley asks Siti to take her to someone who knows how to bring her daughter back. Again Siti's reply that this is black magic and 'no good' is not taken seriously. In further flashbacks throughout the film, we see how Ashley summons her deceased baby back into the world via a ritual that involves, among other procedures, the creation of a talisman, and Asley's repeatedly calling 'Anna di Angelo come stay with me.' The ghost child is born. She wears a flaming-red dress and plays with a red ball. In addition, she is only visible to Ashley and Siti, who have now bonded because of this secret summoning. Once a month the ghost child needs to be fed raw meat and blood. Only gradually is this situation discovered by the others, even if they sense her presence unknowingly. Bill thinks that he imagines the footsteps of a child in the house, as if their baby was born. Naomi senses a foul smell in the house and begins to investigate; she experiences sudden flashes of her ghostly apparition, just as Ashley's mother soon understands that something is wrong. The ghost child becomes more obsessive in wanting to have her mother all to herself when a new baby threatens to take her place. Combined with ignoring the magical rituals, this leads to an unnerving chain of deadly events that Ashley cannot undo, however much she struggles to again reject her ghost child.

In the final moments of the film we find Ashley in an isolation cell of a psychiatric ward. A doctor is discussing her case with students: 'She exhibits signs of paranoia, combined with bouts of severe depression that can last for several weeks, she has moments of psychotic manifestation

Figure 4.3 *Blood Child* (Jennifer Phillips, 2017).

which include hearing voices, delusions, hallucinations.' When one of the students remarks that something terrible must have happened to her, the doctor explains that her entire family perished in a house fire and that she has been in the hospital ever since. Regarding the red-dressed doll she is holding, he explains: 'She believes that is her child. She suffered a miscarriage but not in the fire. We believe that that is what triggered her psychotic break.' Clover argued that in many of the possession films of the 1970s, female-connoted black magic is pitted against masculine white science, and is always in the service of the transformation of a male figure in crisis who has to open up (Clover 1992: 97–113). In *Blood Child*, 'white science' is given as the only rational explanation for Asley's behaviour, proposing that everything that we saw before was her delusions. However, the deaths in the (actual) story were real, and in the film we see Siti visiting Ashley, looking anxious, and then walking away holding the hand of a little girl wearing a red dress. Ghost children must be helped to pass on; they will not just dissipate of their own accord. While the woman who loses a child and remains delusional, holding a doll as her child, has been a common way of expressing the grief of a miscarriage since early cinema, *Blood Child* introduces the chilling reality of other practices that might be non-scientific but have real consequences nevertheless. 'Mommy don't leave me' are the last words we hear before the credits appear. Anna di Angelo remains with Ashley, just as she had wished.

Frozen Blood: Suffocating Mothers without Subjectivity

Doubts and fears about motherhood itself are the next hurdles in gynae-horror that have often found their translation in the language of horror.

Clearly, the mother's powers can be considered as abject or castrating, as Creed discusses. Another version of psychoanalysis from the second wave of feminism that deals explicitly with motherhood, and that should be brought back into focus when discussing the poetics of horror and motherhood, is Luce Irigaray's revision of Freud's mother–daughter relationship. As is well known, Freud argued that mother–daughter relationships are only strong in the pre-oedipal phase (until the age of about four), after which the girl discovers that her mother is 'castrated' and she turns towards the father as love object to compensate for this genital 'lack'. Irigaray has criticised this allegedly typical 'penis envy' of girls, first of all by indicating that female sexual organs lack nothing: women have lips, clitoris, vagina, womb, breasts (Qiu 2009: 32). By giving up all this in favour of the father, the girl must completely relinquish her own subjectivity, Irigaray argued.

However, she also indicates that the mother–daughter relationship can be an ambivalent and inharmonious one. In her short but still very powerful article 'One Does not Stir without the Other', Irigaray observes how, because of their subordinated place in patriarchy, mothers do not have a subjectivity of their own, and hence they can become suffocating for their daughters: 'With your milk, Mother, I swallowed ice . . . You flowed into me, and that hot liquid became poison, paralyzing me. My blood no longer circulates to my feet or my hands, or as far as my head. It is immobilized, thickened by the cold' (Irigaray 1981: 60). Irigaray gives a sharp diagnosis of the potentially poisonous symbiotic relationship between mother and daughter that does not provide either with room for an independent existence. She observes that mother–daughter relations often lack true communication, creating an abyss between them that keeps the daughter captive in the mother's confinement, as 'one does not move without the other'. Irigaray concludes her essay with a cry from the daughter: 'When the one of us comes into the world, the other goes underground. When the one carries life, the other dies. And what I wanted from you, Mother, was this: that in giving me life, you still remain alive' (1981: 67).

Traditionally the melodrama has been the place where complex mother–daughter relations have been explored, most famously in films such as *Stella Dallas* (dir. King Vidor, 1937), *Mildred Pierce* (dir. Michael Curtiz, 1945) and *Imitation of Life* (dir. Douglas Sirk, 1959). Many excellent studies have analysed how the melodrama shows that 'home is where the heart is', that this is the designated place for women, and that if they want to be 'something else besides a mother' they must tragically renounce either their daughter or their own life (Williams 1984b; Gledhill 1987). In *Imitation of Life*, we see how the black mother–daughter relationship is even more complicated because of the racism that accretes on top of patriarchal structures. In Sirk's melodrama the light-skinned daughter of a black woman who works as a housekeeper for a white woman and her daughter wishes to pass for white, and devastatingly rejects her mother because of her darker skin. Conversely, in her short film *The Body Beautiful* (1991), Ngozi Onwurah (whose *Welcome II the Terrordome* was discussed in Chapter 1), as a black daughter, pays tribute to her white mother, whom, as we hear Onwurah herself say in voice-over, she 'always considered sexless, shapeless and safe but never saw as a woman with her own body and her own desires'. Onwurah's actual mother, Madge, performs in the film. After the birth of her younger brother, Onwurah's mother underwent a mastectomy. The relationship between Onwurah herself, a beautiful young black woman who had a modelling career (played by Sian Martin in the film) and her mother, an older white woman with a scarred body, is not a symbiotic one. However, the film provides the mother with agency and a desiring and desired body (she has a young black lover), and the embrace between mother and daughter at the end is a moving expression of this interracial mother–daughter relationship. The daughter concludes in a way that reflects what Irigaray calls for: 'She had moulded me, she fought for me, protected me, I am not in her image but reflected in her soul.'

Very often mother–daughter relations remain difficult. In the horror genre, the epitome of the possessive and destructive mother–daughter relationship is, of course, *Carrie*, discussed in the introduction of this book. In Kimberley Peirce's remake of *Carrie* we have seen that the daughter already has more space to move, more agency and subjectivity of and for herself, reflecting and resonating with societal developments that give more room for girls' subjectivity, even if they have now often internalised the constraints of social media and ideals of perfection.[10] Irigaray's observations about suffocating mother–daughter relations are explicitly taken up from a female subjective point of view in Debora Haywood's fantasy-horror feature debut *Pin Cushion* (2017). The film is shot in an extremely expressive colour palette that gives everything a crisp, candy store glazing, which nonetheless fails to obscure the biting tragedies that lie beneath the luscious images.[11] At the beginning of the film, mother Lyn (Joanna Scanlan) and daughter Iona (Lily Newmark) arrive in an English village. They form an idiosyncratic and awkward couple, dressed in outlandish and colourful clothes, walking hand in hand to their new house. Their relationship is completely interdependent in the exact tragically suffocating way Irigaray described. The mother, insecure and socially awkward, is always trying to take care of her daughter, watching her, protecting her. The daughter, pale, ginger-haired and totally inexperienced, wants to take care of the mother. Things go wrong the moment Iona senses that 'something begins to stir in her' (Irigaray 1981: 60). At her new school Iona meets some 'frenemies', the coolest but meanest girls who seem to allow Iona into their clique but in fact have chosen her as their bullying target. Her sexual awakening (involving among other things an electric toothbrush that one of the girls applies to her panties) confuses her, and her naivety gets her into a lot of trouble. She is drawn into a poker game that leaves her naked and exposed online, and her name is shamed. She begins pouring whiskey into her water bottle, which obviously brings her more profound problems.

Her mother, in the meantime, suffers her own insecurities and bullying. She passively undergoes the humiliating behaviour of her neighbour and her desperation overshadows her simplicity and gawkiness. When she discovers her daughter's online pictures, she joins a women's group, wearing a T-shirt with the awkward text 'Lick me till Ice Cream.' Her introduction to the unwelcoming group is comical but terribly bitter and desperate: 'Hi, I'm Lyn, my daughter is a sexual maniac and I need some friends. It's my fault because I used to dress up and walk at night hoping I'd get raped so I could have a child, so I could have someone.' The women send her away, telling her they are not there to be a freak show.

Horror elements seep into the visual candy-coloured poetics when Lyn takes a hacksaw, cleans it in hot water and begins to apply it to her hunchback, attempting to sever the hump when she takes a bath. Blood is dripping into the water when Iona comes in and rescues her mother. At other moments, Iona escapes into dream fantasies, and at one point she hears the sound of howling wolves (the pack of bullying friends who do not stop harassing her) and then gunshots. Her mother enters covered in blood, saying, 'Don't worry, I've killed them darling.' When her daughter is almost burned in one of the assaults, Lyn finally takes control and in the only revenge she can manage, she ensures that Iona's most persistent bullies witness her suicide, turning herself into a haunting ghost (and a white cat). Iona is cared for by the only black girl in the gang, Chelsea (Bethany Antonia), who all along did not feel good about the bullying but did not dare to do anything. Iona wakes up in a room of her own in her friend's home; a white cat jumps onto her bed.

With this perfect blend of fantasy and horror, Haywood not only tells the story of 'one who does not stir without the other', but also reveals the complex network of emotions around this stifling mother–daughter relationship, which gives them both a subjectivity, albeit a tragic one, and brings to light the problem of bullying. It also shows that the bullying girls have their reasons; in one scene, Keeley (Sacha Cordy Nice), her greatest bully, explains to Iona that she must put on a show to keep her image intact. It is a confessional moment; however, it does not prevent her from continuing her brutish games.

The film was shot in Swadlincote, South Derbyshire, Haywood's home town, and much of the filming took place in the same school where as a young girl she was herself bullied, and where the walls were emblazoned with her name. This was the first time she had returned for many years. It worked as a healing process: 'What I found most healing', Haywood said,

> was when I was doing research, I realized that if you're a bully you're not in a good place yourself. Somebody sorted and happy doesn't need to behave like that. So, it did give me empathy toward [bullies] because I think they're acting out of their own unhappiness. One of the things I like to do in my writing is ask, 'Who's the person behind the label?' And the film gave us an opportunity to really explore who those people are. (Sears 2018)

Pin Cushion is a colourfully dark fairy tale that extends the poetics of horror to show its heartbreaking mother–daughter heroines trapped in each other's vulnerability, addressing an emotional reality that is recognisable for many.[12]

Scared and Scary Mothers under Pressure

In her book *Maternal Horror Film*, Sarah Arnold analyses the American horror film through the lens of the maternal melodrama and focuses on the psychoanalytic script of the self-sacrificing 'good mother' versus the selfish and demonic 'bad mother', arguing that the maternal horror film 'perpetuates an ideology of idealized motherhood' versus the 'evil or transgressive mother' (2013: 4), even if this is not an entirely stable construct. Both Harrington in her book on gynaehorror and Schubart in her study of horror cinema as a place to master fear refer to Arnold's division between good and bad horror mothers, arguing that these two opposed figures are a script (or a myth) that may translate deeply engrained popular and cultural discourses about motherhood, but that has nothing to do with the complexities of motherhood as actually experienced. Both Harrington and Schubart present *Grace* (dir. Paul Solet, 2009) and *The Babadook* (dir. Jennifer Kent, 2014) as examples of maternal horror films that show how these discourses of motherhood compete, and ultimately that 'where monstrous mothers may fail to mother properly, the monstrous maternal is not just an expression of maternal monstrosity; indeed it is also the inability – of any mother – to conform to the rigid (and monstrous) demands of ideal motherhood' (Harrington 2018: 209). *The Babadook* is a striking female-directed horror film that demonstrates how horror aesthetics can be stretched across the emotional spectrum into a deeply complex and moving narrative of mourning, grieving, caring and coping. Because so many excellent things have been written about Kent's extraordinary film, which won a lot of critical acclaim, I will keep my own observations brief, in favour of talking about a few other films related to motherhood, children and parents.

As Harrington argues, *The Babadook* locates 'terror and monstrosity deep within the heart of a mother' (2018: 180). Amelia (Essie Davis), who according to one critic plays both Jack Nicholson and Shelley Duvall in Kubrick's *The Shining* (Murrian 2019), is a single mother working at a care facility for elderly people who lives with her son Samuel (Noah Wiseman) in a rather gloomy and gothic-looking house; everything in the house and in Amelia's behaviour speaks to her exhaustion. Sam has trouble sleeping and as the day of his seventh birthday approaches, Amelia finds it more and more difficult to cope with him. Amelia lost her husband in a car accident on the way to the clinic where she gave birth to Sam, leaving her with the care of a baby and no room to grieve.

The Babadook of the title is a monstrous black figure from a blood-red pop-up book that keeps appearing in the house, no matter what Amelia does to dispose of it. For Harrington, the film is an example of the pressures any new mother faces, provoked by discourses of ideal and bad mothers, which are monstrous in themselves – simply because no one can live up to that ideal (Harrington 2018: 216). Schubart, too, argues that Amelia struggles with how to be a good mother, rejecting 'the mother script handed her by society, represented by [her sister] Claire and Claire's friends, and by the school. From trying to be a good mother, [she] has become a bad mother' (Schubart 2018: 200). Schubart analyses how *The Babadook* offers what she calls a 'meta-play', the 'emotional engagement with fiction' that allows one to face one's shadowy side (2018: 193). The horror aesthetic functions as a 'protective frame' for the spectator (as we know there is no actual danger), but it can prime us to see the real monster that lies beneath the horror form. Schubart focuses on the son who, while at the beginning he seems to be the problem, actually coaches his mother (through his monster plays and his demands that she face the monster) into finally acknowledging her grief, facing the trauma of loss and slaying the monster.

I concur with Harrington and Schubart that *The Babadook* is an extremely powerful film that incrementally forces us to experience the exhaustion of (single) motherhood. The film brings us into Amelia's mental world and translates the desperation of doing your best but seeing that things do not work out; the heartbreak of seeing your child bullied for being different (epitomised in a harrowing party scene where Sam is pushed away by his cousin); the slow paranoia that blurs the lines between reality and fiction, perception and hallucination; the confrontation with the 'black bile' of sorrow and grief that will not go away, but that will be kept in a safe space of the house/mind. This is beautifully expressed at the end of the film, when Amelia descends to the basement to give the Babadook (a shape-shifting figure that ultimately represents her deceased husband) some worms to eat, but remains calm. It is perhaps one of the most moving metaphors of grieving and coping to be translated into a poetics of horror.

The troubled relations between mothers and sons are at the centre of several other psychological horror films that address the problem of good or bad motherhood. In *We Need to Talk about Kevin* (dir. Lynne Ramsay, 2011) a mother, Eva (Tilda Swinton), is torn apart by feelings of guilt for having brought into the world her son, Kevin (Ezra Miller), who commits a horrific crime, killing his classmates, his father and sister. In a non-linear stream-of-consciousness narration, we remain in the traumatised mind of the mother and see how, from her pregnancy onwards, she was unable to handle her son, not knowing how to play with him and being truly scared of him. We do not know how much of this is actually true, as the aesthetics of the film keep us close to her perspective. The film opens with a nightmare in which Eva is drenched by the red flesh and juice of a Spanish Tomatina, then awakes to discover that angry neighbours have covered her house and car in red paint. Dream, memory, reality – everything is coloured by her fear of her son, and the horrific questions of doubt, guilt and remorse combined with grief. Yet still, something that could perhaps be called 'love' remains, albeit of a terrifying kind. When Eva visits Kevin in prison on the second anniversary of the terrible acts he committed, for the first time ever he looks at her, and shows a sign of doubt about what he did; for the first time Eva really embraces him; still frightened, she walks out of the prison into a white light. The film leaves the viewer with questions about whether pure evil exists, and the responsibilities of parenthood. There is no unambiguous answer.

Goodnight Mommy (2014), directed by the aunt–nephew duo Veronika Franz and Severin Fiala, presents a mother–son story from the perspective of the son, or rather sons, as we are dealing here with 10-year-old identical twins Lukas and Elias (played by Lukas and Elias Schwarz) who reside in a luxurious, modern, Austrian country villa surrounded by cornfields, swampy lakesides and woodlands. They are playing hide and seek out in the fields (*Ich Seh, Ich Seh*, the German title of the film, meaning I see, I see, refers to this game) when their mother returns from having been away to undergo facial plastic surgery. Her head bandaged and her behaviour rather distanced, moody and short-tempered, they do not recognise their loving mother: 'She is so different, she is not like our mommy', they whisper to one another in the dark. She also seems cruel, only preparing food for Elias, refusing to talk to Lukas. From this point onwards, they put the mother (Susanne Wuest) to the test, to prove that she is their real mother. However, she does a poor job of convincing them. While playing a guessing game with a sticky note attached to her fore-head that reads 'Mummy', she fails to provide the correct response. The clue from the twins telling her 'You have two children' is rejected: 'How can I possibly know everyone who has two children?' The children grow increasingly suspicious, and their observations are mixed with nightmar-ish visions of their mother going out into the woods, stripping naked and superhumanly twisting and contorting her head, which metamorphoses into alien features. At other moments, they observe her in the bathroom, catching her red bloodshot eyes in a magnifying mirror with a frightening shock. They experience all this as horrific and creepy, like a thin thread of terror underlying every image.

In an interview Franz and Fiala talked about the origins of the story. The broader interest in the (hidden) power relations of family structures is evoked by a tongue-in-cheek pre-credit scene with a mischievous refer-ence to a family like the Von Trapps from *The Sound of Music*, singing a sweet lullaby to wish everyone a good night's sleep, and their awakening from 'so-many-layered-dreams'. Nevertheless, the main premise of the film is the fact that children often doubt if their parents really are their parents. Sometimes it is a desire for other parents, as in *Pin Cushion*, where a daughter dreams of her sad, hunchbacked mother being replaced by a beautiful, loving and freedom-giving stewardess kind of mother. Franz recalls her own childhood hide-and-seek games, when her mother covered with a blanket was really scary: 'I thought: This is a monster now; she's not my mom. She's showing her true side and the monster is coming out' (Buder 2015). Another moment that Franz and Fiala mention as a starting point is when they were watching a television reality makeover show, in which mothers were taken away from their families, sometimes for even a month or two, to return completely transformed:

> They get a new mouth, new teeth, new cheekbones, new haircut, and new clothes. When the family is reunited, what is positioned to be a magical, music-swelling red carpet moment is subverted by unmistakable horror. If you look closely at the

children, their eyes are horrified. There was even one moment when a girl grabbed her father's arm and said, 'This is not our mother.' (Buder 2015)

That feeling of alienation, broken trust and dissociative identity is where the film's plot emerged from.

All the horror elements related to the children's doubts and suspicions could be explained in a natural way, especially when we learn that there was a divorce that would explain the absent father, as well as the empty spaces in the photo album that the boys find bizarre; even the facial surgery can be explained, as the mother (who is a television presenter) is under pressure to remain young and attractive. All this simmers in the background while her presence remains haunting, just like the shadowy pictures on the living room walls that keep spooking the boys. However, there are also events that slowly but surely make us doubt our allegiance to the boys' point of view, when additional horror elements penetrate the *mise en scène*. We see the boys placing a large beetle on their sleeping mother's bandaged face; it crawls into her mouth, and a few moments later they cut open her belly and hundreds of beetles crawl out. It is part of their nightmares but it is also a foreshadowing of the intensity with which the boys intend to pursue the search for their real mother.

In the last part of the film, the mood changes from crawling terror to chilling bodily horror when the boys decide to bind their mother to her bed and begin to torture her with household items such as bandages, a magnifying glass (with which they burn her skin by focusing the rays of the sun), tape, superglue and a pair of scissors. During the first hour of the film, the blinds were closed throughout the entire house and everything took place in shadowy darkness; now there is full light and no escape from the gruesome torture that the boys inflict on their mother. One begins to realise that it is rather strange that Lukas never speaks to anyone except his brother. Moreover, with a shock we remember that at the beginning of the film, we often saw Lukas disappearing into a black void, Elias calling his name at regular intervals without reply. It is only at the very last moment (and too late) that the mother talks to Elias, promising that she will play the game with him of pretending his brother is still alive, that he should not feel guilty about the accident that killed Lukas. Correspondingly, we realise that we have been in the mind of Elias, who can still see his brother. As a final test he asks his mother to tell him what Lukas is doing (he is holding a burning candle near the curtains), but the mother shouts in utter desperation that she cannot see what he sees. This is another children's guessing game (I see, I see what you cannot see . . .) that is entwined in the German title. As the directors explain: 'Our film is about this clash of perspectives and people not communicating clearly or talking to each other. That's what maybe links us to Austrian cinema, where crises arise because people aren't talking to each other' (Myers 2015). I would say that this problem of communication is not just part of Austrian cinema, but also an enormous problem in many of the family dramas exposed by horror films.

A Further Note on Parents and Other Blood Ties from Hell

Before proceeding to the final film in this chapter, which takes the question of pregnancy, mothers and children to an entirely different dimension, I want first to mention a few other horror films that address child–parent relations in the language of horror. Lucile Hadžihalilović's short feature *Mimi* (1996), Marina de Van's *Dark Touch* (2013) and Nora Fingscheidt's *System Crasher* (2019) translate the dreadful phenomenon of everyday domestic child abuse into horror aesthetics. Veronica Kedar shows her rage against the dysfunctional family that is drenched in the violence of the state (of Israel) in her bloody portrait *Family* (2017).

The original French title of *Mimi* is *La Bouche de Jean-Pierre* (Jean-Pierre's Mouth) which sounds more menacing than the English title. Mimi (Sandra Sammartino) is a young girl whose mother tries to commit suicide when her husband leaves her. Everything tells us that this is not the first time Mimi's parents have had a fight, and that it is also not the first time her mother has resorted to this desperate act. Mimi is taken into the care of her aunt Solange (Denise Aaron-Schrofer). In her cramped apartment, she is literally assigned a place in a cupboard where she sleeps behind a yellow curtain. On the first night in the strange bed she hears Solange's boyfriend Jean-Pierre (Michel Trillot) arriving and sees how they make love in a rather passionless way, almost as if they are staging it for the little girl behind the curtain. The atmosphere is gloomy; Solange is irritated by the presence of her niece (an ugly feeling in Ngai's terms) and directs her to the communal stairwell of the building when she needs to make a telephone call. Mimi is taken in by a young Arab neighbour who is playing music with some friends. They are very gentle with her, understanding her loneliness, allowing her just to sit with them. When Solange finds her there, she sends Jean-Pierre to threaten the boys; a strand of racism gives the whole narrative a bleak undertone. While Solange is at work, Jean-Pierre makes a pass at the girl; he tries to kiss her but stops angrily when she freezes, holding her doll in her hands. Nothing really happens, but the threatening atmosphere is terribly depressing. Mimi now has nowhere to go, not even to the friendly neighbour who no longer opens the door now that he has been threatened.

The colour palette in this film is striking: everything is yellow with some greenish-brown glows and details. The absence of red actually indicates the absence of hope, the absence of anger and action. The total dreary and depressing loneliness and isolation of the girl is palpable in every image, every detail of the *mise en scène* and the concise script, which makes it understandable that her only way out and back to her mother seems to be to imitate the path that her mother has chosen. Mimi swallows a handful of pills and is taken to the hospital. Solange and Jean-Pierre travel home by bus. We are left with the understanding that this is not the last time Mimi will end up in a situation similar to her mother's tragic incapacity to handle life.

The situation in *Dark Touch* is even more sinister. De Van's horror drama, shot in dark colours (black, brown and grey dominate the chromatic palette), has been described as 'quiet drama and visceral gore [that] don't mix' (Robertson 2013). However, I think this mixture of the underlying real trauma of child abuse and the expression of resistance through the generic horror elements are actually the strength of the film. In *Dark Touch* the central heroine is 11-year-old Niamh (Missy Keating), who survives an attack on her family home that kills her parents and baby brother by hiding in a cupboard. While she claims that it was the house itself that began to operate of its own violent volition, the police consider it an attack by vandals. Niamh is offered shelter by a neighbouring couple, Nat (Marcella Plunkett) and Lucas (Pádraic Delaney), who lost a girl of the same age a few years earlier.

Niamh slowly discovers that when she is afraid things begin to move on their own. Her telekinetic powers make her another contemporary sister of Carrie. But De Van's film also takes us much further into the mind of the girl, as we learn from several scenes throughout the narrative that the bruises on her body and even on her baby brother's belly must be from abusive parents: both the father and the mother seem to have a habit of inflicting violence on their children, while on the surface they are completely normal and reasonable. This makes it understandable that Niamh does not trust her new carers, especially when she sees pictures of the deceased daughter, who is covered with bruises caused by her disease. To Niamh these are signs of abuse. She cannot be touched, cannot connect to others and is unable to allow anyone into her traumatised physical and mental space. The only person in the film who understands this is the (pregnant) social worker, who simply talks to her, and who recognises the abuse. There are two other children in her class who are typical victims of domestic violence. They are neglected, unwashed and wearing dirty clothes; the other kids in class harass them for this. Niamh recognises their situation in solidarity. In a nightmarish ending, when the foster parents learn about the child abuse that happened within the walls of their neighbour's house, the children take bloody revenge on both them and the other adults who they indiscriminately hold responsible for the traumas inflicted on them.

De Van shot the film in Ireland, not being able to find financial support for it in France; the French authorities even wanted to forbid the making of the film (Vely 2014). Stories of real child abuse might be too horrific to tell; even the 'safety' of the genre's aesthetics is probably not enough to translate the actual damage to the lives of the many children who are traumatised by monstrous adults in real life.

Nora Fingscheidt manages to translate this immensely tragic topic in a very powerful way in her debut film *System Crasher* (2019). Pink, a vivid, ferocious shade of pink, is the colour that expresses the heavily trau- matised mind of nine-year-old Benni (Helena Zengel). We never know exactly what happened, but incest or abuse by her desperate mother's boyfriend might be part of the backstory that has made Benni an unman- ageable and uncontrollable fury. She is moved from a foster home to several youth care houses, from special education institutions to hos- pitals, but everywhere she 'blows a fuse': she is a system crasher. Her favourite colour is pink, and in the entire *mise en scène*, she appears as the only pink figure in her surroundings. On the one hand this indicates her softer side, the longing for her mother who cannot deal with her and keeps rejecting her (in a heartbreaking scene not even the echo responds to her scream of 'Mommy'), and her brief moments of caring for others. On the other hand, pink also appears as a violent and fluorescent hue in traumatic image flashes that engulf the screen when she snaps, gets angry and becomes dangerous. Benni does not partake of her fate passively like Mimi in pale and painful yellow, nor does she have any dark telekinetic powers like Niamh. However, she does possess rage. We understand that soon, when her body begins to change, the screaming pinks will turn to fiery reds.

The tragedy in *System Crasher* is that everybody understands that Benni's intense and dangerous rage is a weapon to protect her from the pain and trauma of her situation. The adults in the film, social workers, most of whom Benni refuses to address by name, instead simply calling them 'caretaker', wish to help but are powerless. One of the youth workers, Micha (Albrecht Schuch), who specialises in guiding aggressive children, takes her on a nature trip in the hope that she will unwind, find some trust and peace of mind. However, when they return, nothing has been solved. The entire film evolves through a series of mini-dramas surrounding this wild and damaged girl who embodies the horrors of trauma and despair, utilising explosive, screaming pinks.

Veronica Kedar directs herself in *Family*. Under the motto 'home is where the hurt is', she presents a family drama in a bold horror script. Lily (Kedar) is a young photographer who literally – but of course we must understand this symbolically – shoots her entire family. In order to make space for herself as a person of her own, she must first unbind her family ties – an epigraph at the beginning of the film presents this in an understatement: 'The cost of growth is always a small act of violence.' In the opening sequence Lily takes a picture of herself surrounded by her family members: father, mother, sister and brother – all dead. Lily then runs to her psychiatrist to confess her deeds to the psychiatrist's daughter Talia (Tommy Baremboem), who, unwillingly at first, understands perfectly what she is talking about. As a child of divorced parents, Lily is met only with hatred from their father, and had to deal with an ailing and complaining mother, a suicidal sister and an abusive brother. The setting of the film is mostly the dark family house, which is difficult to escape from except by violence. References to the military and political violence in Israel are dispersed throughout the narrative. The brother returns home in military clothing, and the father carries a gun. The only moment when he takes his daughter seriously (her ambitions as photographer are completely denied) is when she asks him to teach her how to operate the gun. He does so gladly. It will soon be used against him. He will end up in the family portrait with a hole in his head; through the aperture in his head we see Lily taking a picture. It is one of the many imaginative and spectacular shots in the film that express Lily's 'small acts of violence' to liberate herself.

Besides addressing family issues, Kedar also uses the language of horror to address the violence in society at large, in particular that of her home country Israel. In an interview, she talked about childhood memories of exploding buses and constant news broadcasts of bodies and blood, which at a young age shocked her. Writing the blood in stories of her own gave her a sense of control, and inserting humour into the violence made it bearable, as she explained further:

> There is so much violence in Israel – even when you just walk down the street. This country who [*sic*] once believed in peace is now thirsty for blood. People are miserable and our values are simply twisted. There is no sense of community. It's each to their own. You become violent in your home when on the outside you are not getting what you need from your government. It sinks in. It's hard to live in a place where your government gets a hard-on from war. (Prestridge 2018)

With these explicit references to political violence, Kedar touches upon a fundamental dimension of the horror genre that will be developed further in the next chapter. Here, I want to emphasise that beyond the horrors of growing bellies and mother–child relationships is the entire family, and all the complex (sometimes abusive) relations between its members and between the family and society.

Pregnant Boys and Non-human Motherhood

To conclude this chapter on motherhood and gynaehorror I want to end with yet another dimension of the horrible fantastic which opens up altogether new perceptions of childbearing and motherhood that could be called posthuman. First, there is Octavia Butler's 'Blood Child', a short science fiction story she wrote in 1984, not to be confused with Jennifer Phillips's film of the same title discussed earlier. Butler's 'Blood Child' is her 'pregnant male story', as she declares in the afterword (Butler 2005b: 30). Gan, a male human child, who is chosen to be impregnated by an alien, a Tic called T'Gatoi, a giant squid-insect-like creature, narrates the story. It is set in the future where a colony of humans have escaped planet Earth and are hosted on the planet Tic, where the Tic have discovered that humans provide excellent hosts for Tic eggs. The Tics and the humans have found a way to respect and love each other, in spite of their huge differences.

Butler insists in her afterword that the story is not an allegory of slavery. Rather it is a confrontation with the fear of an insect, in particular the bot-fly that has 'horror-movie habits' (Butler 2005b: 30) of laying eggs in wounds left by bites from other insects and then devouring the surrounding flesh. Another key motivator of the story was the idea that humans would not be able simply to go and colonise some other planet as they had colonised the Earth, but would have to make 'some kind of accommodation with their um . . . hosts. Chances are that this would be an unusual accommodation' (Butler 2005b: 32). In 'Blood Child' all these layers come together in the story of Gan and T'Gatoi; when Gan must assist with another boy's horrific caesarean section, the cut-open body of the male host reveals 'red worms crawling over redder human flesh' (Butler 2005b: 17). Gan becomes scared, and no longer wants to be a host for the Tic zygotes, but in the end he decides to allow himself to be impregnated anyway, and accepts the love and protection of T'Gatoi.

Mixed with science fiction fantasy, we recognise in Butler's story many of the horrifying anxieties about impregnation and giving birth that we encounter in gynaehorror. The theme of male and alien pregnancy is also taken up in *Evolution* (2015), directed by Hadžihalilović. Hadžihalilović addresses monstrosity in terms of striking and strange horror aesthetics in her own idiosyncratic way. I am not sure if 'Blood Child' was on her mind while making the film, but I want to acknowledge the posthuman elements that Butler introduces, which were picked up by Donna Haraway in her cyborg and Chthulucene theories of the post- or transhuman (1991, 2016), and which seem to be a part of the poetics of horror as a new poetics of relation in contemporary cinema. In their book *Squid Cinema from Hell*, William Brown and David H. Fleming mention *Evolution* as one of these typical cephalopod-like films that go beyond human binary relations and transcend the human and non-human in tentacular ways (Brown and Fleming 2020). However, let us first look at the poetics of the film.

In her director's statement, Hadžihalilović articulates that one of the inspirations of the film was the work of Giorgio de Chirico.[13] Like the mysterious green/reddish nightmarish paintings of de Chirico, *Evolution* contains elements of mystery, mythology and menace. The striking formal elements of the same colour palette and abstraction infuse Creed's notions of monstrous motherhood with new elements of ambiguity and ambivalence, addressing the feminine and female in non-human ways. The film is set in a remote microcosmos, a seaside village, and was filmed along the black rocky shores of the Canary island of Lanzarote. The village is uniquely populated by pre-adolescent boys, each of them living with a mother who might not be their biological mother. The women have a special connection to the sea: they are all dressed alike in sober, light-brown dresses, wet hair worn in a tight ponytail, with something alien in their black 'vaguely cetacean' eyes (Combs 2016: 71). At the beginning of the film, Nicolas (Max Brebant) is swimming in the blue-green sea when he sees among the waving orange-red coral a glimpse of the drowned body of a boy, a starfish affixed to his belly. Frightened, he runs home, where his mother (Julie-Marie Parmentier) tells him that 'the sea makes you see strange things'. A little later, she swims to the surface with a huge bright-red starfish as proof that he had imagined things. (We later see her carrying a dead body, surrounded by other mothers, so we know Nicolas is not just imagining things.) She feeds him with slimy black-green seaweed and makes him ingest a black substance that is his medication, 'because at your age your body is changing and weakening like lizards or crabs'. The eerie qualities of the setting and the figures who populate this coastal commune evoke horror scenarios in our mind, but fail to fit any well-known template or affective response.

The starfish is an important and recurrent figure in the film. Besides its compositional bright-red colour (to which I will return), it signifies among other things the Virgin Mary as Stella Maris (Star of the Sea), and as protector and guarantor of safe conduct over troubled waters (Combs 2016: 71). It thus connects the sea (*la mer* in French) to motherhood (the Virgin Mary, the mother, *la mère* in French) and to the language of the unconscious, the sea being a powerful force of nature and symbol for unconscious imagination – which we of course also know from Woolf's *The Waves*. Moreover, if Marguerite Duras, who frequently described *la mer/la mère* in poetic connection to the unconscious of her abstract characters, had ever made a horror film, she could perhaps have made *Evolution*.

The starfish, however, also indicates a more non-human conception of the unconscious, reproduction and sexuality. One of the characteristics of starfish is that they can reproduce both sexually (by spawning, releasing sex cells into the water, usually in groups) and asexually (by dividing equally and regenerating the missing parts). Hadžihalilović has indicated in an interview that the film does not address sexuality, rather it addresses a pre-sexual unconscious (Prigge 2016).

Therefore, while the images that suggest 'archaic motherhood' in the first instance are more poetic and less horrific (the sea, the starfish rather than an alien monstrous creature), Creed's notion of monstrous femininity is still relevant, albeit with another twist. As already indicated, the boys receive some kind of medication to prepare them for 'changes in their body'. After the starfish incident, Nicolas becomes suspicious of his mother and follows her when she leaves the house at night. From behind a rock, he observes how the women of the village have grouped their naked bodies in a star-shaped pattern, crawling on the rocks like fish on dry land, seemingly giving birth to strange small creatures, or perhaps spawning. There is definitely some form of non-human sexuality and reproduction going on; the women groan and cry, almost like the calls of a siren or mermaid. Shocked and horrified, Nicolas runs back home. When he later sees his mother taking a shower, he notices strange suction cups on her back, revealing her squid-like cephalopod nature. Nicolas begins to rebel (drawing pictures, asking questions about the medication, openly doubting whether his mother truly is his mother). As a punishment, he is taken to a gloomy hospital where all the doctors and nurses are also women. Here he undergoes an operation on his belly and is impregnated (much like the male child in Butler's story). The boys in the clinic, not all of whom survive, give birth either on the operating table or in some kind of water-filled vessel.

Here, we are in the full nightmare of phantasies about the monstrous feminine, archaic and parthenogenetic motherhood, and fearsome

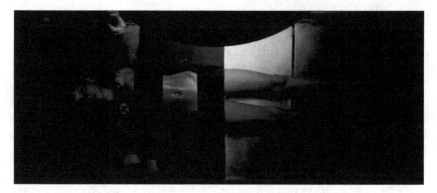

Figure 4.4 *Evolution* (Lucile Hadžihalilović, 2015).

powerful women. Through the operations on the boys' bellies and their giving birth to some kind of creature, the bodily horror is all rendered in a very quiet way, subdued by the unmoved faces of the nurses who are watching the caesarean operations on a screen. This is also true of the boys, who are afraid but remain very calm. There is no screaming that would invite the audience to do likewise. At the same time, also contrary to male horror films about frightening motherhood and primal birthing fantasies, it is a boy's body that undergoes the scary transformation. While for Hadžihalilović the choice of young boys had more to do with the pre-pubescent, gender-neutral perspective that she wanted to convey, she realised that choosing a girl would have brought in other kinds of cultural connotations, as discussed extensively in relation to menarche and vampirism in Chapter 2 (Prigge 2016). Hadžihalilović was also inspired by the idea of the hospital as a place where 'the body is given over to an all-powerful staff and can be subjected to a variety of bizarre practices'.[14] However, regardless of the neutral sexuality she intends, the fact that these are all boys in the hands of scary mother figures, and that they seem to undergo typical female experiences, does address a man's worst nightmare in embodying monstrous femininity.

However, there is more. The boys regain strength on the ward. One of the nurses taking care of Nicolas (Roxane Duran) is kind and protective of him and helps him escape from the hospital and the island. Using her own cetacean mermaid body as an oxygen tank, they swim underwater in an ambiguous embrace, an 'underwater odyssey that is also a kind of mating' (Combs 2016: 71). Perhaps it could even be argued that *Evolution* presents us with a thwarted tale of a 'final boy' who manages to escape, if only with the help of a not-completely-human friend. The nurse takes Nicolas to a boat far from shore, where she dives back into the water, leaving him behind. It is only at this moment, at the end of the film, that he shouts her name and we learn that she is called Stella, thereby recalling the starfish from the beginning of the film and closing the dreamlike, nightmarish loop. Hadžihalilović commented in an interview that *Evolution* is an 'intimate and psychological story' (Prigge 2016). So even if the film addresses something that we could call a collective unconscious, drawing on the symbolic images of the sea and the starfish, Hadžihalilović also constructs a dreamy, nightmarish world, borrowing elements from the horror genre, but completely transforming its aesthetics, opening to a wider array of emotions and an ambiguous, open-ended meaning.

As in almost all of the films discussed in this book, the colour red is the formal element in the *mise en scène* that constructs all these layered and ambivalent meanings. Jean-Luc Godard's famous 'not blood, just red' and 'not red, just blood' comes to mind (Barry 2012: 4).[15] In *Evolution*, most of the settings are in dark or bleak de Chirico colours: the black volcanic rocks of the island; the sand-coloured dresses of the mothers; the white houses of the village at night covered in yellowish points of light; and the green of the walls in the hospital matching the colour of the deep sea in the underwater scenes, sometimes filtered with yellow sunlight, rendering the hospital as an underwater space of the unconscious (this also gives the impression that the scene where Nicolas gives birth in a water tank could also be a dream). Additionally, in these monochromatic fields, red speckles, dots and splashes stand out. The red starfish in close-up at the beginning of the film covers almost the entire screen, like a gigantic and almost hallucinatory pool of red. Nicolas is the only boy who wears a red swimsuit, and when he runs on the rocks in a long shot, his body is seen almost as a moving red blood drop. In the hospital, a dark-red blanket covers the boys, drenching their bodies in the subdued but still violent colour of dried blood. Nicolas has a brown notebook and charcoal pencils to make his drawings, but Stella gives him a red pencil which he uses to colour the starfish on the belly of the boy in his drawings, and the curly vermilion hair of a female figure (his real mother perhaps?) that he draws, which seems to be inspired by the trails of wavy coral that he has seen in the deep sea. Like Gan in Butler's story, he willingly connects to something other than his human self, and we can assume that when he perhaps finds a new shore at the end of the film, he has grown and changed into a new (post)human being.

All these formal elements in the *mise en scène*, and especially the construction of colour as both dangerous and trivial, nightmarishly mythical and mundane, add to the intimate, dreamlike, private unconscious dimensions of the film, in which the inner and outer worlds seem to merge and where the non-human and human seem to combine in a posthuman universe.[16] This creates new dimensions of the monstrous-feminine where perhaps not everything is negative, and not every story needs to end in a frenzy of violence. The formal use of the colour red creates a psychological inner environment that invokes both danger and wonder. We see here how the notion of abjection as a liminal space between dream and reality, between human and non-human, moves beyond Freudian psychoanalysis, perhaps into a non-human, mythical, collective consciousness that is lurking below sea level. In the next chapter this idea of the posthuman will return, but only after we first 'stay with the trouble' of the current world (Haraway 2016).

The Tentacular and Modular Spectrum of Procreation

The female-directed films discussed in this chapter cover a wide range of issues and themes connected to gynaehorror, at least 'eight-legged' indeed, showing modulations and changes in questions relating to pregnancy, mother–child relationships and family issues that have often been treated in the modern horror film as the monstrous-feminine or connected to possessed woman and occult practices. Through a reading of the poetics of these films, I hope to have revealed that especially in these most typical female topics it does make a difference when the perspective is that of a woman's eye behind the camera lens. The physical and mental experience of pregnancy, childbirth, miscarriage and doubts about motherhood are all fundamental issues addressed in different ways. Obviously, this does not make male-directed films any less valuable, but it opens the spectrum of horror to a range of other emotions beyond fear and disgust, also allowing doubt, despair, irritation, rage and wonder, sometimes achieved by mixing horror with psychological drama or opening up psychological drama to the screaming of horror. Moreover, the textures, figures and colours of the materiality of these films and the drama of the narratives are interwoven with actual stories related to the fundamental questions of procreation, even beyond the human race.

CHAPTER 5

Political Gutting, Crushed Life and Poetic Justice

Shattering Political Evil

Besides explicit references to female monstrosity, gender and feminism, many horror films can be considered as allegories or commentaries on sociopolitical situations. History itself is in some significant ways a horror story of war, genocide, famine and other gruesome events. The 'incidents of vicious, macabre torture' involved in the violence of colonialism have often found translation in the aesthetics of the horror film (Smith 2015), albeit for a long time mostly seen from the point of view of the coloniser, or addressed only obliquely, as a sort of generic background for the horror adventures of its white protagonists. As Carol Clover indicated in *Men, Women and Chain Saws*, in many possession films white science is pitted against black magic, associated with a fear of the revenge of the repressed for the genocide on which many colonies and empires were built. The dread of the coloniser for the colonised is present in many voodoo films where the oppressed natives have a tendency to strike back with occult power or return as ghosts or zombies. I want to mention here *I'll Eat Your Skin*, also known as *Zombie Bloodbath* or *Voodoo Bloodbath* (dir. Del Tenney, 1964) and the Blaxploitation voodoo-zombie film *Sugar Hill* (dir. Paul Maslansky, 1974) as some of the many examples of this kind of horror sub-genre. And of course Stanley Kubrick's *The Shining* (1980), whose haunted hotel is built on a sacred ancient Native American burial ground, can also be considered in this light. Zombie films of the 1970s and 1980s, most famously George Romero's *Dawn of the Dead* (1978) entirely filmed at night in a shopping mall that brings out the dead, comment on capitalist consumer culture. Finally, there are the disaster films that illustrate how 'nature strikes back': *The Poseidon Adventure* (dir. Ronald Meam, 1972), *Earthquake* (dir. Mark Robson, 1974), *The Towering Inferno* (dir. John Guillermin, 1974), *Hurricane* (dir. Jerry Jameson, 1974) and *The Swarm* (dir. Irwin

Allen, 1978), to name but a few examples of the natural elements or the animal world that exemplify the revenge of nature.

For this final chapter, my question again is how these and other socio-political themes are picked up by the form of horror aesthetics in films made by women. While the issues addressed in the previous chapters are obviously not disconnected from their sociopolitical contexts, and while the subjects that could be included explicitly as political are countless, I will focus on three different thematic fields. I will look at the implications of the horrors of colonialism: genocide, slavery and racism; the focus will then shift to the contemporary legacies of these political events in stories about outlaws and the forgotten 'on the margins of' our contemporary society; and finally the issues of environmentalist and eco-politics will be explored. I will examine the work of some early female filmmakers who explicitly took up these political issues. As in the other chapters, I will begin by recalling Virginia Woolf, considering her attitude towards politics, war and slavery and the role of women.

As indicated in the introduction, Isabel Stenger and Virgini Despret have referred to Woolf's political legacy and invited women to pick up the baton; and as I argue in this book, female horror directors can be considered as Woolf's unruly daughters of sorts. However, Woolf has rarely been seen as a political writer. The focus has often been on her aesthetics (lyrical style, interior monologues, modernist experiments with narration) but not on the political subtext in her novels, except for her open feminist invitation to women to create a room of their own. In her excellent article 'To Crush Him in Our Own Country', which serves as my main reference here, Berenice Carroll focuses on the 'bolts of iron beneath the surface of Woolf's novels' (Carroll 1978: 103). She indicates how certain male critics have dismissed Woolf's references to India as being quite imprecise. In *The Waves* Percival dies in India; in *Mrs Dalloway* Peter Walsh spends most of his life there. One of the critics complains: 'It seems that she did not know enough about business and about India, if by enough we mean enough to mount a scene with the furniture of action' (Chambers quoted in Carroll 1978: 104). However, Carroll rightly argues that this 'completely misses the point of Woolf's frequent references to India, Egypt, Africa and the "doings" of the men who rule these domains of the British Empire' (1978: 104). In fact, she continues, Woolf was unusually well informed about matters of history and politics, but she had no intention of extolling the work of the patriarchal imperial rulers; as she argues in *Three Guineas*, the best strategy is to 'maintain an attitude of complete indifference . . . for it is far harder for human beings to take action when other people are indifferent than when their actions are made the center of excited emotion' (Woolf quoted in Carroll 1978: 108).

In *A Room of One's Own* we find other elements of criticism when Woolf reflects on the patriarchs, a criticism that returns in *Three Guineas* (where there are portraits of certain representatives of patriarchal power: 'a general', 'heralds', 'a university procession', 'a judge' and 'an archbishop'):

> True, they had money and power, but only at the cost of harboring in their breasts an eagle, a vulture, forever tearing the liver out and plucking at the lung – the instinct for possession, the rage for acquisition which drives them to desire other people's fields and goods perpetually; to make frontiers and flags; battleships and poison gas; to offer up their own lives and their children's lives. Walk through the Admiralty Arch . . . or any other avenue given up to trophies and cannon, and reflect upon the kind of glory celebrated there. Or watch in the spring sunshine the stockbroker and the great barrister going indoors to make money and more money and more money when it is a fact that five hundred pounds a year will keep one alive in the sunshine. (Woolf quoted in Carroll 1978: 107)

While Woolf was critical of patriarchy and all its political institutions, she also recognised that women often submitted to the place assigned to them, and as such also imposed it on other women (Mrs Ramsey, inspired by Woolf's own mother, is a case in point, embodying the stereotypical 'mystique of womanhood'); and that, for most, it was difficult or even impossible to speak out. 'Women have served all these centuries as looking-glasses possessing the magic and delicious power of reflecting the figure of man twice its natural size', Woolf writes in *A Room of One's Own*, adding that when she finally begins to tell the truth, the figure in the looking glass shrinks. 'How is he to go on giving judgement, civilizing natives, making laws, writing books, dressing up and speechifying at banquets, unless he can see himself at breakfast and at dinner at least twice the size he really is?' (Woolf quoted in Carroll 1978: 100).

And so in answer to the question 'how do we prevent war' when fascism and Nazism were gaining increasing momentum in the 1930s, in *Three Guineas* Woolf explains that 'if you insist upon fighting to protect me, or "our" country, let it be understood, soberly and rationally between us, that you are fighting . . . to procure benefits which I have not shared and probably will not share; but not to gratify my instincts, or to protect myself or my country' (Woolf quoted in Carroll 1978: 124). She advises that the best way to prevent war is by not repeating the same words and methods, but by finding new words and creating new methods, teaching people to understand each other instead of preparing to fight. She adds that it would be strategically useful to first battle 'the dictator' at home:

'Should we not help to crush him in our own country before we ask her to help us crush him abroad?' (Woolf quoted in Carroll 1978: 127). Woolf's tools of pen and paper, used to create a new language, new methods, and alternative perceptions, are therefore profoundly political. They have been picked up by other writers and by an increasing number of film-makers who I turn to now.

Tortures and Terrors of Colonialism and Racism

First, I should mention Octavia Butler, whose alternative worlds and visions of mutualistic relationships between humans and non-humans have already been mentioned in previous chapters in relation to the revised vampire story in *Fledgling* and the male-alien pregnancy in 'Blood Child'. One of her most famous novels, *Kindred*, is a time-travel story that explic-itly deals with creating an understanding of what it meant to be a slave in pre-Civil War America. Described by Butler herself as a 'grim fantasy', we encounter in this novel Dana, an African-American writer who lives in Los Angeles with her white husband Kevin, who is also a writer. The year is 1976. Both their families are opposed to their mixed-race marriage, but they are deeply in love and marry anyway. On Dana's twenty-sixth birth-day, all of a sudden she feels dizzy and finds herself transported back in time, specifically to Maryland, around 1815. Here, she saves a red-haired white boy named Rufus from drowning. When a white man points a gun at her, she dizzies back to 1976, where she tries to explain her sudden disappearance and reappearance to Kevin. In 1976 she had only been away for a few minutes, whereas she spent several hours in pre-Civil War Maryland. From then on Dana, who takes Kevin with her at some point, disappears for longer periods into her ancestors' world, as it becomes clear that Rufus and a black free woman forced into concubinage are her ances-tors. Dana and Kevin become inhabitants of antebellum America, where their marriage is completely inconceivable; Dana is considered chattel and is 'owned' by Kevin in that setting. They live and work (with a double temporal consciousness) on Rufus's father's plantation, witnessing and experiencing – with the hindsight of 1976 – the cruelties and profound injustices of slavery and deep racism, the whippings, the rapes, the sales of slave children, the constant fear of random beatings. Dana, who is the narrator and focaliser of the story, will not leave the past unharmed (as well as a scarred back, she will also lose an arm in the terror of the past). At the same time, without taking anything away from the horrors of slavery, the fact that the story has two interracial 'couples' offers a prospect for a future world that is less divided.

One of the first female directors to take up the issue of slavery and the wounds of hateful racism related to colonialism in her films was Euzhan Palcy.[1] In 1984 she directed *Sugar Cane Alley*, set on a sugarcane plantation in Martinique in the 1930s that is pervaded by racial inequalities. The film focuses on the story of a young boy and his courageous grandmother, who is determined to offer her grandson an education that will allow him to escape the dire conditions of poverty. It won many awards, which made it possible for Palcy's next project, *A Dry White Season* (1989), to become the first film directed by a woman of colour to be produced by a major Hollywood studio. *A Dry White Season* is set in 1976, the same year as Butler's *Kindred*. It takes us to the Soweto riots in South Africa and addresses the atrocities of the apartheid regime. Palcy adapted the screenplay from the novel of the same name by André Brink and travelled (not without danger, evading the South African secret service by disguising her identity) to South Africa to understand the situation in the townships and create an accurate picture of apartheid. Marlon Brando decided to support Palcy's project by returning from his self-imposed retirement to play a supporting role as a human rights lawyer. It was the only feature film that opposed apartheid to be made during the twenty-seven years that Nelson Mandela was imprisoned. Palcy met with Mandela the year after he was liberated. While the film does not explicitly address black femininity but focuses rather on general racial inequality and injustice during apartheid, I wish to zoom in on Palcy's film for the particular racial violence it addresses and the 'poetics of horror' it entails, as well as the call for a 'poetics of relation' that it proclaims.

During the opening credits of *A Dry White Season*, a black boy and a white boy are shown playing football on the lawn of a large lush garden. The next scene brings us to the reality of 1976 South Africa during the Soweto uprisings: white policemen are beating up and arresting black men and boys in a public place. The beatings are intercut with a football match, introducing Ben Du Toit (Donald Sutherland), a South African schoolteacher at a whites–only school, and his family. They return to their beautiful home and enjoy their garden. The scene is interrupted when Ben's son Johan sees the gardener, Gordon Ngubene (Winston Ntshona), arriving with his son Jonathan. Johan and Jonathan were the black and white boys we saw playing together during the credit sequence. However, Jonathan can now barely walk, having been beaten by the police because he was participating in a peaceful demonstration for better education for black people. Gordon asks for help, but Ben, blind to the realities of apartheid, answers that there is nothing he can do. Jonathan then disappears and is killed by the police during another riot. When Gordon is taken

Figure 5.1 *A Dry White Season* (Euzhan Palcy, 1989) and *White Material*
(Claire Denis, 2009).

by the police and tortured to death, and Gordon's wife Emily (Thoko
Ntshinga) also loses her life to violence, Ben begins to investigate. Little
by little he loses his white ignorance and becomes politically conscious.
He asks human rights lawyer Ian McKenzie (Marlon Brando) for help in
taking Gordon's case to court, but ultimately loses the case. As he becomes
more politically active, the story reveals the ever-deeper atrocities of the
apartheid regime.

As a white woman of Dutch descent, I find it extremely painful to watch
A Dry White Season. The injustice and immense cruelty of the repression
and violence against black people is intolerable and truly horrific. Hearing
Dutch and Afrikaans as the languages of tyranny makes me cringe with
collective shame for the colonial heritage of the Netherlands. As *A Dry
White Season* is not simply fiction but is completely interwoven with the
tapestry of historical reality, it can also be read as an allegory for Western
colonialism and the struggle of black people all over the world against the
injustices of domination. While some of these struggles can be compared
to the struggle for education, wages and the vote on the part of feminists

of the first wave, there are differences that are precisely those pointed out by black feminists such as bell hooks, who have argued that gender and race cannot simply be equated. This too, is a painful point made in *A Dry White Season*. Ben slowly awakens to the reality and decides to join the resistance. This resonates with the history of anti-apartheid movements in the Netherlands and other Western countries, which between 1960 and 1994 demonstrated and advocated for an independent South Africa and Mandela's exoneration. In the film, Melanie Bruwer (Susan Sarandon), a white journalist who works for an anti-apartheid newspaper, helps Ben. He is ashamed of his obliviousness, or 'white innocence' as Gloria Wekker has termed the coexistence of blindness to or even denial of racial discrimination alongside colonial violence (Wekker 2016). Ben knows his insights come too late; he will be killed, but the fight will go on.

However late opening his eyes, Ben's son supports him and helps him hide incriminating testimony from the regime, which provides hope for the next generation. However, the white women in the film defend the status quo of racial apartheid. When Ben wants to file a civil lawsuit against the police, his wife Suzette (Susannah Harker) tells him to back off, because 'it is not your son who died'. She then continues her rant, expressing the true fears of the colonisers, claiming rights to the country and the necessity of retaining it by force:

> Listen to me Ben. I heard what the police did and I am not saying that everything was right. But you think the blacks wouldn't do the same to us and worse if they had half a chance? Do you think they would let us go and live our quiet peaceful lives if they win? They'll swallow us up. It's *our* country Ben, we made every inch of it.

She urges him to choose a side, as in a war: 'You *have* to choose *your* people or you'll have no people.' When Ben replies that they must choose the truth, Suzette leaves him. Some time later, his daughter will betray him. Clearly, we are to understand that the intersections of gender and race can be intricate and are never self-evident, and that white womanhood can side with the imperial gaze that has nothing to do with the black experience, let alone black femininity.

The cinematographic poetics of Palcy's film 'create and express a shared reality' (Müller and Kappelhoff 2018: 36) that brings about a complex set of reflections on the historical and contemporary realities that the film addresses and the affective reactions that these raise in relation to questions of race. Like *Jeanne Dielman* and *A Question of Silence*, discussed in Chapter 1 as early feminist films that employ a 'poetics of horror' in some of their aesthetics, *A Dry White Season* is a film that violently breaks the silence regarding the truth of racial power relations. Unlike the first two films, however, the power imbalance does not lie between the sexes but is interracially determined. Together with Ngozi Onwurah, the director of *Welcome II the Terrordome* (also discussed in Chapter 1), which addresses some of the same issues, Palcy is among the powerful pioneering female voices who have not been afraid to passionately speak the truth about the injustice they observe, using a camera as their weapon of choice.

In *A Dry White Season* the most brutal white man, Captain Stolz (Jürgen Prochnow), who tortured Gordon and murders Ben, is killed by Stanley Machaya (Zakes Makae), Ben's black driver, who is part of the resistance. Importantly, however, the film itself functions as an image of agential resistance, as it stabs the silence. And as painful and powerful as the film is, and as clear as the positions of truth and justice are (even if the judicial system is blind to this), the poetics and aesthetics of the film language open an intersubjective encounter with the viewer that also invites a 'poetics of relation', as called for by Edouard Glissant. It is in the encounter with these shocking, stabbing images, the movement in the stories, the gestures, silences and resistance of the characters – in short it is in this poetics of horror that we can be moved in turn and be touched by a poetics of relation that might lead to a different future. Glissant expressed this as follows:

> despite seeing the political leap that must be managed, the horror of hunger and ignorance, torture and massacre to be conquered, the full load of knowledge tamed . . . and the exhausting flashes as we pass from one era to another . . . at the bow there is still something we now share: this murmur, cloud or rain or peaceful smoke. We know ourselves as part and as crowd, in an unknown that does not terrify. We cry our cry of poetry. Our boats are open, and we sail them for everyone. (Glissant 1997: 9)

Glissant's poetics of relation allows for an engagement with the fabric of fiction and reality in the film text that gives us insights and perspectives not easily otherwise gained. This does not mean that *A Dry White Season* offers a solution; it shows that the battle for justice needs to be fought in interracial solidarity and that white people cannot claim innocence or ignorance.

In her short film *Coffee Colored Children* (1988), Onwurah makes it painfully clear that for the children of an interracial couple it is often difficult to find a place in society. Before she made *The Body Beautiful*, discussed in the previous chapter, *Coffee Colored Children* took up the racism her family encountered while she was growing up in Newcastle in an all-white environment. Living without their father, her white mother and the three mixed-race children met unbearable racism. Onwurah produced this auto-biographical film together with her brother Simon. In the opening sequence people of all colours are dancing and singing together. However, in the next sequence a young white man smears dog faeces on their front door. 'Why do big boys put dog shit on our door? Mother cleans it all. Mothers with white children don't need to do this,' Simon wonders in voice-over. We hear children's voices ask how their mum can be white while they are black. In the image, a black girl covers her face in white powder; a black boy scrubs his skin with Vim detergent in the bathtub: 'I scrubbed and I scrubbed, sometimes I scrubbed until I bleed. I scrubbed to make my skin go white, to make the black go away. The only way I could think of to make her my mum.' The images hurt, the scrubbing sound of the harsh brush against soft skin makes one ache. 'When I grow old, I wanna be white', we hear the young girl exclaim several times. 'I lost my childhood in a blur of self-hate', Onwurah declares moments later on the soundtrack. At the end of the film Onwurah and her brother, now adults, make a big fire and throw the cans of Vim and bottles of bleach into the flames, and with them their self-hatred, finding strength in the knowledge that 'no-one can ever again hurt me as much as I have hurt myself'. Onwurah addresses herself as a little girl, as well as her unborn daughter. While the flames destroy the whitening detergents and other objects of pain, we hear again the little girl's voice, with a slight difference: 'When I grow old, I wanna be.' It could not have been said more powerfully.

More recently, a new generation of black female filmmakers have taken up their cameras to explore the dreadful and horrifying dimensions of the legacies of slavery and institutionalised racism. Dee Rees's epic *Mudbound* (2017) is set in the Mississippi delta during the late 1930s and post-war period, and shows the difficult relationship between a white and a black family, equally poor but still in unbalanced power relations. Their respective male family members, Jamie (Garrett Hedlund) and Ronsel (Jason Mitchell), both return from fighting in the Second World War heavily traumatised, suffering from PTSD and escaping into alcoholism. They develop a friendship. When the racist *paterfamilias* of the white family discovers that Jamie and Ronsel are in a friendly relationship, and that the black man Ronsel has a child with a white German woman back in Europe, he rounds up the Ku Klux Klan to punish Ronsel for miscegenation. He also assaults his son Jamie, and forces him to choose Ronsel's punishment: to lose either his eyes, tongue or testicles. If Jamie refuses to make a choice, Ronsel will be lynched. In a gruesome scene Ronsel's tongue is cut out. Jamie leaves his family in disgust; a mute Ronsel reunites with his son and girlfriend in Europe.

These historical scenes must be seen as real life horror, and are increasingly addressed by this new generation of black women directors. Ava Duvernet, who directed *Selma* (2014) about the anti-racist and black suffrage protest marches led by Martin Luther King in 1965, has been a prominent and influential voice in African-American filmmaking. Her influential Netflix series *When They See Us* exposes the horrors that shattered the lives of the Central Park Five, who were unjustly convicted and incarcerated for assaulting a white woman jogging in Central Park in 1989 (McDonald 2019). Duvernay is currently working on a television series based on Octavia Butler's *Dawn*.

There are many other young black filmmakers and women of colour who have taken up the horrors of (the legacies of) the dark side of history.[2] Among white female directors who have addressed colonialism, I want to mention Claire Denis, whose *Chocolat* (1988) was another pioneering film.[3] Denis grew up a white French child in Africa where her father worked as a colonial administrator in Cameroon in the late 1950s, towards the end of colonial governance. While set during the same period, *Chocolat* is not autobiographical in the details of the story nor in the depiction of the rigid parents (Gregory 2018). It does, however, translate the more general and absolute racial dividing lines, called the invisible but real '*ligne d'horizon*' in *Chocolat*, that were part and parcel of the colonial system, seen through the eyes of a small girl, France (Cécille Ducasse), and her friendship with the family's servant Protée (Isaach de Bankolé).

Twenty years later Denis returned to Cameroon to film *White Material* (2009). While her first film has something of a nostalgic feel that shrouds the tensions (especially the impossible sexual attraction between Protée and France's mother), *White Material* is an unflinchingly brutal account that clearly shows how strange and problematic the white presence in the former colonies still is. The film is set in an unnamed French-speaking African country where Maria Vial (Isabelle Huppert) refuses to leave the family coffee plantation, even though all the workers are fleeing in fear of an erupting civil war. While we know from the beginning that things will end very badly and that the film's narrative is circular, the tension and terror are primed to erupt at any moment. The atmosphere is menacing in every detail, aided by an ominous soundtrack and the fact that for the first fifteen minutes there is practically no dialogue; we can only attempt to discover, along with the main character played by Huppert, what exactly is going on. While she tries to return to the plantation, we seamlessly enter a flashback depicting very recent past events, through which the story is conveyed. We see rebels, among whom are many child soldiers, arming themselves with machetes, while the mayor of the nearby town is preparing a militia. The local radio preaches revolution and the execution of 'white material', specifically taking aim at the Vial plantation where Maria lives with her ex-husband André (Christopher Lambert), her father-in-law Henri (Michel Subor) and her son Manuel (Nicholas Duvauchel).

Most of the film follows Maria while she walks around with a red purse filled with money in search of new workers to finish the coffee harvest. The redness of her purse stands out among the otherwise subdued dusty colours of the yellowy landscape and reddish soil. It certainly signals the perversion of Western money, which is also mentioned by one of the militiamen. Maria is undaunted when she finds the rebel leader (again played by Isaach de Bankolé), who is taking shelter in a barn because he is wounded. However, this causes the new workers to leave immediately, for fear of being seen as collaborators with the rebels. Maria is a tenacious and fearless woman who drives a motorcycle, a pick-up truck and a tractor and harvests the coffee herself. Her only soft spot is for her lazy son, who is slowly but surely going insane, especially after two rebel youths (sexually) assault him. We do not see the assault itself, but they leave him naked in a field and walk away with his red underpants as a flag fluttering on their spear. Red underpants taken as a violent trophy in a terrible situation literally flags up more horror to come. The horror aesthetics hit us at the end of the film when we discover (with Maria) that the dead bodies that we saw at the beginning of the film are all the people who were on the plantation. The house is littered with the corpses of rebel child soldiers killed by the militia; André is dead on the floor, the family's passports beside him; Manuel is nothing more than carbonised residue; but Henri is still walking around, until Maria picks up an axe and kills him in a blood-splattering attack. The final image is of one of the rebels running across the fields with his head bleeding while holding the red beret of the deceased rebel leader.

While there is certainly not an unambiguous symbolism to the three red objects (the purse, the underpants, the beret) in this film, they are all linked to postcolonial violence. This is brought together by Denis and her co-writer Marie N'Diaye as an assemblage of varying events occurring in Africa today, ranging from the French army departing the Ivory Coast (an image recalled at the beginning of the film), to the pursuit and killing of white farmers in Zimbabwe, and civil wars (whether instigated by foreign forces or not) in Sierra Leone, Nigeria, Sudan and other places. Most of all, as Denis affirmed in an interview, *White Material* seeks to invert the idea of intrusion: not of black migrants in Europe, but of white bodies in Africa, which is also a form of intrusion and related to the question, Who am I, because I am here?[4]

A final dimension of the horror of colonialism that I want to discuss in this section is related to the genocide and marginalisation of Native Americans.[5] As indicated above, in the horror genre there are many films that obliquely refer to the violent history of the founding of America, but usually only as a source of anxiety that allows a return of the repressed to haunt its white protagonists, who actually suffer from a different problem, which transposes the Native references into metaphorical instigators of grief and loss, at best; more often the Native American experience is just a source for scary story framing. One of the most famous horror films in this sub-genre of haunted Indian burial grounds is *Pet Sematary*, directed by Mary Lambert (1989).[6] The film is based on a Stephen King novel and addresses the fear of losing a child, which is certainly a horrifying thought for anyone. The film focuses on a family with two young children who move into a new house. The house is situated between a dangerous road full of menacing red trucks, and a pet cemetery that obscures another space, a Micmac Indian burial ground that has gone sour and needs to remain untouched. When the youngest child, Cage, is run over by one of the red trucks while following a red kite, the father is so grief stricken that he decides to inter Cage on sacred Micmac ground. This indeed reanimates the boy, but as an evil force. While the film certainly combines an explicit horror aesthetics of gutted ghosts and abject zombies with the psychological mechanisms of coping with grief and loss, it does not touch upon the grief and loss of Native Americans whose sacred burial grounds are all that seem to be left if we take a tour through the horror films that address the issue at all.

Hence, while not strictly a horror film, I want to highlight Chloé Zhao's heartbreakingly powerful *Songs My Brothers Taught Me* (2015) as one of the very few feature films that address the grim situation of Native Americans today. The film is set on the Pine Ridge Indian Reservation in South Dakota and follows a Lakota Sioux brother and sister, John and Jashaun Winters (John Reddy and Jashaun St John). John has a special bond with his sister of whom he is the carer, as their mother is mostly under the influence of alcohol or seeking attention from male companions. He sells illegal alcohol so as to save for a car and leave the reservation with his girlfriend Aurélia (Taysha Fuller). Around this plotline, Zhao creates an authentic picture of life on the reservation, head-on depicting the devastations of poverty and alcoholism. She also has an eye for the beauty of the connections between people and the landscape, the south-western Badlands: the bond between brother and sister, the intimacy of boyfriend and girlfriend and the determination, sorrow and wisdom of the faces in close-up, interchanging with wide shots of the figures in vast, barren and overwhelming landscapes.

Zhao, who is of Chinese descent, has found a way to get close to the authenticity of the characters and life on the reservation, carefully 'navigating fact and fiction'.[7] While the original screenplay that she worked on for three years lost its funding, she decided to continue with a much smaller budget, which would turn out to be a blessing in disguise:

> Even before funding fell through, I was feeling trapped by the script. Once we had nothing – no money, no pressure, almost no crew – we had to go with truth in front of the camera. Because truth was all we could afford. My job was to capture authentic moments Pine Ridge and my cast were giving me and try to navigate a story around it.[8]

The main actor, John Reddy, explained that his character was about 80 per cent drawn from his own life. Furthermore, the house that burned down (and in the film kills Karl, the father of John and Jashaun, and twenty-three 'brothers of other mothers') was the actual family home of Jashaun St John, which unexpectedly burned down during the film's production. Her return to the site was therefore doubly heart wrenching.

At the beginning of the film we see John riding and breaking a wild horse, while we hear in voice-over his reflections: 'The thing about breaking horses, don't run them all the time because running them all the time might break its spirit. Anything that runs wild got something bad in them and you wanna leave some of that in it because they need it to survive out here.' This 'something bad needed to survive' we see in John's face when he bootlegs alcohol, but it is mixed with the fondness he has for his sister and his love for his girlfriend. In a scene when they make love, authenticity is also part of the aesthetics, because his girlfriend is menstruating and needs to remove a tampon, which occasions some blood on his hands, which he simply smears on the bedsheet; there is none of the sensation of abjection commonly associated with monstrous femininity.

Throughout the film demonstrations against alcoholism, abandoned children, crime and imprisonment do not prevent real connections between people. When Jashaun finds out about her brother's plan to leave, she is terribly saddened, but she befriends Travis, a tattoo artist who sells clothes and drawings to meet expenses. Jashaun is going to help him; when she asks about the frequent use of the number '7' in his artwork, he answers that besides holy numbers in the Bible and Indian culture, 'Crazy Horse said that everything seems to end here at Wounded Knee, but it will all begin again at the 7th generation.' And looking at 11-year-old Jashaun, he says 'That's you.'

At the end of the film, John decides not to leave with Aurelia but instead to remain on the reservation. While all along there are many 'songs' and lessons that his brothers have taught him, and he has taught his sister a few lessons himself such as to fight and protect herself, in the end he learns from his sister to embrace life on the reservation. Compared to the haunted Indian cemetery in the modern horror film, *Songs My Brothers Taught Me* is a deeply moving and insightful film that reveals the horrors of history in a subdued and subtle way. Like in *Coffee Colored Children*, brother and sister have found their self-respect without any judgement from others.

Surviving on the Margins of Society

Another sociopolitical dimension that has been approached by women directors using formal elements of the horror film could be grouped under the heading of surviving on the margins. Houda Beyamina's *Divines* (2016), a Netflix original that won the Caméra D'Or at the Cannes Film Festival, should be mentioned here as a realistically raw portrait of two friends in a Parisian suburb, Dounia and Maimouna (Oulaya Amamra and Déborah Lukumuena), who drop out of school, hustle, steal money and begin to work for a black female gang leader. As a female '*banlieue* film' which depicts the harsh conditions of life in the suburbs of large French cities where many migrants from France's former colonies in the Maghreb and Africa live (some of these suburbs are not even drawn on city maps), it paints a penetrating picture of life on the margins of society.[9] However, because of the prominent deployment of a poetics of horror, I instead focus on three other films in this section, Ana Lily Amirpour's *The Bad Batch* (2017), Issa López's *Tigers Are Not Afraid* (2017) and Mati Diop's *Atlantics* (2019).[10]

After her 'Iranian vampire Western' *A Girl Walks Home Alone at Night* (discussed in Chapter 2), Amirpour's second film *The Bad Batch* was less well received, and even considered a failure.[11] Nevertheless, I tend to agree with Lindsay Decker who emphasises the political dimensions of this 'extremely trippy cannibal horror film':

> Horror films like *The Hills Have Eyes* (Wes Craven, 1977) and *The Texas Chainsaw Massacre* (Tobe Hooper, 1974) made the cannibal into a figure of underclass or working-class terror for the suburban middle class protagonists (and audiences). Amirpour's film instead presents a critique of the systems that pit economically and socially marginalised people against one another in a man-eat-man system. This manifests in part because of the way *The Bad Batch* refuses to answer the questions it poses and in part because the film prevents viewers from pegging a character as entirely bad or good. (Decker 2018)

Accordingly, this sometimes creates uncomfortable viewing situations that do not allow easy identification or allegiance, forcing the spectator to remain on alert at all times and question their feelings towards the main characters and the director's choices.

At the Texas border, a girl, Arlen (Suki Waterhouse), whose neck has just been tattooed with the number BB5040, is deported to a fenced-in area of the desert, where, as the sign reads, the laws of the United States no longer apply. It is an area to which all of society's undesirables are deported. In the desolate, unforgiving, sun-dried landscape, two older women in a golf cart chase Arlen, and within the first ten minutes of the film she has lost an arm and a leg to the cannibals who capture her. The leader of this pack of man-eaters, who practise bodybuilding and live in an aeroplane junk yard, is Miami Man (Jason Momoa). He is introduced while he is creating a painting of his young daughter Honey (Jayda Fink), whom he obviously loves; and we then see him preparing a barbecue for himself and his wife Maria (Yolonda Ross) from one of his human victims; a 'family man' of sorts. Yet the cannibals are not portrayed as purely evil, but rather as desperate survivors. In a way this reminds us of the super-heroine Jen in *Revenge*; Arlen manages to escape their settlement for a friendlier walled enclave called Comfort. Comfort, a sort of Burning Man-style off-the-grid raver community for the lost and rejected, is run by a creepy cult leader The Dream (Keanu Reeves), who surrounds himself with a harem of pregnant women who also constitute his army. With these ingredients, Amirpour builds a story that brings the most unlikely horror characters, cannibal and final girl, together in a twisted romance.

The Bad Batch deploys many tropes from the horror genre while turning them upside down. Arlen can certainly be considered a final girl who, no matter how bizarre the circumstances she finds herself in, will execute her survival skills in an extreme way. Amirpour herself described her in an interview as 'dumb but brave'.[12] In fact the image of a girl, 'discarded by society and mutilated by her peers' was the starting point of Amirpour's scenario for the film, following a heartbreaking event that made her feel mutilated: 'I thought of that girl in the desert, chopped up, bleeding, in pain, barely alive, but she was going to live. And she was going to *live*. That was the beginning of the story' (Yamato 2017). The film's mutilated heroine can thus be seen as a metaphor for the reinvention of oneself after losing something or someone dear and 'feeling amputated' and totally alone but still wanting to survive.

When Arlen is lying on the dusty floor, missing an arm and a leg, she uses another typical form of abjection to trick her capturers. Using her own excrement to render her flesh literally disgusting, she profits from the fact that she is dragged to a place where she can be washed and manages to escape. Pulling herself across the desert on a skateboard, she is found by a mute hermit (Jim Carrey, whom one would absolutely not recognise), who roams the desert helping whomever he encounters in his idiosyncratic way. He delivers her to Comfort, where we meet Arlen again five months later, when she has a prosthetic leg, and imagines herself with a complete arm by cutting the arm from a picture of a nude model and holding it in front of the mirror, matching it to her own body. She longs to leave the huge, shipping-container-enclosed Comfort, and one cannot help but see the opening in the red wall of containers as a 'vaginal portal' (described by Creed as a monstrous image in, for instance, films such as *Alien*), sucking you into the powerful protection of Comfort. However, it is a womb that the girl leaves, entering the harsh and cruel outside desert world that she nevertheless prefers. There are several other elements in the *mise en scène* that connect Comfort with a (perverse) womb-like space, especially the cult of armed pregnant women who protect The Dream and live off the various forms of drugs they produce, ranging from marijuana to XTC and LSD, which are fabricated in great quantities inside The Dream's mansion.

Arlen leaves the protection of Comfort armed with a gun, looking to exact vengeance on the people who mutilated her; it first seems that she will simply go on a revenge quest, as we know them from the rape-revenge genre. The first people she encounters are the cannibal's wife and daughter, Maria and Honey, foraging through toxic waste to acquire useful materials. Arlen kills the mother in front of her daughter's eyes, in spite of Maria's plea: 'We are all alike, we are all bad batch.' It is a doubly difficult moment in the film, not only because, blinded by her desire for revenge, Arlen disregards the traumatic effects of her deed on the little girl, but also because Maria is a black woman and Arlen is white; the weight of colonial history immediately enters the fiction. It is a difficult scene to watch, especially when Arlen replies, 'No we are not the same.' In the logic of the film, this makes sense because, regardless of the colour of her skin, Maria belongs to the cannibal tribe (even if only reluctantly, as we see her expressing her dismay about their diet of human flesh). It is not surprising that this scene caused controversy, especially among black audiences in Los Angeles where criticism was voiced at the ease with which Amirpour allows the black woman's place to be taken by a white woman, as Arlen joins Miami Man and Honey in an unlikely sort of 'new family' at the end of the film (Yamato 2017; Decker 2018). The scene raises difficult questions about the justification of violence and the levels of metaphorical reading that horror tropes allow. Amirpour, of immigrant descent herself, declared, 'I am brown myself', and did not give any further explanation, other than that she certainly did 'not wish to offend anybody but to spark deeper examination' (Yamato 2017). The vengeance question cannot simply be transposed from the level of the film world to the real world without confronting questions of power imbalance and political, social and poetic justice on different levels of fiction and reality. It may be that skin colour should not make any difference at the level of the film, as Amirpour seems to suggest, but the fact is that on the level of cultural representation as well as in sociopolitical reality, the killing of a black person is still too familiar to be 'neutral' in a fictional setting.

On the other hand, if *The Bad Batch* is an allegory for contemporary America, it is truly a man-eat-man world. Questions regarding the levels of fiction and reality haunt one's mind while watching the film, which then goes on to ask, how do we survive in such barren conditions? Perhaps it is significant that the vengeance story that we are familiar with from the rape-revenge plot soon turns into what one critic calls an 'anti-revenge plot of mercy' (Derrickson 2018). Arlen does regret her deed, or at least she takes the child with her to Comfort, buys her a rabbit, but then loses sight of her during a night-time, LSD-induced psychedelic trip where she feels as if she could touch the star-littered desert sky (visually quite stunningly rendered). It is during this hallucinatory journey out in the desert that she meets Miami Man who, having found his wife dead in the scrapyard, is looking for his daughter. Their encounter has several twists before Arlen rescues Honey from The Dream's cult and they end up outside Comfort in the desert, father and daughter reunited, with Arlen proposing to 'hang out' in spite of his people having taken her arm and leg, and she having taken the life of his wife. However, it remains an ambiguous ending because it seems that there is nowhere left to go after they have eaten the little girl's rabbit.

Undeniably, the film is a political commentary on the sociopolitical situation in the United States (and indeed the entire world) today. Amirpour comments:

> This notion of people that are getting systemically pushed into corners, it can be as literal or as metaphorical as someone needs it to be. I'd go downtown and wander around 6th Street; it looks just like a refugee community . . . I get confused when people say [*The Bad Batch*] is post-apocalyptic, because where are you looking? Where is your attention focused? I see homeless people. Every single person that lives on the street, I cannot *not* see them. But I feel that people habitually don't see them. (Yamato 2017)

Rather than being post-apocalyptic, Amirpour sees her film as pre-apocalyptic. In this respect, it might be insightful to read Octavia Butler's

Parable of the Sower (1993) alongside the *The Bad Batch*. Butler's story is post-apocalyptic but is set in the mid-2020s and actually addresses the same sociopolitical problems as Amirpour. Butler's heroine, Lauren Oya Onamina, is a black girl who survives in the man-eat-man world of dystopian California, where living in a protected community is one's only option for survival, though even that is not enough to remain safe. The world that Butler depicts is dystopian, but also comes to resemble an eerily current reality. In Butler's California, climate change has made water scarce and expensive, and jobs unavailable; omnipotent companies that own everything allow the reintroduction of company towns and debt slavery while the numbers of people who fall in desperation off the grid grows every day. Lauren's community grow their own vegetables and her father is the minister of a Baptist church and a teacher. But they cannot leave the compound's gates without being menaced by scavengers, murderers, the police and groups of drug-addicted 'pyros' who get off by setting fires, which will eventually engulf the entire Californian coastline. When her compound is attacked and all her family members killed, Lauren departs with two other solitary survivors, a white man and another black woman. She decides to travel as a man, walking up north. Along the way, they are joined by several other people, all of mixed colour and background. They must be constantly on the lookout, trying to avoid being abducted, attacked, raped, murdered and eaten (at one point Lauren's ragtag group passes a collection of children devouring a human leg).

Unlike Arlen, Lauren is not dumb at all. Being the daughter of a minister but not believing in religious dogma, she begins to create her own 'religion', Earthseed. The God of Earthseed is Change, the most powerful force there is in the world, as Butler declared in an interview about *Parable of the Sower* (Butler 1993: 336). Under the wisdom of Change, persistence and adaptability, the heroine knows how to survive. While kindness and diversity are part of Earthseed's rules, it does not mean that its members will not kill anyone who threatens their well-being. They possess guns and knives to defend themselves, and when somebody dies, they purloin their belongings, food and money. What is most striking about *Parable of the Sower* is that it is a world that seems not much removed from our own reality. While *The Bad Batch*'s Comfort is similar to the community of people who live at the margins of society in Slab City on the Salton Sea in California (where the film was shot), Butler's world of drought, fires and the increasing power of a few wealthy companies is equally eerily close. While Butler's visionary portrait of the future includes a hopeful new vision of how to begin reforming and changing the deadly routes we are following today, Amirpour keeps us in the desert with mixed feelings, albeit with more mercy than the unforgiving surroundings would seem to allow. Nevertheless, the point both Butler and Amirpour make with their fiction is that the horror of the contemporary world is right in front of our eyes, and needs to be addressed. The alienating consequences of neoliberal capitalism and the devastation of climate change and environmental pollution that are the backdrop of these stories will be further developed in the following sections, but next I want to examine another harsh realistic setting of outcasts on the other side of the United States-Mexican border in Issa López's *Tigers Are Not Afraid*.

When Outlaws Take Over

Tigers Are Not Afraid opens with a clear political statement that in the last ten years drug and gang violence have taken the lives of 160,000 people with 53,000 disappeared, and that it is not known how many children are left without parents. Immediately after this, we are in a classroom where children are being asked to write a fairy tale, when loud gunshots just outside the school force the children and teacher to take cover on the floor. To distract and console her, the teacher gives the girl next to her, Estrella (Paola Lara) three pieces of chalk to make three wishes. While Estrella walks home from school, she sees a dead man in the street in a pool of blood. As she walks by, a thin stream of blood follows her into the house where she lives with her mother. Her mother is not home; the blood creeps inside, in a thin line, it travels over the surface of the walls and stains one of her mother's dresses hanging to dry: something bad must have happened. From this beginning, fear and dread pervade the overall mood, even if there are also some lighter moments of coping and hope in the film.

Estrella waits for her mother, and the wish she whispers to the first piece of chalk is for her mother to return. The wish is granted, albeit in a horrific way: her mother returns as a ghost, frightening the girl out of the apartment. She joins a gang of street waifs, whose leader Shine (Juan Ramón López) only reluctantly accepts her. The others, Tucsi (Hanssel Casillas), Pop (Rodrigo Cortes), and especially the youngest Morro (Nery Arredondo), who carries around a stuffed tiger, are more welcoming. The tiger comes to life at several points, first as a graffiti tiger that Shine sprays on a wall, which becomes animated and escapes to another wall (attacking the drawn images of the children); then after Morro dies, his stuffed tiger returns as his ghost, helping Estrella find the place where one of the local drug gangs buried the murdered bodies of the children's parents (which leads to another horrifying scene when the ghosts of the dead grasp

Figure 5.2 *Tigers Are Not Afraid* (Issa López, 2017).

Estrella by her ankles); finally at the end of the film there is a real tiger, living in the rundown and abandoned buildings of the collapsing city. There is an element of the Peter Pan fairy tale in the gang of lost children, turning Shine and Estrella into Peter Pan and Wendy, and there is even a sort of dark sister of Tinkerbell in the form of black dragonflies that seem to embody the soul of Estrella's mother, which subtly return at magical moments throughout the film. At the beginning of the film, we see how Shine steals a phone from gang member Caco (Ianis Guerrero), which contains compromising photographs and videos of the criminal leader El Chino (Tenoch Huerta), who is also running as a political candidate in his upper-world life. The phone also has images of Shine's mother, who was murdered by Chino's gang. There is also a gruesome video of Estrella's mother, who can be recognised by her bracelet of black dragonflies.

In an interview at the Brussels International Fantastic Film Festival, López talked about the levels of reality mixed with the fantastic and the horrific.[13] While *Tigers Are Not Afraid* is not a true story, the reality of gang- and drug-related violence is very real, and the fact that nobody cares about the horrors of those who are left behind, orphaned and traumatised, is also a bitter truth. In fact, reality is often more brutal than the film, with its fantastic elements and its violence filtered through the poetics of horror. Having lost her mother at the age of eight in different circumstances, López clarifies that there is also the personal reality of feelings of loneliness and shock, of returning home and not finding your mother, who has disappeared, without having been able to say goodbye. Many of the fantasy elements are drawn from her love of comic books, and from the digital mood boards she creates for every film (which brought her, for instance, the image of an abandoned warehouse with a pool of goldfish). The more geeky horror elements in her work she credits to the influence of Japanese horror films from the 1980s (which inspired the movement of the ghosts) and the work of Guillermo del Toro (who is also producing her next film, a werewolf Western).

The phantasmatic trail of blood that is bound to Estrella's imagination seems to have real consequences: every time the thin red line appears something bad happens, especially to the person who is touched by the blood. When Estrella herself is followed, she draws with her magic chalk, just in time, a white line that halts the progress of the bloody line. The other wishes she whispers to the pieces of chalk are also granted in ugly ways. After the gruesome 'return' of her mother, when she is put to the test by the boys by being told to murder the gang member Caco, Estrella's second wish is that she should not need to kill him. She discovers Caco in a pool of blood: he has already been shot; another wish perversely granted. Shine asks her to make a third wish: to compel the scars on his face to disappear. Fearing that something bad might happen to him, she refuses. However, when at the end of the film they form a close friendship and bond, she erases his red scars with the white chalk. The bloody line appears and touches Shine. His face turns entirely red from the bullet he receives from Chino. Then Estrella meets the real tiger and steps into a dreamlike, green-coloured landscape. It is precisely the contrasting mixture of reality and fantasy, tied with the poetics of horror, that makes López's film so devastating and a horror story of reality in contemporary Mexico that is not often told.

Zombies and Ghosts for Poetic Justice

In *Atlantics* (2019), Mati Diop presents an equally deeply moving adoption of horror elements in which reality and imagination blend. A Senegalese political zombie-ghost romance film, Diop's was the first film by a black female director to be entered at the Cannes Film Festival, where it won the Grand Prix in 2019.[14] Set at the seaside of Senegal's capital Dakar, the film tells the story of Ada (Mame Bineta Sane) who is in love with Suleiman (Traore), in spite of the fact that she is engaged to be married to another man. The main protagonist, however, is actually the sea, to which I will return in a moment. At the beginning of the film we see builders working on a gigantic luxury skyscraper, the Meijiza Tower. Rising high over its surroundings, it stands as a symbol of exploitation, as the workers have not been paid for four months. The tower is created using CGI, which enforces its haunting and symbolic value, looming over the inhabitants of the seaside city.

The workers, one of whom is Suleiman, ride in the back of a pick-up truck along the coast. Then we see the first magnetic images of the sea in a sequence that immediately draws one into the picture because of its waving rhythm, which is composed by the long camera movement taken from the back of the truck. The camera shows the sea, interchanged with the men in the truck, slowly finding its focus on Suleiman's sad-eyed face. The soundtrack consists of four layers: ambient rippling music with an ominous undertone (composed by Fatima al Qadir); traffic sounds; the chants of the men (except Suleiman); and the murmuring of the sea, which is a sound that is present in the background or foreground of many scenes. The sea is a milky hazy blue, calmly rolling its white crests to the sandy beach. A mysterious sadness spread across the entire sequence that grips one. In the next scene Suleiman and Ada meet on the beach. Now the sea is closer and seems sensual, voluptuous even, constantly murmuring. 'You only have eyes for the sea', Ada says. However, they are clearly deeply in love and promise to meet again later, in the middle of the night, at a beach club. The sea is now completely still, glistening like a slightly undulating mirror. But when Ada and her girlfriends arrive at the club that night, they hear that all the men have left on a boat, trying to cross the ocean to reach Spain. The sea is dark, deep and menacing. Ada is inconsolable and shows no interest in her well-to-do husband-to-be.

From this moment onward the love story, and the poetics of the sea which will remain a constant presence in many different guises and colours, are blended with elements from the detective and the supernatural horror genres. On Ada's wedding night, the preposterously luxurious wedding bed suddenly catches fire, and a detective Issa (Amadou Mbow) is tasked with investigating the case. In the meantime, the wealthy owner of the construction site receives a visit from a group of twelve women. Their eyes are of a milky blueish-whiteness, like the sea; they claim their wages for the past four months, a form of poetic justice. We understand that the ghosts of their men have returned through the bodies of the women. During his investigations, Issa seems to suffer from inexplicable feverish ailments and he does not get very far with his search for the bed-fire culprit. He has a close look at Ada's wedding video and notices a figure in the background who makes his heart skip several beats; he sees himself, with milky blueish-white eyes, and realises that Suleiman has returned, taking possession of his body. In the very affective final part of *Atlantics*, one of Suleiman's ghost friends (in the body of his girlfriend) tells Ada about Suleiman's last moments at sea, just before a gigantic wave swallowed their boat, sending them to the deep. They sit with the other women who carry the ghostly spirits of their deceased men on the veranda of the beach club. Then the sun sets again, and the sea becomes blood red. Ada returns to the beach club and finally has an encounter with her lover, Suleiman, in the body of Issa. He tells her that he saw her eyes and tears in the wave that devoured him. They make love. The sun rises; the sea is enveloped in a wispy foggy pink. Ada wakes up and looks into the camera. 'Some memories are omens', she says. 'I am Ada to whom the future belongs.'

In a beautiful and hard to describe entanglement of the supernatural, the sacred and the invisible, the gothic and the romantic, Diop tells a tale at once both personal and political. Born in France to a French mother and a Senegalese father, Diop has spoken about her double cultural and racial heritage (Joyard 2019). The supernatural, the sacred and the power of the invisible belong to her African roots, and the gothic and the romantic are part of her European legacy. Furthermore, Ada is for Diop 'a way of experiencing the African adolescence that she hadn't lived' (Aroesti 2019). Part of the film presents elements of her girlhood in Senegal, which implies among other things the importance of virginity, religion, patriarchy and girlfriends.

In 2009 Diop made another film in Senegal, the short film *Atlantiques*, in which a young man talks about his dangerous experience crossing the sea. After that Diop began to observe the sea, perceiving it as a grave. The magnetic attraction of the sea, and the tragic stories it enfolds, are also part of this early film. Diop's family is a very artistic one. Her mother is a photographer, her father a musician, who left for France shortly after he collaborated with his brother on another famous Senegalese film about the desire for the sea, *Touki Bouki* by Djibril Diop Mambéty (1973).[15] While *Touki Bouki* has been widely recognised as a Senegalese New Wave film, the seamless blending of horror poetics with other genres makes Diop's film an important exponent of the new blood of female horror films and characteristic of our contemporary age.

Some final reflections on the sea. Its overwhelming material presence in *Atlantics* enfolds thousands of stories of migration, one of which the narrative in this film recounts. But it also raises countless other stories of migrations, both in our contemporary age, and reaching back to the ancestors of the Middle Passage, the crossing from Africa to the Americas in slave ships. During the fifteen to twenty interludes of the sea in *Atlantics*, it obtains a metaphysical or supernatural power itself. The sea becomes a ghost. One feels the presence of all the perished lives, hears the whispering of countless voices through its murmuring, their screams in the howling wind and the fierce force of the waves. And though Woolf lived in a very different place and time, and her criticism of colonial Britain was only part of the subtext of many of her works, perhaps her sea interludes were also something like an omen, as when she writes in *The Waves*:

> Now the sun had sunk. Sky and sea were indistinguishable. The waves breaking spread with their white fans far out over the shore, sent white shadows into the recesses of sonorous caves and rolled back sighing over the shingle . . . As if there were waves of darkness in the air, darkness moved on, covering houses, hills, trees, as waves of water wash round the sides of some sunken ship. Darkness washed down the streets, eddying round single figures, engulfing them . . . Darkness rolled its waves along grassy rides and over the wrinkled skin of turf, enveloping the solitary thorn tree and the empty snail shells at its foot . . . and girls, sitting on verandas . . . Them too, darkness covered. (Woolf 2015b: 141–2)

Girls sitting on verandas, covered in darkness, like the ghosts of the men in *Atlantics*. Perhaps, in a poetics of relation, in the ocean of *Atlantics* one of the voices we hear softly whispering is that of Woolf, who drowned herself in 1941, in a river leading to the sea.

Eco-Horror and Resistance

While there are many other political issues that would translate into the language of the horror genre, and which have been taken up by women, I must limit myself here to one last urgent theme that concerns us all, to be addressed in an innovative way: our earthly environment.[16] In *Parable of the Sower* Butler presented climate change and ecological destruction as the basis of the total disruption of society, and the importance of ecological issues features in the films I discuss in this last section. In the modern horror film, eco-horror has often been channelled through the female body, in apocalyptic narratives where women give birth to the anti-Christ or need to save the world by bearing the Christ child. Erin Harrington discusses, for instance, *Prophecy* (dir. John Frankenheimer, 1979), which presents a stereotypical image of Native Americans who are victims of industrial mercury poisoning to indicate how the pregnant woman's subjectivity is completely erased in favour of her body becoming the endangered environment for her baby as well as a stand-in for the environment itself: 'She exists in the film only to-be-pregnant, to be an ecological litmus test, and to be the container for a something that will invoke both pity and horror' (Harrington 2018: 111). One can think also of apocalyptic horror films such as *The Seventh Sign* (dir. Carl Schulz, 1988) or *The Johnsons* (dir. Rudolf van den Berg, 1992). The question is, once more, are there other ways of addressing eco-horror?

In *Spoor* (2017) Agnieszka Holland, who co-directed the film with her daughter Kasia Adamik, provides a positive answer to this question. Based on the book *Drive Your Plough Over the Bones of the Dead* by Polish writer Olga Tokarczuk, Holland herself describes the film as an anarchist feminist eco-thriller with elements of black comedy.[17] Amy Taubin called it 'at once a phantasmagorical murder mystery, a tender late-blooming love story, and a resistance and rescue thriller' and 'the most resonant political film of the century' (Taubin 2018). These descriptions do justice to the rich aesthetics and mosaic experience that the film offers, and in addition, I would argue that the film presents its own idiosyncratic and completely original poetics of horror. The opening of the film is mysterious, as the camera seems to operate of its own accord, hovering over the majestic forest (filmed in the Kłodzko Valley in south-western Poland, one of Europe's last remaining primordial forests). While the night birds sing their last songs before dawn, and a 'propulsive orchestral score' (Taubin 2018) sets an epic, enigmatic and threatening tone, the camera's eye flies us over and through the mist-covered pre-dawn landscape. The headlights of a moving car appear, approaching other cars that congregate in a clearing in the woods (the hunters' cars, we will soon discover). The camera moves to a house, and we find two dogs waking up an elderly woman, Janina Duszejko (Agnieszka Mandat), who takes them out for a walk in the morning glory of the surrounding nature. 'Lea' and 'Bianca' the woman calls them repeatedly. Duszejko (she insists on being addressed by her last name) is a retired construction engineer who now lives in a remote location near a small village where she sometimes teaches English to schoolchildren. The ominous atmosphere of the film is constantly contradicted by the intimate ease by which Duszejko blends in with the animals, plants and the changing seasons. She is interested in astrology, living among the cycles of the moon, stars and planets.

Duszejko is a rebel and a fighter. When her two dogs do not welcome her home one day when she returns from the village, she embarks on a mission to find out precisely what has happened to them. Neither the Major, a cruel businessman (and fox breeder), nor even the police or the priest listen to her. They consider her a crazy old woman, even a witch perhaps, but certainly not someone to take seriously. They begin to preach to her, arguing that the commandments ('Thou shall not kill') do not apply to animals, that man needs to control nature, and so on. The point of view is with Duszejko, and as she listens, the mouths of these defenders of patriarchal values appear in grotesque close-up, indicating her disgust for their double standards. She refuses to remain silent, expressing her anger about the loss of her dogs and the breaching of the hunting laws, when hunters kill animals outside the legal hunting seasons; this is something that she obsessively keeps track of as the film progresses through the changing seasons.

Duszejko is also a very warm woman, whose thoughts we hear at certain moments in close-up. When she picks up Dobra (Patricia Volny), a girl from the village who is the fox breeder's girlfriend and works in his shop, we hear her mental voice reading the girl's horoscope (where Venus and Jupiter meet, combining Love and Law) and deciding to like her. She also befriends a young clerk at the police station, Dyzio (Jakub Gierszal), who is epileptic and afraid of being dismissed if anyone were to discover his condition. Dobra and Dyzio will form a relationship, with a slight suggestion that Duszejko is a 'love witch' of the matchmaking kind. As an older woman, Duszejko herself has men who love her; both her sturdy neighbour (Wiktor Zborowsky) and an entomologist who specialises in insect pheromones (Miroslav Krobot), who beds her first. She and her neighbour go giggling to a masquerade party in the village; he is dressed as an oversized Little Red Riding Hood and she as the wolf, a comic inversion of traditional gender roles and perhaps also an indication the animal–human bond, of which Duszejko reminds us (Freccero 2017).

The two sides of *Spoor*'s heroine are summarised by Taubin:

> The film's emblematic image is of Duszejko, crouching over the body of a young wild boar that has been shot through the lungs, trying to give it comfort in its dying moments, but deserving equal weight is the scene in which she and the two men who love her sit around a campfire, smoking pot, laughing uproariously, and singing House of the Rising Sun. (Taubin 2018)

To see an older woman in a different role than mother or grandmother is remarkable in itself, and her fight against the hunters cannot but be seen as a critical and political statement against Poland's current government, which is exploiting its natural resources 'by ignoring all [European] regulations, particularly around hunting and logging' (Taubin 2018).

The horror elements commence when the hunters begin to be found murdered. One after another is discovered brutally slashed in the wilderness, or eaten by insects. Duszejko claims to know the murderer: a nature that strikes back. A trail of deer hooves near the first victim, for instance, would prove her case.[18] Nevertheless, we have to follow the trail of red in the *mise en scène* to get at the real force that strikes back. As in many of the other films discussed in this book, the colour red is of special emotional and symbolic value. Of course, there is the bloody red of the slashed, gutted or half-eaten victims in the woods. However, there are also a few other red pointers. In the winter and autumn months, Duszejko wears a bright red bonnet, first with a blue coat. It signals her liveliness, sorrow

Figure 5.3 *Spoor* (Agnieszka Holland, 2017)

and rage about the lost dogs when she goes around the village putting up 'missing' notices in the hope of retrieving her animals. Then, after she and her neighbour find another neighbour dead in his cabin (deceased in his sleep), she puts on a red-striped winter coat that she repairs with a patch when it is torn, which coincides with her greater effort to fight for the animals that are being killed gruesomely and illegally. Thereafter, during a Mass for St Hubert, the first ecologist to protect nature, when the priest insists that man must subdue the earth, she snaps and interrupts the sermon in a fit of rage. Furiously she leaves the church and when she is outside, looking up at the sun, the entire image becomes coloured red. This filtered red light leads to a series of flashbacks in which we return to winter, where we see Duszejko again in her red-striped coat and red bonnet, killing the hunters herself, laying animal spoor, setting free the foxes from their cages. While dressed in her wolf suit, we see her feeding the drunken Major, who was actually the one who shot her dogs, giving him insect pheromones that lead to his death when he loses consciousness in the woods. At the same time, while investigating the murders, Dyzio and Dobra discover the repair-patch from her red coat, and the neighbour and entomologist find out what she did. 'Don't worry, we won't abandon you', they tell her. She explains that on the night when the other neighbour died, she found a trophy picture in his cabin, in which all the hunters were shown laughing behind a whole range of dead animals, her dogs prominently to one side of the picture, bled dead by the bullet wounds.

Duszejko's four friends help her escape the village police and the film is wrapped up with a utopian image where the five of them, and a young son of Dyzio and Dobra, live together as an alternative family in another place surrounded by nature. It is summer again, and while Duszejko's voice-over muses, 'Things will change again when Aries meets Uranus, a new cycle will begin, and reality will be reborn', she walks into the field, and then suddenly disappears from the image. It is a utopian ending of hope for another way of life, which emphasises the political dimensions of the film.

In an interview in the *Guardian* Holland indicated that she had not set out to create a political allegory about the divided nature of her country (and the wider world), but that she had inadvertently ended up telling a story about a male authoritarian agenda that attacked women's rights and environmental protection, thereby reflecting the wider reality that became all the more pronounced after the populist government came to power in 2017 (Connolly 2017). In Poland, Holland is called a traitor who has made an 'anti-Christian' film. Holland sees it as a 'fairy tale about [the] anger' of her generation of women, who were scientists and engineers and believed the world would change after the fall of communism, but who became very disillusioned. The anger is channelled through the prism of a hunting story. Holland explains:

> The hunt is quite often the place where important political decisions are made. It's like a boys' club – I went to several hunts as research for the film and I saw a woman maybe once. The men are together and they feel free to talk, like Donald Trump does to his buddies about women and power. They can execute their power in a very direct way, by killing living creatures. They also take their sons with them so that they are sure to pass on the flame. (Connolly 2017)

Besides seeing *Spoor* as a political allegory of contemporary Poland (and many other countries in the world) where the destruction of the environment is part of a larger political struggle between conservative patriarchal values and all kinds of 'minoritarian' struggles for planetary survival, including the rights of women (of all colours) and non-human actors such as animals and plants, it is also possible to read the film as a speculative New Materialist turn towards 'staying with the trouble', such as Donna Haraway and Anna Tsing would espouse. Duszejko can be seen as a particularly Harawayan heroine who is conscious of humankind's entangled relationship with all kind of 'critters', as she calls them (Haraway 2016). Or, in Tsing's words in *The Mushroom at the End of the World*, Duszejko could be considered a mushroom picker, following the unpredictable and rhizomatic tracks of nature, fungal spoors, animal prints, fully aware of the interdependence of humans and non-humans, acknowledging the life of animals and plants, the life of the forest, all the actors that are world builders and co-developers of ecologies.[19] One way of acknowledging this codependency is to look for drama and adventure that does not put the human protagonist at its centre. This, Tsing argues, is not common, as 'allowing only human protagonists into our stories is not just ordinary human bias; it is a cultural agenda tied to dreams of progress through modernization' (2015: 155). On this view, other kinds of stories with different protagonists are seen as blocking progress: 'talking animals are for children and primitives' (Tsing 2015: 155). Alternatively, they are for old ladies or madwomen, as the patriarchs in *Spoor* consider Duszejko. 'Their voices silenced', they 'imagine well-being without them', forgetting that 'collaborative survival requires cross-species coordination' (Tsing 2015: 156).

A Monstrous Plant that Makes You Happy

There are two other films that address 'posthuman' environmental politics in a more speculative way that I would like to discuss in this section: Jessica Hausner's *Little Joe* (2019) and Shin Su Won's *Glass Garden* (2017). Both deal with female, Frankenstein-like scientists who experiment with biochemistry, resulting in extreme consequences. In both films the colour red is accompanied by or even replaced by striking green hues. *Little Joe* opens in a huge greenhouse laboratory where scientists dressed in mint-green lab coats have gathered around a display that contains trays of single-budded plants that betray just a tiny glimpse of the still-closed red flower about to burst open. 'The first mood-lifting, anti-depressant, happy plant', the leader of the laboratory proudly announces. The plant is the creation of genetic engineer Alice Woodard (Emily Beecham), who visually stands out from the mint-green environment by virtue of her red hair. The sterile-looking but colourful environment, composed of green with red elements, is immediately striking, sparkly and amusingly eccentric, both familiar but (because of the restricted colour palette) also eerie.[20] This eeriness is reinforced by the soundtrack, composed of a high-pitched beep that seems to surround the plants, hypnotic and strange Japanese drums and flutes from composer Teiji Ito that arrive at regular intervals, and at certain moments later in the film more nightmarish sounds from barking dogs. Ito was the composer of the soundtrack of Maya Deeren's classic surrealist film *Meshes of the Afternoon* (1943), a black-and-white film that influenced Hausner's *Little Joe* with its oneiric and magic qualities (Schiefer 2019). In connection with the horror genre

Shelley's *Frankenstein* has already been mentioned, as the happy plant seems to provoke strange side effects in the people who inhale its wonderful scent; an effect that is reminiscent of that other classic plant horror *Invasion of the Body Snatchers*, filmed by Don Siegel in 1956 and by Philip Kaufman in 1978. The first time we notice this reference is when one of the older laboratory workers, Bella (Kerry Fox), is convinced that her dog Bello, who spent a night locked up in the greenhouse with the plants, is no longer her dog. Bella is actually a sort of Duszejko in a more sci-fi setting, who tries to warn everybody that something is wrong. Nobody believes her.

However, Hausner's film is of a very different order and approach than Holland's eco-thriller and updates the Frankenstein and body-snatcher stories to the present day, where the problems and questions have shifted, and where answers to those questions seem to be less clear-cut and open to multiple interpretations. The issues that *Little Joe* addresses in a smart and subtle way relate to motherhood, to science and to the problem of truth. Alice is a workaholic and a mother. Her son Joe (Kit Connor), wearing bright red shoes, comes to pick her up from the greenhouse laboratory and complains that she has more eyes for her plants than for him. Alice brings one of the experimental plants home, and suggests calling it 'Little Joe', telling Joe that it needs to be kept warm and talked to, as it is a living being and needs attention and affection. Joe welcomes Little Joe and soon enough he changes too, becoming more independent of his mother. At first Alice does not want to notice this as it implies that something is wrong with her other child, Little Joe. She also feels guilty about not being a good enough mother to Joe, something that percolates to the surface in brilliant sessions with her therapist throughout the film. These sessions make it possible that the entire science-fiction dramaturgy could be read as Alice's guilt-ridden mind, as a worried mother who finds it difficult to see her son (who is entering puberty) grow up. 'So you're a good mother but which of your children will you choose?' is the question put to Alice explicitly by her co-worker Chris (Ben Whishaw).

In terms of contemporary scientific questions, *Little Joe* obviously refers to the genetic modification of plants. Little Joe is modified by a virus and enhanced with a growth hormone oxytocin, the mother hormone, which makes you love the plant like your child. While this is not very likely to happen, there are nevertheless some elements that might occur in reality. In an interview, Hausner explained that she and co-writer Géraldine Bajard talked to many scientists, and visited several laboratories and greenhouses to research the scientific background and possible plausible side effects that genetic modification might entail. Plants are sometimes modified with little pieces of viruses, and it is not unthinkable that these viruses might mutate and have effects on humans. In the film, this is presented through the plant's scent, which finds an olfactory pathway to the brain. However, this is not presented as an undeniable truth. There are many places of doubt, especially embodied by Alice when she is confronted with the mixed legacy of her creation. Everyone who is infected by Little Joe's scent begins to care about nothing else but protecting the plant itself. It is suggested that for safety reasons, the plant is modified in such a way that it cannot self-replicate; it therefore produces a side effect that compels people to care for its growth and reproduction. Nevertheless, it does make everybody who does so very happy; a devilish trick of the plant.

In terms of questions of truth, *Little Joe* does not give an answer to the vexed question whether genetic modification is good or bad. As Hausner comments, if you do a simple search on the internet, you find as many pro answers as you do con. In that sense *Little Joe* resonates with our time of multiple truths, in which it is hard to navigate and we have to think, feel and decide for ourselves. Even science has no answer, because there also, the results are mixed. Also on other levels, the truth is multiple. I have already indicated how the entire film can be seen as a figment of Alice's guilt-ridden mind or Bella's paranoia, her burned-out mental state which is also hinted at during some points in the film. But it may also be a New Materialist cautionary tale that makes us rethink the entangled relations between human and non-human actors in our world, as Karen Barad has most famously and rigorously argued in *Meeting the Universe Halfway* (2007). In any case, like Barad, Haraway and Tsing, Hausner does not argue that all is lost and that we must either comply or die, but rather that we somehow need to find ways to cope with the eerie possibilities of our times and the mind games our inventions play with us, even if it means that 'happiness is a business'. At the end of the film orders for 'Little Joe' are received from all over the world, even from the European Union; a Brexit joke on the cusp of a new world order.

As a last set of remarks about *Little Joe*, I want to zoom in on the plant itself. As a plant, Little Joe is a character in itself. Its gorgeous alluring visuals are outstanding, making the film iconic. Hausner explained that from the beginning she had a red flower in mind, but not exactly in all its visual details. They could not use real flowers, as they would have to remain quite stable throughout the production of several weeks. During her research, Hausner found a red flower called *Scandoxus haemantus*, whose striking, bright-red, feathery-headed flower served as inspiration for the design of Little Joe. *Scandoxus haemantus* grows only in warm climates and some of its variants are extremely poisonous. Components of the plant have been used to poison arrowheads or as fish toxin. Nevertheless, it is also used for medication. Hence, *Scandoxus haemantus* is what Derrida would call a *pharmakon*, the Greek word to designate both poison and medicine, depending on its use or context (Derrida 1981).

Little Joe was designed by art director Marko Waschke and a team of twenty people who created hundreds of flowers in four different stages of development: closed, half-open, open in the centre and completely open. Furthermore, for its articulation and the proliferation of its scent, it was digitally animated to give the flowers a feeling of being alive (Schiefer 2019). As an iconic image, Little Joe is fitting for what the film conveys: it refers at the same time to a real plant and to its phantasmatic doppel-ganger; it is at once dangerous and beneficial. With its stark, sparkling-red colour it signals a whole spectrum of feelings, ranging from doubts about motherhood to maternal love, and from paranoid fear and anxiety to seduction, attraction and love. The common designation for the real flower that inspired Little Joe is quite appropriately the 'Blood Lily'.

The Green Blood of the Future

Let me turn now to the last feature film I want to discuss here, a film that equally addresses posthuman issues in a New Materialist way that transcends the borders between the human and the non-human. In *Glass Garden* we encounter Jae-yeon (Moon Geun-Young), a shy biologist with a clubfoot, who works in a scientific laboratory. The film opens with the overwhelmingly green hues of a lush summer forest, and filtered sunlight is reflected on the surface of a green-coloured lake. A close-up of one of the trees reveals that it is wounded, a green liquid oozing from it. Then there is a cutaway to the blue light of a computer screen and a voice-over speaking words as they are typed: 'She was born in the forest, with bones of firm wood and flesh of fibre. One day green blood started to run in her veins.' We cut back to the forest, and then to a laboratory where Jae-yeon is observing test tubes filled with green liquids, injecting a zebra fish with the substance. Then we move to the writer of the opening sentences, the little-known novelist Ji-hoon (Kim Tae Hoon), who is stuck in his new novel which is supposed to be about 'the foundations of life from the perspective of the soil'. From this beginning the narrative is set up as a 'double helix' between speculative science and speculative fiction. Ji-hoon gets into an argument with a famous novelist whom he publicly accuses of plagiarism, which is in fact true; however, as his publisher tells him, 'If you're successful no one questions you.' As *persona non grata*, and evicted from the house by his ex-girlfriend, he begins to observe his opposite neighbour Jae-yeon. Jae-yeon, in turn loses all faith in humanity and the scientific world when her lover and the leader of the laboratory, Professor Jung (Seo Tae-Hwa), takes off with her colleague Soo-hee (Park Ji-soo) after she has stolen Jae-yeon's research findings to give them an immediate industrial application in the cosmetics industry. Jae-yeon retreats to a house (the glass garden) in the forest; Ji-hoon follows and observes her from a distance, fabulating her story into a successful online series.

As Andrew Mathews argues in an essay on ghostly forms and forest histories, the forest is the place where 'people, trees, and other nonhumans have been entangled for a very long time' (Mathews 2017: G145). As a woodland anthropologist Mathews has traced 'ghostly forms' as traces of past cultivations, but also as ways of imagining new environmental futures. His method is to walk and observe the forest closely, paying attention to 'form, texture, and color, and constant speculations as to pattern' (2017: G147). Mathews argues that this attention to our material surroundings is full of speculative politics, and that we need to find new ways of connecting to our environment for planetary survival.

In a similar way, Jae-yeon is following patterns of nature in unconventional scientific ways. For her, the forest is a place full of ghosts indeed; she was born there and her father was a logger who stopped felling trees because her mother died when she was born. Her father believed that the trees had souls and cursed them. Jae-yeon listens to the trees and plants; they talk to her. The blood she synthesises is what she calls 'the green blood of the future'. Transplanting chlorophyll into red blood cells, she creates green blood cells that have the capacity for plant-like photosynthesis, eliminating the need for external oxygen; they would produce their own oxygen. This would be a way of improving and extending human life. This is a Frankensteinian ideal indeed, comparable to the desire of Victor Stein, the AI specialist in Jeanette Winterson's novel *Frankissstein* (2019), who wants to preserve the human brain by cryotechnics, computer power and Artificial Intelligence. While the prototype green blood cell seems promising, the zebra fish she injects with the substance does not survive. Furthermore, it would take many years of fundamental research to take it anywhere applicable. Hence, the financers of the laboratory move ahead with the youth-enhancing cosmetic products. Jae-yeon's work remains speculative.

In the forest, the double helix of Jae-yeon and Ji-hoon, the scientist and the writer, becomes even more entwined as he steals and writes her story and she lets him do so to prove somehow to the world that she is not crazy. The whole narrative suggests that Jae-yeon's speculative green blood will perhaps one day be the real solution for Ji-hoon, who suffers from a sudden stiffening of his body produced by a genetic disease that causes a constriction of the blood flow to his brain, meaning that his brain does not receive enough oxygen. He, too, feels as though he is becoming a tree. Visually there are several moments when *Glass Garden* expresses this parallel. Most strikingly, this is rendered in the overflow from the branching dendrites and blood vessels of Ji-hoon's MRI scan, which slowly transform into branching trees that have open spaces at the exact locations of the brain vessels. The white colour on the MRI scan transforms into the blue-white of the sky between the leaves, where we discover a small figure in the tree (Jae-yeon); then the blue-white 'arteries' of the trees slowly turn red, like blood vessels filling up, suggesting by 'form, texture, and color, and constant speculations' the pattern of a solution for the stiffening of a body. However, that promise of experimental science is not fulfilled.

Slowly but surely the film becomes increasingly monstrous. First, the colour green, besides designating the green of oxygen-producing plants, the verdant hue of the green movement, is also nature's monstrosity, as Dorion Sagan argues in 'Beautiful Monsters' (Sagan 2017). This is because of the (green-coloured) cyanobacteria that live in water and grow in higher temperatures, polluting the water by mass reproduction: 'The green beings spread across the surface of the planet in a kind of green fire that has still not stopped burning. We – human civilization – are of the latter-day flames' (Sagan 2017: M169). Sagan calls this global pollution crisis the 'Cyanocene' (as opposed to the much-used Anthropocene), which is inaugurated by the cyanobacteria that 'contain the possibility for some of its energy-feeding forms to grow rogue, to become teratological,

Figure 5.4 *Glass Garden* (Shin Su-Won, 2017).

monstrous growers that threaten the wholes from which they have sprung' (Sagan 2017: M171). In addition, Jae-yeon becomes monstrous, a mad scientist in a way, when she is caught by 'the green fire' that does not stop burning. First, like a sort of eco-Frankenstein, she tries to bring the professor back to life by injecting him with her green blood from the test tubes. The professor had come to visit her in the glasshouse to ask for the return of the petri dish that she stole from the laboratory (the sample they need to use in reduced concentrations in the patented cosmetic products), and on his way back he was taken by the forest, slipping on a tree root and falling into the cyanic water. She keeps him in a wheelchair, infusing him with green liquids. He turns green, which might just be the decay, mould and rotting of his flesh; then branches begin to grow from his head.

Finally, Jae-yeon injects herself with green blood and transforms into a tree. When Ji-hoon returns to the forest years later, walking with a stick and hampered, he finds a tree that was previously dead (and that Jae-yeon tried to revive with her sacs of green infusions) now fully in bloom. Pondering in front of the enormous tree, we hear his closing words:

> One day I met her again in the woods, wild grass amongst the weeds, chattering birds; they all had names but she did not. One day her tender bark swelled, the branch split into two arms, and white flesh appeared like a woman's breast. White liquid dripped like milk. A branch below sprouted and rooted itself to form a leg. Now people could call her by her name. She was at last a tree.

In rich imagery Won's *Glass Garden* presents a speculative fiction about speculative science that nevertheless tells us that the red blood of human life might one day be overgrown by green, when the Anthropocene gives way to the Cyanocene.

'When All You Love is Being Trashed'

All the protagonists in the films discussed in this chapter are in one way or another confronted with the terrors of sociopolitical circumstances, 'when all you love is being trashed' (Rose 2017: G51). The tropes of the fantastic and the horror genre are a way of addressing and redeeming these political circumstances, as much as they sometimes offer a route via the imagination to critique and to cope. The blood of colonial and racist violence, the battle for survival when pushed to the margins of society and the search for reconnection in new 'monstrous' ways to nature are all part of these films. In many cases, a poetics of horror is introduced to create forms of poetic justice, but also to invite us not only to stay with the fascination for horror aesthetics and powerful stories, but to address the most urgent political questions that are at stake in our contemporary age, inspired by and expanding a poetics of relation into New Materialist and imaginative futures.

Bloody Red: Poetics, Patterns, Politics

Where there is blood there is life.

(Woolf 2018: 213)

Poetics

Red is a signal colour, it flags something in the image as important: something has happened, something is happening, something will (or might) happen. In the works discussed in this book, this vivid outstanding colour has appeared in the guise of numerous tints, tinges, shades and intensities, as elements in the *mise en scène* (red filtered light, a scarlet sea star, a Blood Lily, red fingernails, a ruby dress or scarlet cloak) and as a trail of blood connected to the poetics, patterns and politics of horror in the work of female directors. Historically, the creative work of women has often been neglected (Korthase 2019), much like the work of Lily Briscoe, the unmarried painter who is a guest at the Ramseys' house in Virginia Woolf's *To the Lighthouse*. In her analysis of this novel, Berenice Carroll focuses on this seemingly trivial character, who is repeatedly described as 'little' and 'insignificant'. As Lily stands before her easel, she hears another guest of the Ramseys, Mr Tansley, repeatedly whispering in her ear: 'Women can't paint, women can't write . . .' (Woolf 2004: 75). She is an unlikely heroine for whom 'there was no hope for badges, orders, or degrees. Her paintings would be hung in the servant's bedrooms. It would be rolled up and stuffed under the sofa' (Woolf quoted in Carroll 1978: 116). Lily nonetheless continues her creative work, and at the end of the book she completes the painting that she has been working on throughout the novel:

> Quickly, as if she were recalled by something over there, she turned to her canvas. There it was – her picture. Yes, with all its greens and blues, its lines running up and across, its attempt at something. It would be hung in the attics, she thought; it would be destroyed. But what did that matter? She asked herself, taking up the brush again

. . . With a sudden intensity, as if she saw it clear for a second, she drew a line there, in the centre. It was done; it was finished. Yes, she thought, laying down her brush in extreme fatigue, I have had my vision. (Woolf in Carroll 1978: 116)

Since we know that for Woolf the central line in *To the Lighthouse* is the lighthouse itself, as discussed in Chapter 3 with regard to Campion's references to the lighthouse and Woolf's novel in her film *In the Cut*, it is fair to imagine that the colour of the line that finishes Lily's painting is, indeed, bright red. In the final pages of this book, I will recall three other 'minor characters' to accompany Lily Briscoe: Lola, Lucy and Lili, who feature in three short films by women that subscribe to the poetics of horror. As 'final girls' in the line-up of Carrie's crimson sisters, they signal the vision and agency of the female creators whose work I have precisely wanted to flag in this book, and not allow to 'hang in the attic' or disappear in the cavernous vaults of film history.

Like Woolf's lighthouse, the colour red, both as a formal element of the blood and guts associated with the horror genre, as well as in all its symbolic values and meanings, has been a guiding line, a literal red thread throughout this book. Every film establishes its own poiesis, weaving together its material and perceptual elements with the content of the stories told, the visibility and movement of its affective dimensions reso-nating with the sociopolitical world it addresses. Ranging from brilliant scarlets, to deep crimsons, translucent rubies, reddish-purples, magentas, soft rosy reds, violent fuchsias, pinks and bloody oranges, the hues of the red colour spectrum are innumerable and its affective and symbolic dimensions operate in various ways on the senses, in every film, in each viewer and under different viewing conditions. Ranging from the 'seeing red' of rage or traumatic memory, as Keir-la Janisse describes her auto-biographic mental topography in relation to horror and exploitation films (Janisse 2012: 94), to the ontological 'blood-image' of the invisible realm beyond the skin or the surface of the image, described by Jean-Luc Nancy in relation to *Trouble Every Day*, the colour red has thus no stable affec-tive quality, but unfolds within the constellation of each film. It emerges as what Sergei Eisenstein in *The Film Sense* famously called the fourth dimension of the feeling of film aesthetics: 'The emotional intelligibility and function of colour will rise from the natural order of establishing the colour imagery of the [part of the] work, coincidental with the process of shaping the living movement of the whole work' (Eisenstein 1947: 151). While the colour red certainly has what Eisenstein calls a 'dynamogeneous' (invigorating) effect on the body and brain of the spectator (as opposed to, for instance, the more 'inhibitive', dampening or calming effect of a colour like blue), there is nevertheless no fixed symbolic meaning to the poiesis of the 'feel of horror' (Brinkema 2019), 'the feel of red'. The most general thing one can say about the colour red is that because of its signalling vivacity, it is intensely present, often as a trail of blood, in the vision of female directors.

Ansuya Blom's short experimental film *Lola Magenta* (2017) gives expression to the painful physical and mental condition of Lola Voss, a patient admitted to Bellevue psychiatric hospital in Kreuzlingen, Switzerland, famously described by her doctor Ludwig Binswanger, a contemporary of Freud, in his case study on schizophrenia (Binswanger 1963). Blom does not refer to Binswanger's report but instead focuses on the 'minor' character of the patient. She brings Voss's own words to life by reading from her letters, in which she speaks with insight and clarity about her situation. The soundtrack consists of Voss's intimate observations about her condition, expressed in a whispering voice ('The only thing is that I now feel contaminated by everything'), combined with haunting and rapidly repeated fragments from *4.48 Psychosis*, the final play by British playwright Sarah Kane, completed shortly before her self-chosen death. The image track of *Lola Magenta* shows parts (the back of a head, hands) of the body of a woman in extreme close-up, all filtered through a magenta-red that changes texture, first becoming fluid like watercolours, then dusty like sparks; sometimes the image becomes completely abstract, like red blood cells moving inside the body seen under a microscopic lens. Black spots seem to contaminate the blood and almost take over the image plane, which then shifts back to magenta. In an interview, Blom indicated that for her, magenta is an abject colour, a colour that is not exactly red, but somehow hurts, as it 'scrapes' the eyes.[1] Even if *Lola Magenta* is not a horror film as such, it does exemplify the poetry and 'feel of horror' that each of the films discussed in this book creates anew. While magenta can provoke different affective qualities, the specific poetics of Blom's assemblage of colour, sound, text, the rhythm of images and words, certainly provokes the dread of an unstable mental condition, which nevertheless also has agency that transpires through the extraordinary perception that the film presents, poetically painful and powerful.

Patterns

While no recipe can be given to understand the feel of horror and the power of the poetics of red, there have been several recurrent patterns that can be observed in the work of female horror directors. Let me return here to the three hypotheses that I put forward in the introduction. First, besides the greater agency that is given to the female protagonists, and certain aesthetic choices regarding the depiction of violence done to women (for instance, not to show sexual violence, as is the case with *Revenge* and *Joy*, discussed in Chapter 1), it is striking that much of the horror is presented from an intimate point of view of inner experience. Appropriating and adapting stylistic elements and tropes from the horror genre, all the directors in this book express thoughts, desires and fears from the darkest corners of the unconscious with a boldness or explicitness that Woolf dreamed of, but was unable to commit to paper in the ways she might have wished, blocked by the demon of patriarchal good manners. Many of the films discussed in the previous chapters take us inside the mind of a woman, exploring the dark corners of the unconscious where confusion and ambiguity of experiences, memories and emotions do not always find clarity or closure. This also implies that the monstrous is not encountered as something out there, monstrously feminine and other than 'I', the abject that can be exorcised in the horror film through a modern defilement rite, as in many of the male-authored horror movies of the 1970s and 1980s described by Clover and Creed. Rather, the new blood in contemporary horror often pivots around recognising, acknowledging and dealing with the monstrosity inside ourselves. They are confrontations with our inner demons and with terrifying emotions.

Chelsea Lupkin's short body-horror film *Lucy's Tale* (2018) tells the story of teenage girl Lucy. Many coming-of-age stories have translated female experience into the language of horror. In Chapter 2, for instance, we saw how the vampire is revisited at at an all-girls' boarding school in *The Moth Diaries* to tell a tale about friendship, jealousy, childhood trauma and suicidal thoughts. Additionally, *Raw* is a ferocious coming-of-age story about the discovery of female lust and sexuality and the acknowledgement of inner monstrosity, as discussed in Chapter 3. The insecure horror heroine Iona in *Pin Cushion*, featured in Chapter 4, illustrates the terror of being bullied by classmates and of being too close symbiotically to the pain and sorrow of the mother to grow into an independent woman. In a concise way, *Lucy's Tale* also explores the high-school anxieties of being an outcast and discovering the physical changes associated with entering womanhood. Lupkin combines references to De Palma's *Carrie* with Cronenbergian body horror and creates a new amalgamation that speaks from the inner experiences of the young heroine. Like Carrie, Lucy is bullied by the popular girls; she is pelted with dozens of red balls in the gymnasium, called a freak and left alone. Like Carrie, she discovers her powers when she seems to be able to make her bullies stumble, get a nosebleed or feel otherwise physically unwell. Alone in bed at night, she watches De Palma's *Carrie* on her laptop in an explicit intertextual acknowledgement of the 'prom queen of blood'. However, unlike *Carrie*, Lucy's mother seems quite normal, even if at the beginning of the film when Lucy is in a fitting room trying on bras, she embarrasses her by asking for a more padded model (which emphasises the small size of her developing breasts and the shame, emotional distress and insecurity this causes). Unlike *Carrie*, the boy who takes an interest in her genuinely seems to like her, precisely because she is different. And unlike *Carrie*, Lucy experiences her bodily transformations as horror when she feels something growing out of her spine, which quite literally transforms 'Lucy's Tale' into 'Lucy's tail'. We are always with her, experiencing the events and especially the bodily transformations through her inner experience of something monstrous growing in (and on) her. However, she cannot mentally process this yet. We are completely within her mind, and the fear that her changing body inspires is translated into visions of horror.

Beside this inner perspective, the second pattern that emerges in connection to the new poetics of horror is that horror is no longer strictly confined to strict genre boundaries. Underneath its bloody, gory, spooky or otherwise dark surfaces, typical horror aesthetics can hide psychological, social or political drama and tragedy. And vice versa, psychological, social or political dramas can embed inside their generic aesthetics the terror and horror that lies underneath. While hybrid genres are not new, many of the contemporary horror films by women mix genres to the point that they are sometimes misunderstood as 'neither horror, nor drama', and therefore easily dismissed. However, I would argue that the quite daring breaks with genre conventions that some women directors propose allow precisely a confrontation with difficult topics and social taboos, which find new ways of expression and therefore advance new social debates. Marina de Van's *Dark Touch*, discussed in Chapter 4, disguises a drama of child abuse within typical horror aesthetics. Dismissed by some critics for its genre mixing (Robertson 2013), it is precisely this rewriting (or should I say underwriting) of the genre that opens it to a larger scale of questions and problems than the horror genre typically allows. And vice versa, Nora Fingscheidt's *System Crasher* (also discussed in Chapter 4) is a psychosocial drama about the same tragic topic of child abuse. Here we see how the aesthetics of a more realistic drama precipitates the terror and dread of the horror genre, especially in its ferocious use of pink which borders the violence of red, so important in the poetics of horror. *Divines* exhibits the horror underneath the harsh living conditions in French *banlieus*. Other films more explicitly mix different genres, such as *Spoor*, which could be described as a feminist crime-story eco-horror melodrama, and *Atlantics*, a political romance zombie-horror ghost film (all three films discussed in Chapter 5). And films such as *I'm Not a Witch* (Chapter 2) and *Evolution* (Chapter 4) defy genre expectations altogether.

Another characteristic pattern that must be mentioned here in connection to this mixing of genres is that horror can be expressed in the most exuberant ways, by spilling gallons of blood, or explicit violence and body horror, or retakes of the slasher genre, the vampire film or cannibals and zombies. Or it can be voiced in much more subdued and restrained forms such as a creeping or eerie menace, a sudden nosebleed, an unexplained scratch, a shiver down one's spine, or a subtle menacing soundtrack, an ominous noise. Moreover, many of the works of the directors from the second wave of feminism of the 1970s that were labelled as experimental or women's films can be reread as horror films within this broader definition of the genre.

This revised conception of the horror genre is connected to the third pattern that recurs throughout the collective body of work discussed in this book, which concerns its emotional spectrum. As indicated at several points, the horror aesthetics goes beyond the variations of fear (dread, anxiety) and disgust (repulsion, loathing), the conventional emotions connected to the genre that can be responded to either with screams, shivers or laughter. Obviously, these emotions remain important reactions to horror. But we have seen that while they remain by and large on the spectrum of negative emotions characteristic of horror, many of the films also include a whole range of more minor 'ugly feelings' such as jealousy, irritation and paranoia. The heroine of *Retrospekt*, discussed in Chapter 1, or Sarah in *Sarah Plays a Werewolf* in Chapter 2, for instance, are often irritated and also provoke irritation in the spectator. The heroine of *Helter Skelter* (Chapter 2) or the mother in *The Babadook* (Chapter 4) could also be considered as paranoid. The bodily transformations of many new horror heroines could be considered on the spectrum of mental distortions coloured by the intensity of the experiences (of growth, of loss, of racism, of political injustice) through which the characters go. More importantly, we see that horror and terror can now be imbued with sadness, mourning and other trauma-related affects. This also invites surprising emotional responses to the horror on screen: not just screams and laughter, but also being moved by the recognition of these underlying affects of sadness, mourning and dealing with ordeal and distress. Discovering at the end of the film that the mother in *The Babadook* has found a way to give the black bile containing her anger and grief (over the death of her husband) a place by locking it in the basement, every now and then feeding it with some attention and then moving on, provokes quite a different emotion than being relieved by the fact that the monster has finally been killed.

Moreover, female-directed horror films present women not just as either victims or their opposite, 'final girls' or 'strong women', but propose a whole array of more flawed characters. As Amelia Moses, director of the short body-horror film *Undress Me*, pointed out in an interview, we need to see more 'women who make mistakes and are emotionally complex'.[2] Horror heroines are not always nice girls, or characters you can sympathise with because they are victims or superheroines. Only when this emotional complexity and imperfection is accepted will there also be room for a less stereotypical female screen presence. We may not always understand them, we may not agree with them, they may remain ambiguous and non-transparent, but they invite us to process this ambiguity, this poetic opacity of not knowing (everything) and an ethics that incubates a poetics of relation that can grow and change, and even extend beyond the human realm, while 'staying with the trouble', nevertheless reaching into a posthuman future.

Politics

It is remarkable that there are so many female directors twisting and turning elements from the poetics of horror into many different variations, scales and political contexts. This can be considered as part of the new third wave of feminism.[3] This latest wave of collective feminist consciousness is loosely grouped around the global #MeToo debates that were ignited by the scandals surrounding Harvey Weinstein, the heretofore untouchable Hollywood producer who fell from grace when in 2017 dozens of women accused him of sexual harassment, assaults and rape over the last thirty years. The accusations raised a multitude of sexual allegations and precipitated a rise in consciousness about power abuse via sexuality all over the world. While men can also be victims of sexual abuse, the gender divide is mostly very traditional in these cases.

In her short film *Lili* (2019), Yfke van Berkelaer presents a poetics of horror in the context of the #MeToo debates, showing the subtle ways in which the abuse of power in the film industry works, and how a poetics of horror slowly but surely creeps into the situation. Against a simple black background, we see an actress (Lisa Smit) attending an audition, performing some lines for a film role. When she presents herself as Lili Buy, off-screen we hear the director (Derek de Lint), who is sitting beside the camera. He tells her that his daughter's name is Lily, too (albeit spelled differently). This seems like a congenial remark to make her feel more comfortable. It could also be a reference to Weinstein's oldest daughter, whose name is Lily.[4] In any case, it is clear that the age difference is an important component to the power balance in this situation (the actress could be his daughter); one has all the power, and the other is young, less experienced and wants a job. Over several takes of the dialogue in which the director in voice-off assumes the counter-part and comments on her performance on each take, we see how, slowly but surely, the situation becomes increasingly awkward. After uttering the lines first as an angry woman, then as a character who seems unaffected and in control, both in very convincing performances, Lili is asked to now play the scene in a more seductive way, like a *femme fatale* who 'is even more in control'. At the same time, she is invited to unfasten her shirt. With a hesitant look, Lili opens the top button of her white blouse and delivers another very convincing performance of the same lines, only this time with much more enticement. However, the director is not yet convinced, and asks her to do it again, to open up more . . . I will not spoil the ending of the film here, but one has to imagine how in only eight minutes we see a confident and competent young woman denigrated, relegated to a position of vulnerability and abuse. At the end of the film, her blouse is no longer white but splashed with bright-red stains. She is also no longer sweet, vulnerable young prey.

Lili exemplifies how a poetics of horror in the work of female directors resonates with the spirit of the #MeToo debates, and demonstrations against the turning back of women's rights to birth control and abortion in several parts of the world, symbolised by the red-cloaked *Handmaid's Tale* demonstrators. During the course of this book, I have discussed films that show how the language of horror can be employed to counter or avenge sexual abuse, as in *Revenge* and *A Girl Walks Home Alone at Night*. It is also a way of exploring female sexuality in itself and for itself, as we have seen, for instance, in *Raw* and other coming-of-age stories: via the exploration of sexuality in *Longing for the Rain* and sexual identity in *Pariah*. Awareness of trauma and family dynamics could also be considered part of contemporary emancipation, in which the films of the female directors discussed in Chapter 4 place the emphasis on the experience of pregnancy in, for instance, *Prevenge*, while terrifying mother–child and family relations are explored in films such as *Pin Cushion*, *Goodnight Mommy* and *Family*.

Clearly, this third wave of feminism that seeks to protect women's rights should be seen in connection and intersection with other battles, especially the #BlackLivesMatter movement against racial violence, discriminatory racial profiling and an unfair justice system, which began in the United States in 2013 and 2014 after brutal police violence in Ferguson and New York. In this sense, *Welcome II the Terrordome* expresses many of today's racial problems. Films discussed in Chapter 5 such as *White Material, Songs My Brothers Taught Me* and *Atlantics* place female agency in a perspective that addresses the sociopolitical contexts of (neo)colonialism and migration as well as racial and ethnic identity more explicitly. *Tigers Are Not Afraid* does the same with respect to children who are lost to the Mexican drug wars. Finally, a third contextual background for today's poetics of horror is the ecological crisis and global climate change protests; questions surrounding nature and technology are examined in the language and tropes of horror, as in *Spoor,* and in different, more Frankenstein-like ways in *Glass Garden* and *Little Joe.*

In view of the real-life young female activists, such as Malala Yousafzai (fighting for girls' education and women's rights in Afghanistan and across the world), Erica Gardner, Brittany Packnett and Alica Garza (activists in the #BlackLivesMatter movement), Emma González (leading demonstrations for stricter gun control laws in the United States), Swati Maliwal (chair of Delhi's Women's Commission who went on a hunger strike to enforce legal measures against the atrocious rape and murder of women in India), Megan Rapinoe (representing LGTBQ+ rights and criticising Donald Trump), Yumi Ishikawa (who started #KuToo in Japan, fighting against the obligation for women to wear high heels as an employment prerequisite), Wei Tingting (a Chinese activist who was imprisoned because she protested against assaults on public transport), Amani Aruri (who changed the law that allowed rapists to marry their victim in Palestine), Joyce Fernandez (who translates her humiliating experiences as a servant – *empregada doméstica* – in Brazil in her rap songs), Olga Misik (who read from the Russian constitution during demonstrations in Moscow), Greta Thunberg (initiator of the Fridays-for-Future student strikes for climate change) and Hilda Flavia Nakabuye (of the same movement, representing millions of African youngsters), it is clear that the female voices that we hear in the films that appear in this book have rebellious and 'unruly' real-life sisters whose fights are multiple, global and fraught with renewed and necessary intensity. Much is at stake as the world is in crisis on many levels. Mati Diop reminds us in an interview given after the realease of her film *Atlantics* that the horror genre is always more popular in times of crisis. She refers to Antonio Gramsci's famous statement, 'The old world is dying and the new world struggles to be born, now is the time of monsters' (Diop quoted in Joyard 2019).[5] We might be on the verge of a new world order, where more female voices will be heard. But as I hope to have been able to indicate, the collective body of female-directed horror films suggests that we will first need to process our nightmares, challenge our inner demons and perhaps change our ideas about monstrosity before this new world can be born.

A final image also comes from Diop's work. Ten years before her feature film *Atlantics* won the Grand Prix at Cannes, she made a short film entitled *Atlantiques* (2009).[6] The film contains the seeds of her later work and investigates the attraction and hardship of the sea for the many young men in Dakar who choose to leave on small boats and travel in search of a better future. Alongside footage of one of the young men, Serigne Seck, registering the dangers they face on the water, we are also offered more abstract images, the grainy contours of a tape recorder it seems, which give the images of the men talking at the seaside an asynchronicity, as if they might be in the past. The voice talks about 'The Siram', waves as tall as buildings (foreshadowing the immense building in *Atlantics* that now metaphorically becomes a wave); about the impossibility of saying goodbye to his loved ones (which is something the men in *Atlantics* also cannot do); and about the fact that there is nothing but dust in his pockets, so he has no choice but to take his chances again. We see a woman, Serigne's mother as we understand from the credits, and we find out that Serigne has gone again, although this time swallowed up by the sea. The final images are again abstract. We read a description of the longing for the sea inspired by another horrific shipwreck, *The Raft of the Medusa*, painted by Théodore Géricault in 1818, followed by an image plane that consists of what seem like rotating blades illuminated by pulsating light. The extreme close-up provides it with an intangible quality. Very slowly we realise that what we are looking at is a lighthouse with its rotating beacon searching for new ways of seeing, for new perceptions, for moving affects, for a poetics of relation 'to awake a being and an awareness of the world, in constant movement, and of the links in it and with it', providing a line of orientation (Glissant in Delpech 2011: 244) – like the bloody red of Woolf's lighthouse that has been the searching line of orientation in this book.

Notes

Introduction

1. The Night of Terror began as The Weekend of Terror in 1984, which became the annual Fantastic Film Festival, and is now part of the Imagine Film Festival Amsterdam: <https://imaginefilmfestival.nl/> (last accessed 18 March 2020).
2. This book is indebted to the editors of *Re-Reading the Monstrous Feminine* (Chare, Hoorn and Yue 2019). My own contribution to this volume appears 'chopped up' and with slight alterations in various parts of this book.
3. See the filmography at the end for an extended list of titles I encountered during my research. See also Peirse 2020.
4. For instance, in *The Neuro-Image* I argued for the shift to inner perspectives and mental landscapes in digital screen culture (Pisters 2012).
5. See <https://wfpp.cdrs.columbia.edu/> (last accessed 18 March 2020) (emphasis in original). I should also mention here the excellent curatorial work of MUBI, which has often chosen films by women for its selections and also offers extended and growing lists of films made by women with over 1000 titles, such as <https://mubi.com/lists/essential-films-by-women> or <https://mubi.com/nl/lists/films-directed-by-women> (last accessed 18 March 2020). See also 100 overlooked films directed by women on the website of *Sight & Sound*, <https://www.bfi.org.uk/news-opinion/sight-sound-magazine/october-2015-issue> (last accessed 18 March 2020). Finally, Mark Cousin's epic documentary series *Women Make Film* (2019) provides a revision of film history by focusing on female directors.
6. The neglect of female creative and intellectual professionals is widespread. In art history, for instance, the work of female painters has often been overlooked in hidden places within archives (or not kept at all), a phenomenon that is also slowly being challenged, for instance in the exhibition *Fighting for Visibility: Women Artists in the Nationalgalerie: Before 1919*, Berlin, 11 October 2019–8 March 2020.
7. In my research into the poetics of female-directed horror movies, I have not encountered many films that explicitly address transgenderism from a new perspective, except perhaps in *A Girl Walks Home Alone at Night* (discussed in Chapter 2). Very often transgendered characters in horror films have been portrayed as monsters, exemplified by Norman Bates in *Psycho* (dir. Alfred

Hitchcock, 1960), Bobbi in *Dressed to Kill* (dir. Brian De Palma, 1980) and Buffalo Bill in *Silence of the Lambs* (dir. Jonathan Demme, 1991). Beyond the horror genre *pur sang*, I wish to note Kimberley Peirce's *Boys Don't Cry* (2000), based on the tragic true story of Teena Brandon, who was murdered because of his transsexual masculinity. In *Sense 8* (2015–18) Lana and Lily Wachowsky, following their transition from male to female, present a vivid celebration of diverse and non-binary sexuality. Claudia Priscilla and Kiko Goifman portray in their documentary *Bixa Travesty* (2018) the incredibly powerful 'tranny faggot' Linn da Quebrada whose body is a political weapon that defies any categorisation of binary sexuality. For more transgender films, see the TranScreen Transgender Film Festival, available at <https://transcreen.wordpress.com/> (last accessed 25 March 2020). In her novel *Frankisssstein* (2019), Jeanette Winterson rewrites Mary Shelley's classic horror story, presenting Ry, a young transgender doctor in Brexit Britain who falls in love with Victor Stein, a leading professor in AI.

8. The other Marys are Mary Beton, Mary Seton and Mary Carmichael, all of whom Woolf identifies with to the point that 'Mary' becomes a generic name for women in history. Obviously one can also think here of Mary Shelley, who as a writer also had to take the name of her husband to get her first work *Frankenstein* published. Woolf does not mention Shelley but does refer to female writers such as Charlotte Brontë and Jane Austen, in whom she finds the freedom of mind to write 'without hate, without bitterness, without fear, without protest, without preaching' (Woolf 2015a: xix).

9. Linda Williams has made similar arguments about the horror genre as simultaneously expressing women's desire and potency while punishing this with the same stroke (Williams 1984a, 1991).

10. SLAB refers to Sausurian semiotics, Lacanian psychoanalysis, Althusserian Marxism and Barthesian textual theory (Bordwell 1989: 385).

11. Kappelhoff does not refer to Deleuze's distinction between movement-image and time-image but uses movement-image as a more general concept of cinema as a moving image of 'visual affect', to use Woolf's term, to propose a new conception of cinepoetics.

12. Glissant, too, implicitly refers to Deleuze, more specifically to Deleuze and Guattari's conception of rhizomatics, the idea of non-hierarchical grassroots connections that lies at the basis of their philosophy developed in *A Thousand Plateaus* (1988). The desire to understand the other in the image of the self is conceptualised by Deleuze and Guattari in the notion of patriarchal state power as a 'machine of capture'. Others have commented extensively on the resonances between Deleuze and Guattari and Glissant (Nesbitt 2010; Kaiser 2012; Yountae 2014). This is just to say that the ghosts of Deleuze and Guattari also linger behind the words of this book.

13. There is another remake of King's story, the television film *Carrie* directed by David Carson (2002). Kat Shea directed a sequel to the original film: *The Rage: Carrie 2* (1999).

14. Peirce's Carrie thus resembles one of the heroines in Naomi Alderman's novel *The Power* (2016), who discover that they have electrical superpowers that they can use (and abuse) to change the gender balance in the world.

Chapter 1

1. Marguerite Duras could be counted as the other female director among the Left Bank new wave filmmakers. As a novelist she began to write screenplays, most famously *Hiroshima Mon Amour* (dir. Alain Resnais, 1955) and later she made her own films. *Nathalie Granger* (1972), for instance, shot in her own house, addresses the confined female spaces of the home. The theme of violence runs in the background of the film through the association of the women with young killers in the woods of Les Yvelines (Pisters 2003).

2. See David Maguire's 'cultography' (2018) for more on this film (originally called *Day of the Woman*) and its remake and sequel by Steven Monroe (in 2010 and 2013), for its historical and political contexts and its polemic status as 'ground zero' for the rape-revenge genre and its countless imitators.

3. 'Je fais de l'art avec une femme qui fait la vaisselle' (INA Archive), available at <https://www.youtube.com/watch?v=X8ohlkEDOyw> (last accessed 18 March 2020).

4. The story of the genesis of the film was told by Gorris in a public interview at the EYE Filmmuseum (6 May 2019). The other telling anecdote that Gorris recounted was the fact that she had to fight with the producer (Matthijs van Heijningen) to get her name as director on the film's poster. The film is not based on real events, but two years after its release there was a famous murder case in The Netherlands named 'the fitting room murder' after the place where it took place, in a fitting room. The victim was the female owner of the clothing shop, killed by (as became evident much later) two male heroin addicts.

5. In a way, this is a call that was also raised in the first feminist wave, in a short story by Susan Glaspell, 'A Jury of Her Peers' (1917). In this story two women hide a crucial piece of evidence (a dead bird) that could incriminate the wife of a murdered man. To the women it is quite clear that she indeed committed the murder, but the story also presents the reasons why they understand her by relating to the experience and psyche of a woman in her home, bullied by an unforgiving husband. The story was filmed by Sally Heckel in 1980.

6. The atrocity of slavery, and the cruel and shocking racism in the practice of lynching, were explicitly and militantly addressed in the writings of black women as early as the nineteenth century, when Ida B. Wells campaigned against lynching in her publications between 1892 and 1895, *Southern Horrors* and *A Red Record* (Wells-Barnett 1997).

7. <https://en.wikipedia.org/wiki/National_Film_Registry> (last accessed 18 March 2020).

8. The film tells the story of a mousy copy-editor who becomes a psychopathic

murderess when she is to be fired. While the film could have cult potential, it is not convincing (the main actress especially seems just weird and psychopathic rather than empowered), and it risks being laughed at instead of being laughed with.

9. All references to the words of the director and the main actress, Mathilda Lutz, are paraphrases from various interviews in which they comment on the film. See <https://www.youtube.com/watch?v=siOQTJ-k5kk>, <https://www.youtube.com/watch?v=t-olS6PdkBU>, <https://www.youtube.com/watch?v=mOO2H5NarWw> and <https://www.birds-eye-view.co.uk/cora lie-fargeat-interview/> (last accessed 4 August 2019).

10. *I Spit on Your Grave* was remade in 2010 by Steven Monroe and had some sequels.

11. The directors appear briefly in the film as two of Mary's first clients, asking her to swap the left arms of each other's body so they will always be literally part of each other. Mary performs the operation without flinching. In her documentary *The Ballad of Genesis and Lady Jane* (2011), about Genesis Breyer P-Orridge and his wife and partner Lady Jane, director Marie Losier gives a moving portrait of the ways in which the couple undergo sexual transformation operations to become part of each other for their 'pandogyne project'.

12. Talia Lugacy's *Descent* (2007) should also be mentioned here as a more psychological take on the rape-revenge story which involves an interracial date rape.

13. See also <https://asiancorrespondent.com/2009/06/why-do-korean-horror-movies-have-only-female-ghosts/> (last accessed 18 March 2020).

14. See TIFF review available at <http://www.cinemablographer.com/2018/09/tiff-review-retrospekt.html>, and Variety review available at <https://varie ty.com/2019/film/markets-festivals/retrospekt-review-1203127677/>. See also interview with Esther Rots (in Dutch), available at <https://filmkrant.nl/interview/esther-rots-retrospekt/> (all last accessed 5 August 2019).

15. *The Handmaid's Tale* (1985), Atwood's classic dystopian novel about women's condition deprived of all rights in a totalitarian near future, has also been adapted into a television series for HBO.

16. See <https://www.newsweek.com/alias-grace-star-explains-why-margaret-atwoods-novels-are-more-important-ever-702861> (last accessed 19 July 2019).

17. In her novel *Beloved*, Toni Morrison takes the perspective of Margaret Garner, an African-American slave who temporarily escaped slavery in 1857 by fleeing to Ohio, a free state. Under threat of being brought back to the plantation in Kentucky, she killed her child. See also Gordon 2008. *Beloved* was filmed by Jonathan Demme in 1997 (with Oprah Winfrey in the role of Sethe, the fictionalised Margaret Garner). But since I focus on female directors, this film will not be discussed. A comparison between the novels *Beloved* and *Alias Grace* would be very illuminating, but this is beyond the scope of this book.

Chapter 2

1. Filmed by Neil Jordan in 1994.

2. Harris's novels are the basis for the television series *True Blood* (HBO 2008–14).

3. Anne Rice's *Interview with the Vampire* novels were also inspired by a traumatic loss. She began writing her vampire tale (which features a child vampire Claudia) while grieving the loss of her daughter Michelle, who died at the age of six. While Woolf compares the sharp pain of vampire fangs to the pain of loss, Rice raises the vampire as a sort of 'cure against death' to process traumatic loss.

4. In the 1980s Corman also hired other women, such as Amy Holden Jones, Deborah Brock and Sally Matison for the *Slumber Party Massacre* trilogy in 1982, 1987 and 1990.

5. The male directors from Corman's 'film school' include Francis Ford Coppola, Ron Howard, Martin Scorsese, Jonathan Demme, John Sayles and James Cameron. Rothman did get other job offers, but only for exploitation films.

6. Rothman wrote the story of the film with her husband Charles Swartz and Maurice Jules.

7. Available at <https://metro.co.uk/2017/07/31/15-things-you-may-not-know-about-buffy-the-vampire-slayer-the-movie-6804028/> (last accessed 26 August 2019). I am not sure if Weldon indeed said 'somebody' since the Kuzuis were also involved in the production of the television *Buffy*. The fact remains that Fran Rubel Kuzui is not well known.

8. More recently in British literature, Sarwat Chadda's Muslim vampire novels *Devil's Kiss* (2009) and *Dark Goddess* (2011) have invented 'Bilqis the vampire slayer' as a new heroine. See Chambers and Chaplin 2013. Black vampire slayers came to the screen with *Blade* (dir. Stephen Norrington, 1998) and its sequels and television series.

9. Hardwicke also directed the first vampire film in the *Twilight* series (2008), based on the books by Stephanie Meyer with a script by Melissa Rosenberg. Another film that presents a variation on the 'Red Riding Hood' theme (and the colour red in the *mise en scène*) is Anne Hamilton's coming-of-age fantasy film *American Fable* (2016).

10. Harron is also known for directing *American Psycho*, *I Shot Andy Warhol*, *The Notorious Betty Page* and *Alias Grace*.

11. The other contemporary vampire film that treats this theme in a sensitive and beautiful way is *Let the Right One In* (dir. Tomas Alfredson, 2008). The friendship between a bullied shy boy and his strange and isolated girl neighbour shows how themes of feeling excluded and misuse can be part of the vampire genre.

12. The figure of the vampire, as well as the werewolf and zombie, also lend themselves to more romantic and comedic adaptations, in which women

directors also have engaged. For lack of space, I here just wish to mention two early works by female directors. Kat Shea's *Dance of the Damned* (1989) and Shimako Sato's *Tale of a Vampire* (1992) present romantic versions of vampire love. And from the younger generation of women, Yfke van Berkelaer's short horror-musical *Zombie Love* (2007) presents a bloodthirsty zombie who falls in love with a girl and tries to disguise his true nature, only to discover that she actually fell in love with his zombie version. Emily Haggins's *My Sucky Teen Romance* (2011) is a vampire high school horror comedy.

13. In South-East Asia vampire stories are often connected to the ghost spirit of women who died while pregnant or during childbirth. The so-called Pontianak in Malay mythology, for instance, features regularly in Asian horror cinema. In her short film *It's Easier to Raise Cattle* (2017), Amanda Nell Eu presents her take on the Pontianak. Unfortunately, at the time of this writing, I have not yet been able to find this film.

14. In the same vein Yun Jae-Yeon's horror film *Yoga Lesson* (2009) has her characters obsessed with beauty and youth, even if the vampire in this film is not so much a bloodsucker as a soul-eating yoga teacher. And in their (rather disappointing) remake of David Cronenberg's *Rabid* (2019), the Sotska sisters set the story in the forever-young-and-happy fashion industry. After a terrible accident that deforms her face, a shy fashion designer gets experimental plastic surgery, which basically turns her into a vampire who contaminates everybody with rabies, even though she now looks splendid and her clothing collection is a sudden success. At the end of the film, she is imprisoned by a mad scientist who will keep her alive simply for his pleasure.

15. Another film that presents an interesting portrait of a ferocious woman is Ngozi Onwurah's short *White Men Are Cracking Up* (1994), in which Onwurah addresses the fetishisation of the black 'feminine mystique'; a mysterious vampiric *femme fatale* (dressed in a bright-red bonnet) seduces and anaesthetises white men with her fatal attraction and induces them into her web-of-death by convincing them to kill themselves. The film is seen through the eyes of a detective who both despises her and falls for her. By keeping the woman a total mystery, Onwurah comments on the media's representation of black women, which (certainly in the 1990s) mainly presents black women in stereotypically flat images, as the absolute unknowable, seductive and dangerous 'other'.

16. Male black vampires appeared on the screen with *Blacula* (dir. William Crain, 1972) and *Ganja and Hess* (dir. Bill Gunn, 1973).

17. See also Beugnet 2007 for the 'Global Transylvania' in contemporary French cinema.

18. Van Abbe Museum 2019. See <https://vanabbemuseum.nl/programma/programma/the-otolith-group/> (last accessed 18 March 2020).

19. Available at <https://www.freethebid.com/nikyatu-jusu-suicide-by-sunlight-pt-1/> (last accessed 3 January 2020).

Chapter 3

1. Other important 'bloody women artists' besides Schneemann include Valie Export whose *Touch Cinema* performance (1968) remains remarkable; Fluxus artist Shigeko Kubota performing her *Vagina Paintings* in 1965; Judy Chicago's *Red Flag* (1971) and *Menstruation Bathroom* (1971–72) depicting menstruation; and Ana Mendieta's blood paint super-8mm works such as *Sweating Blood* (1973), *Blood Writing* (1974), *Blood Sign* (1974), *Body Tracks* (1974), *Blood and Feathers* (1974) and *Blood Inside Outside* (1975). See Green-Cole 2015; and for Mendieta, see Lukkas and Oransky 2015.

2. In the 1970s Ana Mendieta also explicitly and fearlessly addressed 'feminist issues like campus rape and domestic violence when they were still taboo' (Rosen 2018). From the 1980s, Lydia Lunch is another noteworthy performance artist and singer who embodies the articulation of frustration over pain and trauma. In an interview in 2009, Lunch explained that men are socialised to turn their violence outwards and women are socialised to 'zip it up', be silent and turn inward, surrounded by unrealistic images of themselves. So turning 'outward' in itself is often experienced as a shocking thing for women to do. Lunch calls this 'positive negativism'. See <https://www.youtube.com/watch?v=E5Vpjax8RlE> (last accessed 16 September 2019).

3. See, for instance, <https://fineartmultiple.com/blog/carolee-schneemann-interior-scroll-masterpiece/> and <https://www.moma.org/collection/works/109934> (last accessed 18 March 2020).

4. Leontine Sagan's *Girls in Uniform* from 1931 was one of the first female-directed films to explore lesbian themes. In 1970 Barbara Peeters and Jack Deerson portrayed the attraction between two bored housewives in the suburbs of Los Angeles in *The Dark Side of Tomorrow*. Patricia Rozema's *I've Heard the Mermaids Singing* (1987) is another film that explores these themes of love between women in a highly imaginative and original way. The film received much acclaim when it premièred but has since disappeared into the shadows of film history. Claire Oakley's *Make Up* (2020) explores the emergent lesbian desire and sexuality of its protagonist in a subtle poetics of horror (including red fingernails, other red elements in the *mise en scène* and literally engulfing emotions) that belongs to the new blood in contemporary cinema under discussion.

5. The title of *The Watermelon Woman* may also hint at Melvin von Peebles's *The Watermelon Man* (1970), a comedy about an extremely bigoted white insurance agent in the 1960s who one morning wakes up and discovers that he has turned black, and now experiences all the (sexual) stereotypes about black men at first hand.

6. In 2019 Wanuri Kahlu presented the first Kenyan lesbian love story in her film *Rafiki*.

7. The make-up stands out to such a degree that there are several 'Love Witch make-up tutorials' online. See, for instance, <https://www.youtube.com/

watch?v=zkn650l4rNM> or <https://www.youtube.com/watch?v=wfVdt
SlgKgQ> (last accessed 18 March 2020).

8. Later on there is another echo of *Marnie* when Elaine and her new victim go
   horseriding.

9. Here a parallel to *Blue My Mind* can be made, where the 15-year-old protagonist Mia (Luna Wedler) finds herself with cravings for fish (she eats the
   fish from the family fish tank) and experiments with drugs and sex. She also
   develops a skin rash, another resonating moment with *Raw*, but her rash is
   the beginning of her slow transformation and becoming-fish as she develops
   scales and eventually a tail. Because of the realism of the film, here too, the
   horror is not that of a fantasy, but provides the feel of what it is to go through
   so many bodily transformations.

10. A version of this analysis of *In the Cut* also appeared in Pisters 2019.

11. The film received mixed reviews, especially from male critics. Philip French,
    for instance, after wittily but flatly summarising the plot, remarked that the
    film simply repeats the plot of *The Eyes of Laura Mars* (dir. Irvin Kershner,
    1978), and concluded rather condescendingly that of course the difference
    is that now, twenty-five years after male directors broke the taboo subject
    (a woman falling in love with a murderer), a feminist director changes the
    style, singing 'non, je ne regretted Ryan' (French 2003). For an overview of
    In the Cut's critical reception, see Butler 2013. For an extended analysis of
    Campion's film, see Onaran 2017: 117–57; and Benoit 2006. For the interna-
    tional reception of *In the Cut*, see Butler 2014.

12. This is an ancient Tibetan Buddhist mantra for compassion and purifica-
    tion from delusions. It means 'Behold the Jewel in the Lotus' and is used to
    help achieve generosity, tolerance and patience, but it also has many other
    meanings. See <https://www.yowangdu.com/tibetan-buddhism/om-mani-
    padme-hum.html> (last accessed 18 March 2020).

13. The vagina trousers, inspired by David Bowie's Yamamoto trousers from 1989,
    were designed by Duran Lantink. Being gay, he had to Google vulva images,
    as Emma Westenberg confesses with a smile when describing the making
    of the video: <https://www.youtube.com/watch?v=4ZNFfYccXLM> (last
    accessed 18 March 2020).

Chapter 4

1. Another example to mention here is David Lynch's *Eraserhead* (1977), a
   film filled with anxieties about pregnancy and a monstrous brood that was
   inspired by his own experiences of becoming a parent.

2. In her novel *Frankissstein: A Love Story* (2019), Jeanette Winterson moves
   between the experiences of Mary Shelley in the nineteenth century and the
   reappearance of her characters as Ry Shelley, a transgendered doctor, and
   Victor Stein, a specialist in artificial intelligence who works on uploading the
   brain, who fall in love. Winterson updates questions of science and technol-

ogy, body and mind, and life and death for the multiple desires and concerns related to artificial intelligence and cryogenics. Ry Shelley's double gender, as both female and male, revives Orlando and resonates with contemporary awareness and the growing acceptance of gender fluidity (which does not mean that Winterson does not also address the aggression with which this is often still met).

3. In *The Hours* (2002), Stephen Daldry paints an insightful portrait of Woolf's struggles with motherhood during her life and work. In this film, we see the parallel lives of three women in different time zones: Nicole Kidman is Virginia Woolf writing *Mrs Dalloway*; Julianne Moore is an unhappy pregnant housewife in the 1950s who decides to abandon her husband and children; and Meryl Streep is a modern-day Mrs Dalloway who organises a party and represents the good wife.

4. A short horror film that is worth mentioning here is *Ink* (dir. Ashlea Wessel, 2016). The film expresses the trauma of a pregnancy gone wrong literally through ink (the ink of tattoos covering her body; an ink bath). In her excruciating grief, despair and feelings, perhaps, of guilt, the woman in the film hallucinates an ink fish growing out of her belly which has 'mother of monsters' tattooed on it.

5. During a 2017 EYE Film Institute public interview, Dutch director Nouchka van Brakel, the first female director in the Netherlands in the 1970s, confessed that Varda's film was an eye-opener to her and gave her the courage to address women's issues in her own films, such as *The Debut* (1977), *A Woman Like Eve* (1979) and *The Cool Lakes of Death* (1982). Equally, during a 2019 panel discussion at the Seoul International New Media Festival, Korean filmmaker Shim Hyejung also mentioned Varda as her example.

6. Other films that Harrington discusses in this chapter are *Demon Seed* (dir. Donald Cammell, 1977), *The Unborn* (dir. Rodman Flender, 1991), *Warlock: The Amargeddon* (dir. Anthony Hickox, 1993) and *The Reaping* (dir. Stephen Hopkins, 2007).

7. In her extended purely formal analysis of *Inside*, Eugenie Brinkema proposes an altogether different reading of the film, a reading that is not concerned with gender but with timing, rhythm and the feel of violence. Brinkema dissects the film into three different parts, each with their own tempo of violence. It is the third part that strikes her most, when the police arrive for the last time and bring along Abdel, a young Arab whom they arrested during riots in the *banlieue*. His murder by la Femme is rendered in such a different way to that of the fourteen others before him that his position as someone from '*l'exterieur*' (as opposed to the '*interieur*' of the belly, the house, Paris) is emphasised and formally connects with the cruelty to his body. It gestures towards the more general feel of horror and cruelty in dealing with issues of interior and exterior matters in society. Brinkema concludes: 'Theory does not abandon the world in a suspension of feeling as embodiment and its insistence on reading horror, cruelty, carelessness towards life, etc. via

radical formalism. The feel of violence is precisely the impersonal play of the arrangement of these inextricable elements that precariously live among each other: Paris, the Arab, the chain, the law' (2019: 77). Brinkema's analysis brings out a completely new dimension of the film, in which, however, female agency is even further eclipsed.

8. Agnieska Holland directed a mini-series remake of Polanski's film, also entitled *Rosemary's Baby* (NBC, 2014). Rosemary is played by Zoe Saldana and Guy by Patrick Adams. The setting is now modern-day Paris, Rosemary is not just a victim but also a strong-willed woman, and the devil appears with the faces of the rich, glamorous and powerful. Another film to mention in response to *Rosemary's Baby* is Karyn Kusama's short film *Her Only Living Son* (2017, part of the *XX* horror anthology project, directed by Jovanka Vuckvic, Sofia Carrillo, Roxanne Benjamin, Annie Clark and Kusama). *Her Only Living Son* could be seen as Rosemary's baby turning eighteen, as seen through her own eyes.

9. Another Asian female-directed horror film that involves children who return as ghosts is the Korean film *Uninvited* (dir. Lee Su-yeon, 2003). The film is not about Toyol, but the haunting past as a child shaman of an architect who discovers the ghosts of two recently murdered girls in his home. It also addresses the theme of adoption (see Seung Chung 2013). See also the short horror film *Ink*, mentioned in note 4.

10. In this sense, *Black Swan* (dir. Darren Aronofsky, 2011) offers another interesting case where we find both an overwhelmingly present mother and external demands to be the best, in this case in a contemporary New York ballet environment, which leads to horrific mental and physical strains and consequences (Pisters 2016).

11. The cinematography by Nicola Daley was inspired by American photographer Alex Prager, and the early colour photos of William Eggleston. See <https://britishcinematographer.co.uk/nicola-daley-acs-on-pin-cushion/> (last accessed 4 October 2019).

12. Another film with a remarkable mother–daughter relationship, one where both mother and daughter have their own subjectivities, is Léa Mysius's intense and playful coming-of-age film *Ava* (2017).

13. Press kit, available at <https://www.wildbunch.biz/movie/evolution/> (last accessed 18 March 2020).

14. Ibid.

15. 'Not blood, just red' was Godard's commentary on the colour scheme of *Pierrot le Fou* (1965); 'Not red, just blood' was what he noted about *La Chinoise* (1967).

16. In *Horror Film: A Critical Introduction*, Murray Leeder recalls H. P. Lovecraft's short story 'The Colour Out of Space', in which Lovecraft describes the polluted consequences of an alien meteorite as a 'colour that was almost impossible to describe' (Leeder 2018: 186). Lovecraft's story then is the starting point for reflections on chromophobia and chro-

mophilia in relation to the construction of fear through colour in horror cinema.

Chapter 5

1. Another pioneering black filmmaker who treats the subject of slavery and rich ancestral traditions is Julie Dash, whose independent film *Daughters of the Dust* was in 1991 the first film directed by an African-American woman to receive a theatrical release in the United States. The film is set in 1902 when three generations of Gullah women are preparing to migrate to the mainland. The story is told in non-linear fashion by the unborn child, and memories of past slavery and future possible lives are interwoven in an intricate poetic narration (see Dash, hooks and Bambara 1992).
2. At the time of writing I have not yet been able to see Kasi Lemmons's film *Harriet* (2019), which tells the story of Harriet Tubman, who escaped slavery and became an abolitionist and rescued seventy other people from slavery. Lemmons's film *Eve's Bayou* is discussed in Chapter 3.
3. Margarida Cordosa's haunting *The Murmuring Coast* (2004) should also be mentioned here as a film that recollects the terrors of colonialism from a white woman's perspective. Cordosa's film is set in the final days of Portugese colonial rule in Mozambique.
4. See the interview with Denis, available at <https://www.youtube.com/watch?v=fizGcvu2u_c> (last accessed 18 March 2020).
5. At the time of writing Jennifer Kent's new film *Nightingale* (2019) was not yet available on DVD and so I have not been able to see this 'Tasmanian gothic' film. As a film about colonial violence perpetrated against Australian Aboriginals that uses explicit images to show this violence, it certainly belongs in this section.
6. See the *Screamography* interview with Mary Lambert about this and her other horror films, as well as her pioneering work as a music-video director in the early 1990s when she directed, among others, five videos for Madonna; available at <https://www.youtube.com/watch?v=FBP1JzE1TsI> (last accessed 15 October 2019).
7. Available at <https://walkerart.org/magazine/navigating-fact-and-fiction-chloe-zhao-on-songs-my-brothers-taught-me> (last accessed 18 March 2020).
8. Ibid.
9. See Tarr 2005 for a study of French *banlieue* films, including *Le Thé au Harem'Archimède* (dir. Mehdi Charef, 1985), *De Bruit et de Fureur* (dir. Jean-Cluade Brisseau, 1988), *La Haine* (dir. Matthieu Kassovitz, 1995) and many more. More recently, one could include *Dheepan* (dir. Jacques Audiard, 2016). The films have long been quite male-centred. Besides *Divines*, Céline Sciamma's *Bande de Filles* (2014) is another example of a more female-centred gaze in *banlieue* films.

10. Another film that I want to mention here which would deserve a wider discussion in this context is *Most Beautiful Island* (dir. Ana Asensio, 2017), which addresses female Spanish and Russian immigrants surviving on the fringes of New York City.
11. Amirpour's third feature film, entitled *Mona Lisa and the Blood Moon*, is due for release in 2020.
12. Available at <https://www.youtube.com/watch?v=CZ6KVl02Hec> (last accessed 18 March 2020).
13. Available at <https://www.youtube.com/watch?v=WP4VM-20c-0> (last accessed 18 October 2019).
14. *Atlantics* was also shortlisted for an Oscar at the 92nd annual American Academy Awards in the International Feature Film category.
15. Diop also made a film about the main actor in *Touki Bouki*, *Mille Soleils* (2013).
16. For instance, the cruelties of capitalism, and especially the requirement for women to remain young and beautiful, are revolted against in *In My Skin* (dir. Marina de Van, 2002). See also Lübecker 2015. The failing of politics as social satire with some horror elements can be seen in *The Party* (dir. Sally Potter, 2017).
17. Available at <https://www.youtube.com/watch?v=gEXgYW5D-Hk> (last accessed 23 October 2019).
18. The English title 'Spoor' means a trail of hoof marks or paw prints. The Polish title 'Pokot' designates the number of animals killed during a hunt.
19. Fungi, for instance, are world builders that provide nutrients not only for themselves but also for all kinds of other organisms, thus sharing environments (Tsing 2015: 138). Tsing explains why this world-building work of fungi received little appreciation: 'Partly, this is because people can't venture underground to see the amazing architecture of the underground city. But it is also because until recently many people – perhaps especially scientists – imagined life as a matter of species-by-species reproduction. The most important interspecies interactions, in this world view, were predator–prey relations in which interaction meant wiping each other out. Mutualistic relations were interesting anomalies, but not really necessary to understand life, Life emerged from the self-replication of each species, which faced evolutionary and environmental challenges of its own. No species needed another for its continuing vitality; it organized itself. This self-creation marching band drowned out the stories of the underground city. To recover those underground stories, we might reconsider the species-by-species worldview, and the new evidence that has begun to transform it' (Tsing 2015: 139).
20. Since her first film *Lovely Rita* (2001), Hausner has collaborated with her sister Tanja, who does the costume design and had a great influence on the *mise en scène* of *Little Joe*.

Conclusion

1. Public interview with Ansyua Blom at EYE Film Museum, 2 December 2019.
2. Available at <https://medium.com/the-muff-society/mini-muff-profile-amelia-moses-820c43ae3f30> (last accessed 18 March 2020).
3. There are numerous debates about the exact contours of the different waves of feminism: whether there are three or four waves; where exactly they begin and end; and the differences across regions and cultures. Angela McRobbie and others, for instance, have identified a 'post-feminist' period (in the 1990s and early 2000s), embodied by the girlie-feminism of *Sex and the City* (McRobbie 2008). In that sense, the current wave of emancipation can be considered a fourth wave. However, for the female directors that I am concerned with, I trace a line from Woolf to the female directors of the 1970s and from there to the contemporary post-millennium age.
4. Lily Weinstein is also known as Remy Weinstein.
5. This quote appears in *The Prison Notebooks*, written between 1929 and 1935 during Gramsci's imprisonment in Italy during Mussolini's fascist regime. The original English translation is 'The crisis consists precisely in the fact that the old is dying and the new cannot be born, in this interregnum a great variety of morbid symptoms appear' (Gramsci 1971: 276).
6. For the Critics Choice programme of the International Film Festival Rotterdam, I made a short video-essay as a reflection on *Atlantics* and *Atlantiques*, also inspired by Glissant's poetics of relation and Woolf. See https://vimeo.com/387154954 (last accessed 18 March 2020).

Filmography

This filmography presents horror films directed by women that I encountered during my research. As presented throughout this book, the poetics of horror is taken to cover a wide spectrum beyond strict genre boundaries, as a continuum from very subdued to most extreme forms of horror; and from realistic to fantastic, phantasmagoric and symbolic terror. Some female directors have occasionally ventured into a 'poetics of horror' while others can be considered as genre directors *pur sang*. Their names will appear more than once in this overview (which does not mean that their filmographies are completely covered in this list).

I have made a distinction between pre- and post-millennial productions. The former include some of the earlier female directors who addressed issues of dread without explicitly subscribing to the horror genre, their work usually designated as experimental and/or feminist films, as well as some early genre films directed by women that are classified as exploitation, cult or B-films. It is remarkable that in post-millennial productions, horror aesthetics can be found in increasingly more mixed-genre and arthouse films. I have also included films (or series) made by female directors that may not be considered horror at all but have been mentioned in reference to other films.

While many of the women directors mentioned here are also writers, producers, editors and/or actors in their films, and they often work with female crew members, I have only indicated the name of the director. Films are listed in alphabetical order by their English title (followed by their original title, if applicable). The list comprises more films than I had room to discuss in this book. This filmography is not complete, but I hope additional studies on this rapidly growing area of the audio-visual landscape will follow and that the presence of these remarkably creative women will become more noticeable and remain visible.[1]

Pre-Millennial

Black Milk / Zwarte Melk (Netherlands 1976, Marianne Zwollo)
Blood Bath (USA 1966, Stephanie Rothman and Jack Hill)
Blood Diner (USA 1987, Jackie Kong)
The Body Beautiful [short] (Nigeria/UK 1991, Ngozi Onwurah)
Boxing Helena (USA 1993, Jennifer Lynch)
Boys Don't Cry (USA 1999, Kimberly Peirce)
Broken Mirrors (Netherlands 1984, Marleen Gorris)

Buffy the Vampire Slayer (USA 1992, Fran Rubel Kuzui)

Child of Darkness, Child of Light (USA 1991, Marina Sargenti)

Chocolat (France 1988, Claire Denis)

Chronic (USA 1996, Jennifer Reeves)

Coffee Coloured Children [short] (Nigeria/UK 1988, Ngozi Onwurah)

Dance of the Damned (USA 1989, Katt Shea)

The Dark Side of Tomorrow (USA 1970, Barbara Peeters and Jack Deerson)

Diary of a Pregnant Woman / L'Opéra Mouffe (France 1958, Agnès Varda)

A Dry White Season (USA 1989, Euzhan Palcy)

Earth (India 1996, Deepa Metha)

Eve's Bayou (USA 1997, Kasi Lemmons)

Fire (Canada/India 1996, Deepa Mehta)

Flame (Zimbabwe 1996, Ingrid Sinclair)

Freak Orlando (Germany 1981, Ulrike Ottinger)

Freddie's Dead: The Final Nightmare (USA 1991, Rachel Talalay)

Fuses (USA 1967, Carolee Schneemann)

Humanoids from the Deep (USA 1980, Barbara Peeters and Jimmy Murakami)

Jeanne Dielman, 23 Quai du Commerce 1080 Bruxelles (Belgium/France 1975, Chantal Akerman)

A Jury of her Peers (USA 1980, Sally Hackel)

Kissed (Canada 1996, Lynne Stopkewich)

The Mafu Cage (USA 1978, Karen Arthur)

Messiah of Evil (USA 1973, Gloria Katz and Willard Huyck)

Mimi / La Bouche de Jean-Pierre [short] (France 1996, Lucille Hadžihalilović)

Mirror, Mirror (USA 1990, Marina Sargenti)

Near Dark (USA 1987, Kathryn Bigelow)

A Night to Dismember (USA 1983, Doris Wishman)

The Night Porter (Italy 1974, Liliane Cavani)

Office Killer (USA 1997, Cindy Sherman)

One Sings, the Other Doesn't / L'Une Chante, L'Autre pas (France 1976, Agnès Varda)

Organ / Orugan (Japan 1996, Kei Fujiwara)

Orlando (UK 1992, Sally Potter)

The Other Side from Underneath (UK 1972, Jane Arden)

Outrage (USA 1950, Ida Lupino)

Pet Sematary (USA 1989, Mary Lambert)

Punishment / Straf [short] (Netherlands 1974, Olga Madsen)

A Question of Silence (Netherlands 1982, Marleen Gorris)

The Rage – Carrie 2 (USA 1999, Katt Shea)

Ravenous (USA 1999, Antonia Bird)

Siesta (USA 1987, Mary Lambert)

The Slumber Party Massacre (USA 1982, Amy Holden Jones)

The Slumber Party Massacre II (USA 1987, Deborah Brock)

The Slumber Party Massacre III (USA 1990, Sally Mattison)

Tale of a Vampire (UK/Japan 1992, Shimako Satō)
Ticket of No Return / Bildness einer Trinkerin (Germany 1979, Ulrike Ottinger)
Uncanny Women / Die Unheimlichen Frauen (Germany 1991, Birgit Hein)
The Velvet Vampire (USA 1971, Stephanie Rothman)
Welcome II the Terrordome (UK/Nigeria 1995, Ngozi Onwurah)
White Men Are Cracking Up [short] (UK 1994, Ngozi Onwurah 1994)
Widow Burning (India 1989, Aparna Sen)
Yakshagaanam (India 1976, Sheela)

Post-Millennial

Abjection [short] (South Korea 2016, Jiyeon Choi)
Alias Grace [mini-series] (Canada 2017, Mary Harron)
Always Shine (USA 2016, Sophia Takal)
Amer (France/Belgium 2009, Hélène Cattet and Bruno Forzani)
American Fable (USA 2017, Anne Hamilton)
American Mary (Canada 2012, Jen and Sylvia Soska)
American Psycho (USA 2000, Mary Harron)
Anatomy of Violence (Canada/India 2016, Deepa Mehta)
Atlantics / Atlantiques (Senegal/France/Belgium 2019, Mati Diop)
Atlantiques [short] (Senegal/France 2009, Mati Diop)
The Attic (USA 2007, Mary Lambert)
The Babadook (Australia 2014, Jennifer Kent)
The Bad Batch (USA 2016, Ana Lily Amirpour)
Bad Girls (Canada 2009, Jen and Sylvia Sotska)
The Ballad of Genesis and Lady Jaye (USA/Germany/UK/Netherlands/France
   2011, Marie Losier)
Belagile [short] (USA 2014, Anastasia Cazabon)
Bixa Travesty (Brazil 2017, Claudia Priscilla and Kiki Goifman)
Black Christmas (USA 2019, Sophia Takal)
Black Metal [short] (USA 2013, Kat Candler)
Bleed with Me (Canada 2020, Amelia Moses)
Blood Child (Canada/Singapore 2017, Jennifer Phillips)
Blood Punch (USA 2013, Madellaine Paxson)
Blood Sisters [short] (Australia 2017, Caitlin Koller)
Blue My Mind (Switzerland 2017, Lisa Bruhlmann)
Bluebeard / Haebing (Korea 2017, Lee Soo-Yeon)
Body (Poland 2015, Malgorzata Szumowska)
The Boogeywoman [short] (USA 2019, Erica Scoggins)
Book of Birdie (UK 2017, Elisabeth Schuch)
By the Time it Gets Dark / Dao Khanong (Thailand 2016, Anocha Suwichakornpong)
Ça Brûle (France 2006, Claire Simon)
Can Go Through Skin / Kan Door Huid Heen (Netherlands 2009, Esther Rots)
The Captured Bird (Canada 2012, Jovanka Vucovic)

Carrie (USA 2013, Kimberly Pierce)

Catcalls [short] (Ireland 2018, Kate Dolan)

Chanthaly (Laos 2012, Mattie Do)

Children of the Dead, The / Die Kinder der Toten (Austria 2019, Kelly Copper and Pavol Liska)

Clip / Klip (Serbia 2012, Maja Miloš)

The Countess / La Comtesse (France/Germany 2009, Julie Delpy)

Creswick [short] (Australia 2017, Natalie James)

Darlin' (UK 2019, Pollyanna McIntosh)

The Day Mum Became a Monster [short] (France 2017, Joséphine Hopkins)

Dead Horses / Chevalls Morts [short] (Spain 2017, Anna Solanas and Marc Riba)

The Dead Outside (UK 2008, Kerry Anne Mullaney)

Dead, Tissue, Love [short] (UK 2017, Natasha Austin Green)

Dearest Sister (Laos/France/Estonia/Slovakia 2016, Mattie Do)

Descent (USA 2007, Talia Lugacy)

Dirty God (Netherlands/UK/Belgium/Ireland 2019, Sacha Polak)

Disco Inferno [short] (Spain 2015, Alice Weddington)

Egomaniac (UK 2016, Kate Shenton)

Electric Children (USA 2012, Rebecca Thomas)

Evolution / Évolution (France 2015, Lucille Hadžihalilović)

The Falling (UK 2014, Carol Morley)

Family (Israel 2017, Veronika Kedar)

Fish Tank (UK 2009, Andrea Arnold)

Gaze [short] (USA 2018, Ida Jogler)

Geography of Fear / Pelon Maantiede (Finland 2000, Auli Mantila)

Girl in the Hallway [short] (Canada 2018, Valerie Barnhart)

A Girl Walks Home Alone at Night (USA 2014, Ana Lily Amirpour)

Glass Garden (Korea 2017, Shin Su-won)

Good Manners / As Boas Maneiras (Brazil/France/Germany 2017, Juliana Rojas)

Goodnight Mommy / Ich Seh, Ich Seh (Austria 2015, Veronika Franz and Severin Fiala)

Hana [short] (Japan 2018, Mai Nakanishi)

Harriet (USA 2019, Kasi Lemmons)

The Headless Woman / La Mujer sin cabeza (Argentina 2009, Lucretia Martel)

Helpless / Hoa-cha (Korea 2012, Byun Young-joo)

Helter Skelter / Herutâ sukerutâ (Japan 2012, Mika Ninagawa)

The Hitchhiker [short] (Australia 2018, Adele Vuko)

The Holding (UK 2011, Susan Jacobson)

Honeygiver Among the Dogs (Buthan 2016, Dechen Roder)

Honeymoon (USA 2014, Leigh Janiak)

I Am Not a Witch (UK/France/Germany/Zambia 2017, Rungano Nyoni)

I Blame Society (USA 2020, Gillian Wallace Horvat)

In My Skin / Dans Ma Peau (France 2002, Marina de Van)

In the Cut (USA/UK/Australia 2003, Jane Campion)

Ink [short] (Canada 2016, Ashlea Wessel)
Innocence / Innocence (France 2004, Lucille Hadžihalilović)
The Invitation (USA 2015, Karyn Kusama)
It Felt Like Love (USA 2014, Elisa Hittman)
The Itching [short] (USA 2016, Diane Bellino)
It's Easier to Raise Cattle / Lagi Senang Jaga Sekandang Lembu [short] (Malaysia 2017, Amanda Nell Eu)
Jennifer's Body (USA 2009, Karen Kusama)
Jezebel (USA 2019, Numa Perrier)
Joy (Austria 2018, Sudabeh Mortezal)
Knives and Skin (USA 2019, Jennifer Reeder)
Last Night [short] (Austria 2017, Juliana Neuhuber)
The Lesson (UK 2015, Ruth Plath)
Lili [short] (Netherlands 2019, Yfke van Berkelaer)
Little Joe (UK/Austria, Jessica Hausner)
Lola Magenta [short] (Netherlands 2017, Ansuya Blom)
The Long Walk (Laos 2019, Mattie Do)
Longing for the Rain / Chunmeng (China 2013, Lina Yang)
The Love Witch (USA 2016, Anna Biller)
Lovely Rita (Austria 2001, Jessica Hausner)
Lucy's Tale [short] (USA 2018, Chelsea Lupkin)
Luna Nera [series] (Italy 2020, Francesca Manieri, Laura Paolucci, Tiziana Triani)
The Lure / Córki dancingu (Poland 2015, Agnieszka Smoczyńska)
LVRS [short] (USA 2018, Emily Bennett)
Lyle (USA 2014, Stewart Thorndike)
Maggie May [short] (Australia 2019, Mia'kate Russel)
Make Up (UK 2019, Claire Oakley)
Malina the Murderer in Four Acts / Marlina Si Pembunuh dalam Empat Babak (Indonesia 2017, Mouly Surya)
The Man who Caught a Mermaid [short] (Australia 2016, Kaitlin Tinker)
Mania (USA 2015, Jessica Cameron)
Mary Queen of Scots (UK/USA 2018, Josie Rourke)
Mary Shelley (Australia/UK/Ireland/USA/Luxembourg 2017, Haifaa al-Mansour)
M.F.A. (USA 2017, Natalia Leite)
Midnight Swim (USA 2014, Sarah Adina Smith)
Mirror / Chermin (Malaysia 2007, Zaruba Abdullah)
Missing / Sarajin Yeoja (Korea 2016, Lee Eon-hee)
Mommy [short] (USA 2013, Heidi Moore)
Mona Lisa and the Blood Moon (USA 2020, Ana Lily Amirpour)
Morvern Callar (Ireland 2002, Lynne Ramsey)
Most Beautiful Island (USA 2017, Ana Asensio)
The Moth Diaries (Canada/Ireland 2011, Mary Harron)

Motif / Motif (Malaysia 2019, Nadiah Hamzah)

The Murmuring Coast / A Costa dos Murmurios (Portugal 2004, Margarida Cardoso)

Mustang (Turkey/France/Germany 2015, Deniz Gamze Ergüven)

My Final Girl: Black Women in American Horror [short] (USA 2016, Kristina Leath)

My Sucky Teen Romance (USA 2011, Emily Haggins)

Nana [short] (China 2017, Yunxuan Wang)

Nancy (USA 2018, Christine Choe)

Never Rarely Sometimes Always (USA 2020, Eliza Hittman)

The Nightingale (Australia 2018, Jennifer Kent)

Nose Nose Nose Eyes! [short] (Korea 2017, Jiwon Moon)

Olmo and the Seagull (Denmark/Brazil/Portugal/France 2014, Petra Costa and Lea Glob)

On Body and Soul / Testről és lélekről (Hungary 2017, Ildikó Enyedi)

The Original [short] (UK 2018, Michelle Garza Cervera)

The Other Lamb (US/UK/Denmark/Ireland 2019, Malgorzata Szumowska)

Our House / Watashitachi no ie (Japan 2017, Yui Kiohara)

Panic Attack [short] (USA 2018, Eileen Omeara)

The Party (UK 2017, Sally Potter)

Pathogen (USA 2006, Emily Hagins)

Petite Avarie [short] (France 2018, Manon Allirol and Leo Hardt)

Pin Cushion (UK 2017, Deborah Haywood)

Playing the Taar [short] (Afghanistan 2008, Roya Sedat)

Post-partum [short] (USA 2015, Izzy Lee)

Prevenge (UK 2016, Alice Lowe)

Puppet Master [short] (Finland 2018, Hanna Bergholm)

PYNK/Janelle Monae (USA/Netherlands 2018, Emma Westenberg)

Queen of Hearts / Dronningen (Denmark 2019, May El-Toukhy)

Rabid (Canada 2019, Jen and Sylvia Soska)

Rafiki (Kenya 2018, Wanuri Kahiu)

Rainha [short] (Brasil 2016, Sabrina Fidalgo)

The Ranger (USA 2018, Jenn Waxler)

Raw / Grave (France 2016, Julia Ducournau)

Ready to Burst [short] (Canada 2016, Ariel Hansen)

Red Riding Hood (USA 2011, Catherine Hardwicke)

The Retelling (USA 2009, Emily Hagins)

Retrospekt (Netherlands 2018, Esther Rots)

Revenge (France 2017, Coralie Fargeat)

Riot Girls (Canada 2019, Jovanka Vucovic)

Saint Maud (UK 2019, Rose Glass)

Sarah Plays a Werewolf (Switzerland 2017, Katharina Wyss)

Saviour Complex [short] (Canada 2008, Ariel Smith)

Scarlet Diva (Italy 2000, Asia Argento)

Shorty [short] (USA 2016, Anna Zlokovic)
Silent House (USA 2011, Laura Lau and Chris Kentis)
Siren [short; part of *Southbound* anthology] (USA 2015, Roxanne Benjamin)
Sixth Floor [short] (USA 2017, Meosha Bean)
The Sleeping Child (Morocco 2006, Yasmine Kassari)
Slut [short] (USA 2014, Chloe Okuno)
Sometimes I Think about Dying [short] (USA 2019, Stefanie Abel Horowitz)
Songs My Brothers Taught Me (USA 2016, Chloé Zhao)
Soulmate (UK 2013, Axelle Carolyn)
Spoor / Pokot (Poland/Czech Republic/Germany 2017, Agnieszka Holland)
Static [short] (Canada 2016, Tanya Lemke)
The Strange Colour of Your Body's Tears / L'Étrange Couleur des larmes de ton corps
  (France/Belgium 2013, Helene Cattet and Bruno Forzani)
The Stylist [short] (USA 2016, Jill Gevargizian)
Suicide by Sunlight [short] (USA 2018, Nikayatu Jusu)
System Crasher / Systemsprenger (Germany 2019, Nora Fingscheidt)
Tick [short] (Canada 2018, Ashlea Wessel)
Tigers Are Not Afraid / Vuelven (Mexico 2017, Issa López)
Touch [short in anthology *Chilling Visions: 5 Senses of Fear*] (USA 2013, Emily
  Hagins)
Tower. A Bright Day / Wieza. Jasny Dzien (Poland 2017, Jagoda Szelc)
Trouble Every Day (France 2001, Claire Denis)
The Truth Beneath / Bi-mil-eun eobs-da (Korea 2016, Lee Kyoung-mi)
Undress Me [short] (Canada 2017, Amelia Moses)
The Uninvited – A Table for 4 / 4 Inyong Shiktak (Korea 2003, Lee Soo-Yeon)
Urban Legends: Bloody Mary (USA 2015, Mary Lambert)
Vaspy [short] (New Zeeland 2019, Hweiling Ow)
Venefica [short] (USA 2016, Maria Wilson)
The Virgin Suicides (USA 2000, Sofia Coppola)
Voyager [short] (Norway 2018, Kjersti Helen Rasmussen)
Vulture [short] (UK 2019, Shweta Chavan)
Wakey Wakey [short] (USA 2019, Mary Dauterman)
Waste [short] (USA 2016, Justine Raczkiewicz)
We Need to Talk about Kevin (UK/USA 2011, Lynne Ramsey)
Weirdo [short] (Canada 2020, Ashlea Wessel)
White Material (France 2009, Claire Denis)
Who is Who in Mycology [short] (USA/Czech Republic 2018, Marie Dvorakova)
wHole [short] (Germany 2014, Verena Klinger and Robert Banny)
The Woman Who Hid Fear under the Staircase [short] (UK 2018, Faye Jackson)
XX [anthology] (USA 2017): *The Box* (Jovanka Vuchovic); *The Birthday Party*
  (Annie Clark); *Don't Fall* (Roxanne Benjamin); *Her Only Living Son* (Karyn
  Kusama)
Yoga Class / Yoga Hakwon (Korea 2009, Yoon Jae-Yeon)
Zombie Love [short] (Netherlands 2007, Yfke van Berkelaer)

Note

1. The list has been compiled by selecting from and combining different sources, ranging from online lists of 'best horror films', 'most scary mothers on screen', 'great films made by women' etc., to searching online VOD platforms (MUBI especially proved to be an extremely useful source), contacting festivals, distributors, film critics, fans and filmmakers directly, as well as following literature references and citations. For short films (which are often difficult to find outside the festival circuit and which I have not always been able to see), the Born of Woman section of the *Fantasia International Film Festival* in Montreal is very helpful (https://fantasiafestival.com/en/program/born-of-woman-2019). The archive of the programmes of the *Final Girls Festival* in Berlin (https://www.finalgirlsberlin.com/), which has been running since 2017, includes a wealth of horror shorts and features (mostly directed by women, though sometimes written or produced but not directed). Also running since 2017, the *Women in Horror Festival* in the USA (https://www.wihff.com/) offers many additional horror film titles by women; the selection criterion for films in this festival is that at least three women must have performed roles in the creative process, not necessarily directing. *Cut-Throat Women: A Database of Women Who Make Horror* (https://www.cutthroat women.org/) is organised by name of director and contains links to the IMDB entries on the directors.

Bibliography

Abbs, Carolyn (2005), 'Virginia Woolf and Gilles Deleuze: Cinematic E-motion and the Mobile Subject', *IM/NASS*, 1, 1–19.

Abdi, Shadee, and Marie Calafell (2017), 'Queer Utopias and a (Feminist) Iranian Vampire: A Critical Analysis of Resistive Monstrosity in *A Girl Walks Home Alone at Night*', *Critical Studies in Media Communication*, 34:4, 358–70.

Aftab, Kaleem (2017), '*I'm Not a Witch* Director on the Modern Persecution of Witches in Zambia and Ghana', *The Independent*, 18 October, <https://www.independent.co.uk/arts-entertainment/films/features/i-am-not-a-witch-rungano-nyoni-a8007081.html> (last accessed 27 March 2020).

Alderman, Naomi (2016), *The Power* (London: Penguin).

Anderson, Ana Christina (2004), 'The Woman as Mother and Artist in Virginia Woolf's *To the Lighthouse* and *Mrs. Dalloway*', Senior Honors thesis, University of Tennessee.

Anonymous (2003 [1959]), *A Woman in Berlin. Diary 20 April 1945 to 22 June 1945*, trans. Philip Boehm (New York: Virago).

Arnold, Sarah (2013), *Maternal Horror Film: Melodrama and Motherhood* (New York: Palgrave Macmillan).

Aroesti, Rachel (2019), '*Atlantics* Director Mati Dio: As a Mixed Race Girl there is a Visible and Invisible Side of You', *The Guardian*, 9 November, <https://www.theguardian.com/film/2019/nov/09/atlantics-director-mati-diop-as-a-mixed-race-girl-theres-always-a-visible-and-invisible-side-of-you> (last accessed 27 March 2020).

Atwood, Margaret (1985), *The Handmaid's Tale* (Toronto: McClelland and Stewart).

Atwood, Margaret (1996), *Alias Grace* (Toronto: McClelland and Stewart).

Bakare, Lanre, and Catherine Shoard (2019), 'Venice Film Festival: Gender Disparity Rages for Second Year', *The Guardian*, 26 August, <https://www.theguardian.com/film/2019/aug/26/venice-film-festival-gender-disparity-roman-polanski-nate-parker> (last accessed 27 March 2020).

Bane, Theresa (2010), *Encyclopedia of Vampire Mythology* (Jefferson, NC: McFarland).

Barad, Karen (2007), *Meeting the Universe Halfway: Quantum Physics and the Entanglement of Matter and Meaning* (Durham, NC: Duke University Press).

Barker, Jennifer (2009), *The Tactile Eye* (Berkeley, CA: University of California Press).

Barry, Robert (2012), 'It's Not Blood, it's Red: Colours of Jean-Luc Godard', *Vertigo*, 30, 1–4.

Beaumont, Peter, and Amanda Holpuch (2018), 'How *The Handmaid's Tale* Dressed Protests Around the World', *The Guardian*, 3 August, <https://www. theguardian.com/world/2018/aug/03/how-the-handmaids-tale-dressed-pro tests-across-the-world> (last accessed 27 March 2020).

Benoit, Catherine (2006), 'Sex and Violence as Phantasm: Eros and Thanatos in Campion's *In the Cut*', *Offscreen*, 10:4, <https://offscreen.com/view/ in_the_cut> (last accessed 27 March 2020).

Berenstein, Rhona (1996), *Attack of the Leading Ladies: Gender, Sexuality and Spectatorship in Classic Horror Cinema* (New York: Columbia University Press).

Beugnet, Martine (2004), *Claire Denis* (Manchester: Manchester University Press).

Beugnet, Martine (2007), 'Figures of Vampirism: French Cinema in the Era of Global Transylvania', *Modern and Contemporary France*, 15:1, 77–88.

Beugnet, Martine (2011), 'The Wounded Screen', in Tanya Horeck and Tina Kendall (eds), *The New Extremism in Cinema from France to Europe* (Edinburgh: Edinburgh University Press), 29–42.

Binswanger, Ludwig (1963), 'The Case of Lola Voss', in *Being-in-the-World: Selected Papers of Ludwig Binswanger*, ed. Jacob Needleman (London: Basic Books), 266–341.

Bodegom van, Fiep (2019), 'Octavia Butler's Science Fiction als Filosofie: Interview met Otolith Group', *Metropolis M.*, August/September, 50–5.

Bollinger, Laurel (2007), 'Placental Economy: Octavia Butler, Luce Irigaray, and Speculative Subjectivity', *Literature Interpretation Theory*, 18:4, 325–52.

Bordwell, David (1989) 'Historical Poetics of Cinema', in Barton Palmer (ed.), *The Cinematic Text: Methods and Approaches* (New York: AMS Press), 370–98.

Bordwell, David (2008), *Poetics of Cinema* (London: Routledge).

Braidotti, Rosi (2013), *The Posthuman* (Cambridge: Polity Press).

Bramesco, Charles (2018), *Vampire Movies. Little White Lies* (New York: Harper Collins).

Brinkema, Eugenie (2014), *The Forms of Affects* (Durham, NC: Duke University Press).

Brinkema, Eugenie (2015), 'Introduction: A Genreless Horror', *Journal of Visual Culture*, 14:3, 263–66, special issue, 'The Design and Componentry of Horror'.

Brinkema, Eugenie (2019), 'Sticky, Nimble, Frantic, Stuck: *A l'Intérieur* and the Feel of Horror', *Literature Interpretation Theory*, 30:1, 62–79.

Brooks, Kinitra (2014), 'The Importance of Neglected Intersections: Race and Gender in Contemporary Zombie Texts and Theories', *African American Review*, 47:4, 461–75.

Brown, William, and David H. Fleming (2020), *The Squid-Cinema from Hell: Kinoteuthis Infernalis and the Emergence of Chthulhumedia* (Edinburgh: Edinburgh University Press).

Brox, Ali (2008), 'Every Age has the Vampire it Needs: Octavia Butler's Vampire Vision in Fledgling', *Utopian Studies*, 19:3, 391–409.

Buder, Emily (2015), '*Goodnight Mommy* Directors on the Value of Violence and How Horror Should Be Challenging', *IndieWire*, 14 September, <https://www.indiewire.com/2015/09/goodnight-mommy-directors-on-the-value-of-violence-and-how-horror-should-be-challenging-58179/> (last accessed 27 March 2020).

Butler, Lucy (2013), 'Too Close to the Bone: the International Critical Reception of Jane Campion's *In the Cut*', *Studies in Australasian Cinema*, 7:1, 9–22.

Butler, Octavia (1993), *Parable of the Sower* (New York and Boston: Grand Central Publishing).

Butler, Octavia (2005a), *Fledgling* (New York and Boston: Grand Central Publishing).

Butler, Octavia (2005b), *Blood Child and Other Stories* (New York: Seven Stories Press).

Butler, Octavia (2018 [1979]), *Kindred* (London: Headline).

Carby, Hazel (1985), 'On the Threshold of Woman's Era: Lynching, Empire, Sexuality in Black Feminist Theory', *Critical Inquiry*, 12:1, 262–77.

Carroll, Berenice (1978), ' "To Crush Him in Our Own Country": The Political Thought of Virginia Woolf', *Feminist Studies*, 4:1, 99–132.

Carroll, Noël (1990), *The Philosophy of Horror, or Paradoxes of the Heart* (New York: Routledge).

Carter, Angela (2015 [1979]), *The Bloody Chamber and Other Stories* (New Delhi: Penguin India).

Chambers, Claire, and Sue Chaplin (2013), 'Bilqis the Vampire Slayer. Sarwat Chadda's British Muslim Vampire Fiction', in Johan Högland and Tabish Khair (eds), *Transnational and Postcolonial Vampires: Dark Blood* (New York: Palgrave Macmillan), 138–52.

Chare, Nicholas, Jeanette Hoorn and Audrey Yue (eds) (2019), *Re-reading the Monstrous-Feminine: Art, Film, Feminism and Psychoanalysis* (New York: Routledge).

Cixous, Hélène (1976), 'The Laugh of the Medusa', trans. Keith Cohen and Paula Cohen, *Signs*, 1:4, 875–93.

Clover, Carol (1992), *Men, Women and Chain Saws: Gender in the Modern Horror Film* (Princeton: Princeton University Press).

Combs, Richard (2016), '*Evolution*', *Sight and Sound*, 26:6, 71.

Connolly, Kate (2017), 'Agnieszka Holland: *Pokot* Reflects Divided Nature of Polish Society', *The Guardian*, 16 February, <https://www.theguardian.com/film/2017/feb/16/agnieszka-holland-pokot-reflects-divided-nature-of-polish-society> (last accessed 27 March 2020).

Cooper, Harriet (2017), 'Alice Lowe's *Prevenge*: a Response', *Studies in the Maternal*, 9:1, 1–6.

Creed, Barbara (1993), *The Monstrous-Feminine: Film, Feminism, Psychoanalysis* (London: Routledge).

Crucchiola (2019), 'The Future of Horror is Black and Female – Ask Nikyatu Jusu', *Vulture*, 13 February, <https://www.vulture.com/2019/02/horrors-future-is-black-and-female-just-ask-nikyatu-jusu.html> (last accessed 27 March 2020).

Dash, Julie, bell hooks and Toni Cade Bambara (1992), *Daughters of the Dust: The Making of an African American Woman's Film* (New York: New Press).

Davis, Angela (1983 [1981]), *Women, Race and Class* (New York: Vintage).

de Beauvoir, Simone (2010 [1949]), *The Second Sex*, trans. Constance Borde and Sheila Malovany-Chevalier (London: Vintage).

Decker, Lindsey (2018), 'Ana Lily Amirpour', *Cut-throat Women A Database of Women who Make Horror*, <https://www.cutthroatwomen.org/amirpour> (last accessed 27 March 2020).

Deleuze, Gilles (1986), *Cinema 1: The Movement-Image*, trans. Hugh Tomlinson and Barbara Habberjam (London: Athlone Press).

Deleuze, Gilles (1989), *Cinema 2: The Time-Image*, trans. Hugh Tomlinson and Robert Galeta (London: Athlone Press).

Deleuze, Gilles, and Félix Guattari (1988), *A Thousand Plateaus. Capitalism and Schizophrenia*, trans. Brian Massumi (London: Athlone Press).

Delpech, Catherine (2011), 'Edouard Glissant: Poetics and Politics of the Whole-world', *First World Humanities Forum Proceedings* (Busan: UNESCO), 244–56.

Del Rio, Elena (2008), *Deleuze and the Cinemas of Performance: Powers of Affection* (Edinburgh: Edinburgh University Press).

Del Rio, Elena (2016), *The Grace of Destruction: A Vital Ethology of Extreme Cinemas* (London: Bloomsbury).

Derrickson, Scott (2018), 'Why *The Bad Batch* is One of the Best Films of 2017', *Balder and Dash*, 7 February, <https://www.rogerebert.com/balder-and-dash/why-the-bad-batch-is-one-of-the-best-films-of-2017> (last accessed 27 March 2020).

Derrida, Jacques (1981), 'Plato's Pharmacy', in *Dissemination*, trans. Barbara Johnson (Chicago: University of Chicago Press), 63–171.

Dunn, George, and Rebecca Housel (eds) (2010), *True Blood and Philosophy* (Hoboken, NJ: John Wiley and Sons).

Early, Frances (2001), 'Staking her Claim: Buffy the Vampire Slayer as Transgressive Woman Warrior', *Journal of Popular Culture*, 35:3, 11–27.

Edelstein, Eric (2014), 'Ana Lily Amirpour Is the Raddest Filmmaker Working Right Now', *IndieWire*, 1–9, <https://www.indiewire.com/2014/11/ana-lily-amirpour-is-the-raddest-filmmaker-working-right-now-67640/> (last accessed 27 March 2020).

Eisenstein, Sergei (1947), *The Film Sense*, trans. Jay Leyda (New York: Harcourt Brace).

Ferreira, Maria Aline (2010), 'Symbiotic Bodies and Evolutionary Tropes in the Work of Octavia Butler', *Science Fiction Studies*, 37:3, 401–15.

Florio, Angelica (2018), 'Janelle Monáe's "PYNK" Video About Female Sexuality Will Make You Feel Like a Goddess', *Bustle*, 10 April, <https://www.bustle.

com/p/janelle-monaes-pynk-video-about-female-sexuality-will-make-you-feel-like-a-goddess-8746306> (last accessed 27 March 2020).

Freccero, Carla (2017), 'Wolf, or Homo Homini Lupus', in Anna Tsing, Heather Swanson, Elaine Gan and Nils Bubant (eds), *Arts of Living on a Damaged Planet* (Minneapolis: University of Minnesota Press), M91–M105.

Freeland, Cynthia (2000), *The Naked and the Undead: Evil and the Appeal of Horror* (Boulder, CO: Westview Press).

French, Philip (2003), '*In the Cut*', *The Guardian*, 2 November, <https://www.theguardian.com/film/News_Story/Critic_Review/Observer_review/0,,107 5896,00.html> (last accessed 27 March 2020).

Freud, Sigmund (1959 [1926]), 'The Question of Lay Analysis', in *The Standard Edition of the Complete Psychological Works of Sigmund Freud, Volume XX (1925–1926): An Autobiographical Study, Inhibitions, Symptoms and Anxiety, The Question of Lay Analysis and Other Works*, trans. James Strachey (London: Hogarth Press), 177–258.

Fusco, Virginia (2014), 'Love and Desire in the Postmodern Era: *The Gilda Stories* or How Black Feminism Challenged Gothic Literary Traditions', *Dossier Feministes*, 18, 245–58.

Gaines, Jane (2018), *Pink Slipped: What Happened to Women in the Silent Film Industry* (Champaign: University of Illinois Press).

Gillespie, Michael Boyce (2016), *Film Blackness, American Cinema and the Idea of Black Film* (Durham, NC: Duke University Press).

Glaspell, Susan (1917), 'A Jury of Her Peers', *Every Week Magazine*, 5 March.

Gledhill, Christine (1987), *Home is Where the Heart is: Studies in Melodrama and the Woman's Film* (London: British Film Institute).

Glissant, Edouard (1997), *Poetics of Relation*, trans. Betsy Wing (Ann Arbor: University of Michigan Press).

Godfrey, Alex (2017), '*Raw* Director Julia Ducournau: Cannibalism is Part of Humanity', *The Guardian*, 30 March, <https://www.theguardian.com/film/2017/mar/30/raw-director-julia-ducournau-cannibalism-is-part-of-humanity> (last accessed 27 March 2020).

Gomez, Jewelle (2016), *The Gilda Stories*, expanded 25th anniversary edition (San Francisco: City Lights).

Gordon, Avery (2008), *Ghostly Matters: Haunting and the Sociological Imagination* (Minneapolis: University of Minnesota Press).

Gramsci, Antonio (1971), *Selections from the Prison Notebooks*, ed. and trans. Quentin Hoare and Geoffrey Nowell Smith (London: International Publishers).

Green-Cole, Ruth (2015), 'Bloody Women Artists', *The Occasional Journal*, November, 1–16, special issue, 'Love Feminisms', ed. Alice Tappenden and Ann Shelton, <http://enjoy.org.nz/publishing/the-occasional-journal/love-feminisms/text-bloody-women-artists> (last accessed 27 March 2020).

Gregory, Alice (2018), 'The Fearless Cinema of Claire Denis', *The New Yorker*, 21 May, <https://www.newyorker.com/magazine/2018/05/28/the-fearless-cinema-of-claire-denis> (last accessed 27 March 2020).

Greifenstein, Saray, Dorothea Horst, Thomas Schreber, Christina Schmitt, Hermann Kappelhoff and Cornelia Müller (eds) (2018), *Cinematic Metaphor in Perspective: Reflections on a Transdisciplinary Framework* (Berlin: De Gruyter).

Grierson, Tim (2017), 'Inside *Raw*: How a Female Filmmaker Made a New Body Horror Classic', *Rolling Stone*, 9 March, <https://www.rollingstone.com/movies/movie-features/inside-raw-how-a-female-filmmaker-made-a-new-body-horror-classic-127028/> (last accessed 27 March 2020).

Hall, Stuart, and Bill Schwartz (2017). *Familiar Stranger: A Life Between Two Islands* (Durham, NC: Duke University Press).

Hammack, Brenda Mann (2008), 'Florence Marryat's Female Vampire and the Scientizing of Hybridity', *Studies in English Literature 1500–1900*, 48:4, 885–96.

Hanich, Julian (2010), *Cinematic Emotion in Horror Films and Thrillers: The Aesthetic Paradox of Pleasurable Fear* (New York: Routledge).

Haraway, Donna (1991), *Simians, Cyborgs, and Women: The Reinvention of Nature* (London: Free Association Books).

Haraway, Donna (2016), *Staying with the Trouble: Making Kin in the Chthulucene* (Durham, NC: Duke University Press).

Harrington, Erin (2018), *Women, Monstrosity and the Horror Film: Gynaehorror* (Abingdon: Routledge).

Harris, Charlaine (2001), *Dead until Dark* (New York: Random House).

Hendershot, Heather (2018), '*The Handmaid's Tale* as Utopian Allegory: "Stars and Stripes Forever, Baby" ', *Film Quarterly*, 72:1, 13–15.

Höglund, Johan, and Tabish Khair (eds) (2013), *Transnational and Postcolonial Vampires: Dark Blood* (New York: Palgrave Macmillan).

Holland, Samantha, Robert Shail and Steven Gerrard (eds) (2019), *Gender and Contemporary Horror in Film* (Bingley: Emerald Publishing).

hooks, bell (1996), *Reel to Real: Race, Sex and Class at the Movies* (New York: Routledge).

Iordanova, Dana (2019), 'Only Two of the Directors Featured at the Venice Film Festival Are Women', *Quartz*, 4 September, <https://qz.com/author/dina-iordanova/> (last accessed 27 March 2020).

Irigaray, Luce (1981), 'And the One Doesn't Stir without the Other', trans. Vivienne Wenzel, *Signs*, 7:1, 60–7.

Irigaray, Luce (1985), *This Sex Which is Not One*, trans. Catherine Porter with Carolyn Burke (Ithaca, NY: Cornell University Press).

Irigaray, Luce (1996), *I Love to You: Sketch for a Possible Felicity in History*, trans. Alison Martin (London: Routledge).

Ito, Robert (2014), 'Shadow in the Chador: Ana Lily Amirpour's *A Girl Walks Home Alone at Night*', *The New York Times*, 12 November, <https://www.nytimes.com/2014/11/16/movies/ana-lily-amirpours-world-a-girl-walks-home-alone-at-night.html> (last accessed 27 March 2020).

Jamison, Kay (1996), *An Unquiet Mind: A Memoir of Moods and Madness* (New York: Vintage).

Janisse, Kier-la (2012), *House of Psychotic Women: An Autobiographical Topography of Female Neurosis in Horror and Exploitation Films* (Godalming: Fab Press).

Jenkins, Henry (2007), 'Exploiting Feminism: An Interview with Stephanie Rothman', <http://henryjenkins.org/2007/10/stephanie_rothman.html> (last accessed 26 August 2019).

Jermyn, Deborah, and Sean Redmond (eds) (2003), *The Cinema of Kathryn Bigelow: Hollywood Transgressor* (London: Wallflower Press).

Jones, Sara Gwenllian (2003), 'Vampires, Indians and the Queer Fantastic: Kathryn Bigelow's *Near Dark*', in Deborah Jermyn and Sean Redmond (eds), *The Cinema of Kathryn Bigelow: Hollywood Transgressor* (London: Wallflower Press), 57–71.

Joyard, Oliver (2019), 'Mati Diop, the First Black Woman Selected in Cannes Film Festival', *Numéro*, 8 October, <https://www.numero.com/en/cinema/mati-diop-cannes-film-festival-atlantique-senegal-grand-prix-dakar-director> (last accessed 27 March 2020).

Juzwiak, Rich (2014), 'The Iranian Vampire Tale of *A Girl Walks Home Alone at Night*', *Gawker*, 21 November, <https://gawker.com/the-iranian-vampire-tale-of-a-girl-walks-home-alone-at-1661607676> (last accessed 27 March 2020).

Kaiser, Birgit (2012), 'Poésie en Étendue: Deleuze, Glissant and a Postcolonial Aesthetics of the Earth', in Rosi Braidotti and Patricia Pisters (eds), *Revisiting Normativity with Deleuze* (London: Continuum), 131–44.

Kanai, Saika (2013), 'Revision of Motherhood: Virginia Woolf's Creative Reproduction in Life and Art', PhD thesis, Hokkaido University.

Kappelhoff, Hermann (2015), *The Politics and Poetics of Cinematic Realism* (Berlin: De Gruyter).

Karras, Irene (2002), 'The Third Wave's Final Girl: Buffy the Vampire Slayer', *Third Space: A Journal of Feminist Theory & Culture*, 1:2, 1–7.

Keesey, Douglas (2017), *Twenty First Century Horror Films* (Harpenden: Kamera Books).

Kermode, Mark (2017), '*I'm Not a Witch* Review – Magical Surrealism', *The Guardian*, 22 October, <https://www.theguardian.com/film/2017/oct/22/i--am-not-a-witch-review-magical-surrealism-margaret-mulubwa-rungano-nyoni> (last accessed 27 March 2020).

Kerner, Aaron Michael, and Jonathan Knapp (2016), *Extreme Cinema: Affective Strategies in Transnational Media* (Edinburgh: Edinburgh University Press).

Kinder, Marsha (1977), 'Reflections on Jeanne Dielman', *Film Quarterly*, 30:4, 2–8.

King, Stephen (1974), *Carrie* (New York: Doubleday).

Korthase, Karolin (2019), 'Kamp um Sichtbarkeit' ('Fight for Visibility'), *Museum. Programheft Staatliche Museen zu Berlin*, October–November–December, 7–9.

Kotzathanasis, Panos (2015), '*Helter Skelter* Review', *Asian Movie Pulse*, 9 October, <https://asianmoviepulse.com/2015/10/helter-skelter-2012-review-mika-ninagawa/> (last accessed 27 March 2020).

Kuo, Chia-chen (2009), 'A Cinematic Reading of Virginia Woolf's "Kew Gardens"', *Concentric: Literary and Cultural Studies*, 35:1, 181–201.

Kwan, Jennifer (2009), 'Cody Exorcises Demons from Jennifer's Body', *Reuters*, <https://www.reuters.com/article/us-toronto-cody/cody-exorcises-demons-from-jennifers-body-idUSTRE58C0ZI20090914> (last accessed 27 March 2020).

Lacey, Lauren (2008), 'Octavia Butler on Coping with Power in *Parable of the Sower*, *Parable of Talents*, and *Fledgling*', *Critique: Studies in Contemporary Fiction*, 49:4, 379–94.

Laine, Tarja (2011), *Feeling Cinema: Emotional Dynamics in Film Studies* (New York: Continuum).

Laine, Tarja (2015), *Bodies in Pain: Emotion and the Cinema of Darren Aronofsky* (New York: Berghahn).

Lakeland, Mary Jo (1979), 'The Color of *Jeanne Dielman*', *Camera Obscura*, 1–2:3–1 (3–4), 215–18, DOI: 10.1215/02705346-1-2-3-1_3-4-216.

Lee, Hyangjin (2013), 'Family, Death and the *wonhon* in Four Films in the 1960s', in Alison Peirse and Daniel Martin, *Korean Horror Cinema* (Edinburgh: Edinburgh University Press), 23–34.

Leeder, Murray (2018), *Horror Film: A Critical Introduction* (New York: Bloomsbury).

Le Fanu, Sheridan (2004 [1872]), *Carmilla* (Holicog, PA: Wildside Press).

Löffler, Marie-Luise, and Florain Bast (2011), 'Bites from the Margins: Contemporary American Women's Vampire Literature', *Kultur & Geschlecht*, 8, 1–19.

Loichot, Valérie (2009), '"We Are All Related": Edouard Glissant Meets Octavia Butler', *Small Axe*, 30, 37–50.

Lorde, Audre (1982), *Zami: A New Spelling of My Name* (New York: Crossing Press).

Lübecker, Nicholai (2015), *The Feel Bad Film* (Edinburgh: Edinburgh University Press).

Lukkas, Lynn, and Howard Oransky (eds) (2015), *Covered in Time and History: The Films of Ana Mendieta* (Minneapolis: Katherine E. Nash Gallery, University of Minnesota in association with University of California Press).

Lysen, Flora, and Patricia Pisters (eds) (2012), *Deleuze Studies*, 6:1, special issue, 'The Smooth and the Striated'.

MacDonald, Scott (2016), 'About *Fuses*. Interview with Carolee Schneemann', *Documents: Cinema/Comparative Cinema*, 4:8, 10–11.

Maguire, David (2018), *I Spit on Your Grave* (London: Wallflower Press).

Majteles, Lily (2018), 'Interview: Katharina Wyss', *Film Comment*, 25 February, <https://www.filmcomment.com/blog/interview-katharina-wyss> (last accessed 26 August 2019).

Malabou, Catherine (2012), *The New Wounded: From Neurosis to Brain Damage* (New York: Fordham University Press).

Margulies, Yvonne (1996), *Nothing Happens: Chantal Akerman's Hyperrealist Everyday*. (Durham, NC: Duke University Press).

Marks, Laura (1999), *The Skin of Film: Intercultural Cinema, Embodiment and the Senses* (Durham, NC: Duke University Press).

Marryat, Florence (2010 [1897]), *The Blood of the Vampire*, ed. Greta Depledge (Brighton: Victorian Secrets).

Mathews, Andrew S. (2017), 'Ghostly Forms and Forest Histories', in Anna Tsing, Heather Swanson, Elaine Gan and Nils Bubant (eds), *Arts of Living on a Damaged Planet* (Minneapolis: University of Minnesota Press), G145–G156.

McDonald, Soraya (2019), 'In "When They See Us" Ava DuVernay Shows the Horrors that Swallowed the Central Park Five', *The Undefeated*, 31 May, <https://theundefeated.com/features/when-they-see-us-ava-duvernay-netflix-central-park-five/> (last accessed 27 March 2020).

McNally, Raymond (1985), *Dracula was a Woman: In Search of the Blood Countess of Transylvania* (London: Hamlyn).

McRobbie, Angela (2008), *The Aftermath of Feminism: Gender, Culture and Social Change* (Thousand Oaks, CA: Sage Publications).

Meehan, Meagan (2018), 'Blood Child: Interview with Writer and Director Jennifer Philips', *Movie Vine*, 30 September, <https://www.movievine.com/interviews/blood-child-interview-with-writer-and-director-jennifer-phillips/> (last accessed 27 March 2020).

Miller, Jennie (2017), 'Pregnancy is the Best Time to Make a Horror Movie', *The Cut*, 24 March, <https://www.thecut.com/2017/03/prevenge-alice-lowe-interview.html> (last accessed 27 March 2020).

Misek, Richard (2010), *Chromatic Cinema. A History of Screen Color* (Oxford: Wiley-Blackwell).

Monks Kauffman, Sophie (2017), 'Lynne Ramsay: "Being a Filmmaker is Like Being a Psychoanalyst"', *Little White Lies*, <https://lwlies.com/interviews/lynne-ramsay-you-were-never-really-here/> (last accessed 27 March 2020).

Morgne Cramer, Patricia (2010), 'Virginia Woolf and Sexuality', in Susan Sellers (ed.), *The Cambridge Companion to Virginia Woolf* (Cambridge: Cambridge University Press), 180–96.

Morgne Cramer, Patricia (2013), 'Woolf and Theories of Sexuality', in Bryony Randall (ed.), *Virginia Woolf in Context* (Cambridge: Cambridge University Press), 129–46.

Morrey, David (2004), 'Textures of Terror: Claire Denis' *Trouble Every Day*', *Belphégor*, 3:2, 1–7, <https://dalspace.library.dal.ca/handle/10222/47680> (last accessed 27 March 2020).

Morris, Bethany (2018), 'Loud Ladies: Deterritorializing Femininity Through Becoming-Animal', in Janae Sholtz and Cheri Lynn Carr (eds), *Deleuze and Guattari Studies*, 12:4, 506–21, special issue, 'Infinite Eros: Deleuze, Guattari and Feminist Couplings'.

Morris, Susana M. (2012), 'Black Girls are from the Future: Afrofuturist

Feminism in Octavia Butler's *Fledgling*', *Women's Studies Quarterly*, 40:3/4, 146–66.

Morrison, Toni (2004), *Beloved* (with new introduction) (London: Vintage).

Müller, Cornelia, and Hermann Kappelhoff (2018), *Cinematic Metaphor: Experience-Affectivity-Temporality* (New York: De Gruyter).

Mulvey, Laura (2009), *Visual and Other Pleasures* (New York: Palgrave Macmillan).

Mulvey, Laura (2016), 'A Neon Sign, A Soup Tureen', *Film Quarterly*, 70:1, 25–31.

Mulvey, Laura, and Anna Beckmann-Rogers (eds) (2015), *Feminisms: Diversity, Difference and Multiplicity in Contemporary Film Cultures* (Amsterdam: Amsterdam University Press).

Murrian, Samuel (2019), 'Five Undeniable Reasons Why *The Babadook* is the Best Horror Movie So Far This Century', *Parade*, 2 August.

Myers, Emma (2015), 'Interview: Veronika Franz and Severing Fiala', *Film Comment*, 9 September, <https://www.filmcomment.com/blog/goodnight-mommy-interview-veronika-franz-severin-fiala/> (last accessed 27 March 2020).

Nancy, Jean-Luc (2005), 'Image and Violence', in Jeff Fort (ed.), *The Ground of the Image* (New York: Fordham University Press), 15–26.

Nancy, Jean-Luc (2008), 'Icon of Fury: Claire Denis's *Trouble Every Day*', trans. Douglas Morrey, *Film-Philosophy*, 12:1, 1–9.

Nayar, Pramod (2012), 'A New Biological Citizenship: Posthumanism in Octavia Butler's *Fledgling*', *MFS Modern Fiction Studies*, 58:4, 796–817.

Ndalianis, Angela (2012), *The Horror Sensorium: Media and the Senses* (Jefferson, NC: McFarland).

Nesbitt, Nick (2010), 'The Post-Colonial Event: Deleuze, Glissant and the Problem of the Political', in Simone Bignail and Paul Patton (eds), *Deleuze and the Postcolonial* (Edinburgh: Edinburgh University Press), 103–18.

Ngai, Sianne (2007), *Ugly Feelings* (Cambridge, MA: Harvard University Press).

Nichols, Mackenzie (2019), '*Jennifer's Body* Turns 10: Megan Fox, Diabolo Cody and Karyn Kusama Reflect on Making the Cult Classic', *Variety*, 11 September, <https://variety.com/2019/film/news/jennifers-body-10th-anniversary-megan-fox-diablo-cody-1203323111/> (last accessed 27 March 2020).

Onaran, Gozde (2017), 'Escaping Entrapment: Gothic Heroines in Contemporary Film', PhD dissertation, University of Amsterdam, Netherlands.

Ong, Amandas (2016), 'The Vengeful Woman and the Changing Face of Asian Horror Cinema', *Little White Lies*, 22 June, <https://lwlies.com/articles/vengeful-woman-asian-horror-cinema/> (last accessed 27 March 2020).

Peirse, Alison (ed.) (2020), *Women Make Horror: Film, Feminism, Genre* (New Brunswick, NJ: Rutgers University Press).

Peirse, Alison, and Daniel Martin (eds) (2013), *Korean Horror Cinema* (Edinburgh: Edinburgh University Press).

Penrose, Valentine (2012), *The Bloody Countess: The Atrocities of Erzsebet Bathory*, trans. Alexander Trocchi (Bangkok: Sun Vision Press).

Perlmutter, Ruth (1979), 'Feminine Absence: A Political Aesthetic in Chantal Ackerman's *Jeanne Dielman, 23 Quoi de commerce, 1080 Bruxelles*', *Quarterly Review of Film Studies*, 4:2, 125–33.

Pisters, Patricia (2003), *The Matrix of Visual Culture. Working with Deleuze in Film Theory* (Stanford, CA: Stanford University Press).

Pisters, Patricia (2007), 'Refusal of Reproduction: Paradoxes of Becoming-Woman in Transnational Moroccan Filmmaking', in Katarzyna Marciniak, Aniko Imre and Aine O'Healy (eds), *Transnational Feminism in Film and Media* (New York: Palgrave Macmillan), 71–92.

Pisters, Patricia (2010), 'Violence and Laughter: Paradoxes of Nomadic Thought in Postcolonial Cinema', in Simone Bignall and Paul Patton (eds), *Deleuze and the Postcolonial* (Edinburgh: Edinburgh University Press), 201–19.

Pisters, Patricia (2012), *The Neuro-Image: A Deleuzian Film-Philosophy of Digital Screen Culture* (Stanford, CA: Stanford University Press).

Pisters, Patricia (2016), 'I Just Want to Be Perfect: Affective Compulsive Movement in *Black Swann*', *Cinefiles*, 10, 1–15, special issue, 'Cinematic Affect', ed. Ann Rutherford, <http://www.thecine-files.com/pisters2016/> (last accessed 27 March 2020).

Pisters, Patricia (2019), 'Carrie's Sisters: New Blood in Contemporary Female Horror Cinema', in Nicholas Chare, Jeanette Hoorn and Audrey Yue (eds), *Re-reading the Monstrous-Feminine: Art, Film, Feminism and Psychoanalysis* (New York: Routledge), 121–37.

Pisters, Patricia, and Wim Staat (eds) (2005), *Shooting the Family: Transnational Media and Intercultural Values* (Amsterdam: Amsterdam University Press).

Prestridge, James (2018), '*Family* Director Veronica Kedar Talks Violence and Life in Israel', *Close-Up Culture*, 20 September, <https://closeupculture.com/2018/09/20/raindance-2018-family-director-veronica-kedar-talks-violence-and-life-in-israel/> (last accessed 27 March 2020).

Prigge, Matt (2016), 'Lucile Hadzihalilovic Doesn't Want to Classify her Film *Evolution*', *Metro*, 24 November, <https://www.metro.us/entertainment/interview-lucile-hadzihalilovic-doesn-t-want-to-classify-her-film-evolution/zsJpkw---ZSB3ZwbWLJ6Wk> (last accessed 27 March 2020).

Qiu, Xiaoqing (2009), 'Luce Irigaray's View on Mother–Daughter Relationship', *Comparative Literature: East & West*, 11:1, 31–43.

Quinlivan, Davina (2009), 'Material Hauntings: The Kinaesthesia of Sound in Innocence', *Studies in French Cinema*, 9:3, 215–24.

Ramanathan, Geetha (2006), *Feminist Auteurs: Reading Women's Films* (London: Wallflower Press).

Reynaud, Bérénice (2017), 'Pan African Dreams: The Dreams that Dance', *Senses of Cinema*, 83, <http://sensesofcinema.com/2017/festival-reports/pan-african-film-festival-2017/> (last accessed 27 March 2020).

Rice, Anne (1976), *Interview with the Vampire* (New York: Ballantine Books).

Rife, Katie (2017), 'Maybe Some Day the World Will Appreciate *The Bad Batch*,

Not Now', *The AV Club*, 22 June, <https://film.avclub.com/maybe-someday-the-world-will-appreciate-the-bad-batch-1798191861> (last accessed 27 March 2020).

Robertson, Adi (2013), 'Review *Dark Touch*: A Heady Horror Film that Never Quite Hits its Mark', *The Verge*, April 20, <https://www.theverge.com/2013/4/20/4242988/dark-touch-heady-horror-film-never-quite-hits-its-mark> (last accessed 27 March 2020).

Robinson, Chauncey (2018), '*Gehenna*: Horror Film Uses Supernatural to Show Terror of Colonialism and War', *People's World Social Media*, 3 May, <https://www.peoplesworld.org/article/gehenna-horror-film-uses-the-supernatural-to-show-terrors-of-colonialism-and-war/> (last accessed 27 March 2020).

Rose, Deborah Bird (2017), 'Shimmer: When All You Love is Being Trashed', in Anna Tsing, Heather Swanson, Elaine Gan and Nils Bubant (eds), *Arts of Living on a Damaged Planet* (Minneapolis: University of Minnesota Press), G51–G63.

Rosen, Miss (2018), 'Ana Mendieta Fought for Women's Rights and Paid with Blood', *Vice*, 30 April, <https://www.vice.com/en_us/article/gym79y/ana-mendieta-fought-for-womens-rights-and-paid-with-blood> (last accessed 18 March 2020).

Rowe, Kathleen (1995), *The Unruly Woman: Gender and the Genres of Laughter* (Austin: Texas University Press).

Sagan, Dorion (2017), 'Beautiful Monsters: Terra in the Cyanocene', in Anna Tsing, Heather Swanson, Elaine Gan and Nils Bubant (eds), *Arts of Living on a Damaged Planet* (Minneapolis: University of Minnesota Press), M169–M174.

Samsonow, Elisabeth von (2019), *Anti-Electra: The Radical Totem of the Girl*, trans. Anita Fricek and Stephen Zepke (Minneapolis: University of Minnesota Press).

Savino, Charlotte (2008), ' "I Hate, I Love": How Mothers Fail in Virginia Woolf's Fiction', Undergraduate Honors thesis, College of William and Mary, <https://scholarworks.wm.edu/honorstheses/783> (last accessed 27 March 2020).

Schneemann, Carolee (1991), 'The Obscene Body/Politic', *Art Journal*, 50:4, 28–35.

Schneemann, Carolee (2003), *Imaging Her Erotics: Essays, Interviews, Projects* (Cambridge, MA: MIT Press).

Schiefer, Karin (2019), 'Sparkling and Strange: Interview with Jessica Hausner', *AFC Austrian Films.Com*, May, <https://www.austrianfilms.com/interview/jessica_hausner/little_joe_ENG> (last accessed 27 March 2020).

Schneider, Steven Jay (2003), 'Suck . . . Don't Suck: Framing Ideology in Kathryn Bigelow's *Near Dark*', in Deborah Jermyn and Sean Redmond (eds), *The Cinema of Kathryn Bigelow: Hollywood Transgressor* (London: Wallflower Press).

Scott, David (2017), *Stuart Hall's Voice: Intimations of an Ethics of Receptive Generosity* (Durham, NC: Duke University Press).

Scott, Jody (1977), *I, Vampire: The Benaroya Chronicles II* (London: Create Space Independent Publishing Platform).

Schubart, Rikke (2018), *Mastering Fear: Women, Emotions and Contemporary Horror* (New York: Bloomsbury Academic).

Sears, Emily (2018), 'Interview: Director Deborah Haywood Puts Herself Out There in the Dark and Whimsical *Pin Cushion*', *Birth Movies Death*, <https://birthmoviesdeath.com/2018/07/20/interview-director-deborah-haywood-puts-herself-out-there-in-the-dark-and-w> (last accessed 27 March 2020).

Seung Chung, Hye (2013), 'Acacia and Adoption Anxiety in Korean Horror Cinema', in Alison Peirse and Daniel Martin (eds), *Korean Horror Cinema* (Edinburgh: Edinburgh University Press), 87–100.

Shannon Miller, Liz (2017), '*Alias Grace*: An All-Women Team Created the Downtown Abbey', *Indie Wire*, 5 November, <https://www.indiewire.com/2017/11/alias-grace-netflix-anti-downton-abbey-american-psycho-1201894315/> (last accessed 27 March 2020).

Shelley, Mary (1992 [1818]), *Frankenstein or The Modern Prometheus*, ed. Wendy Lesser (New York: Everyman's Library).

Sholtz, Janae, and Cheri Lynne Carr (eds) (2018), *Deleuze and Guattari Studies*, 12:4, special issue, 'Infinite Eros: Deleuze, Guattari and Feminist Couplings'.

Shuttle, Penelope, and Peter Redgrove (1978), *The Wise Wound: Eve's Curse and Everywoman* (New York: Richard Marek).

Silver, Brenda (2000), *Icon, Virginia Woolf* (Chicago: University of Chicago Press).

Smelik, Anneke (1993), 'And the Mirror Cracked: Metaphors of Violence in the Films of Marleen Gorris', *Women's Studies International Forum*, 16:4, 349–63.

Smelik, Anneke (1998), *And the Mirror Cracked: Feminist Cinema and Film Theory* (New York: Palgrave).

Smith, Ariel (2015), 'Indigenous Cinema and the Horrific Reality of Colonial Violence', *Decolonization, Indigeneity, Education and Society*, 13 February, <https://decolonization.wordpress.com/2015/02/13/indigenous-cinema-and-the-horrific-reality-of-colonial-violence/> (last accessed 27 March 2020).

Sobchack, Vivian (2005), 'Waking Life: On the Experience of *Innocence*', *Film Comment*, 41:6, 46.

So-young, Kim, and Chris Berry (2000), 'Suri suri masuri: The Magic of Korean Horror Film: A Conversation', *Postcolonial Studies: Culture, Politics, Economy*, 3:1, 53–60.

Stengers, Isabelle, and Vinciane Despret (2014), *Women Who Make a Fuss: The Unfaithful Daughters of Virginia Woolf* (Minneapolis: Univocal Publishers).

Stoker, Bram (1993 [1897]), *Dracula* (London: Wordsworth).

Swinton, Tilda (ed.) (2019), *Aperture*, 25, special issue, '*Orlando*'.

Tarr, Carrie (2005), *Reframing Difference: Beur and Banlieue Filmmaking in France* (Manchester: Manchester University Press).

Tarr, Carrie (2012), 'Introduction: Women's Film-Making in France 2000–2010', *Studies in French Cinema*, 12:3, 189–200.

Taubin, Amy (2018), 'Mother Earth', *Film Comment*, March–April, <https://www.filmcomment.com/article/spoor-agnieszka-holland/> (last accessed 27 March 2020).

Taylor, Kate (2007), 'Infection, Postcolonialism and Somatechnics in Claire Denis' *Trouble Every Day*', *Studies in French Cinema*, 7:1, 19–29.

Thomas, Lou (2017), 'I'm Fed Up with the Way Women's Sexuality is Portrayed on Screen', *BFI News*, <https://www.bfi.org.uk/news-opinion/news-bfi/interviews/raw-director-julia-ducournau> (last accessed 27 March 2020).

Tsing, Anna (2015), *The Mushroom at the End of the World: On the Possibility of Life in Capitalist Ruins* (Princeton: Princeton University Press).

Tsing, Anna, Heather Swanson, Elaine Gan and Nils Bubant (eds) (2017), *Arts of Living on a Damaged Planet* (Minneapolis: University of Minnesota Press).

Vely, Yannick (2014), 'Interview: La *Dark Touch* de Marina de Van', *Paris Match*, 23 March, <https://www.parismatch.com/Culture/Cinema/La-Dark-Touch-de-Marina-de-Van-555346> (last accessed 27 March 2020).

Wedel, Michael (2019), *Pictorial Affects, Senses of Rupture: On the Poetics and Culture of Popular German Cinema, 1910–1930* (New York: De Gruyter).

Weinstock, Jeffrey Andrew (2012), *The Vampire Film: Undead Cinema* (New York: Columbia University Press).

Wekker, Gloria (2016), *White Innocence: Paradoxes of Colonialism and Race* (Durham, NC: Duke University Press).

Wells-Barnett, Ida B. (1997), *Southern Horrors and Other Writings: The Anti-Lynching Campaign of Ida B. Wells, 1892–1900*, ed. Jacqueline Jones Royster (Boston: Bedford Books).

White, Dennis (1971), 'The Poetics of Horror: More than Meets the Eye', *Cinema Journal*, 10:2, 1–18.

White, Frances (2001), *Dark Continent of Our Bodies: Black Feminism & Politics of Respectability* (Philadelphia: Temple University Press).

White, Louise (2000), *Speaking with Vampires: Rumor and History in Colonial Africa* (Berkeley and Los Angeles: University of California Press).

Wigley, Sam (2016), 'Mika Ninagawa on *Helter Skelter*', *BFI in Focus*, 4 April, <https://www.bfi.org.uk/news/in-focus-mika-ninagawa-helter-skelter> (last accessed 27 March 2020).

Williams, Linda (1984a), 'When the Woman Looks', in Mary Ann Doane, Patricia Mellencamp and Linda Williams (eds), *Revisions: Essays in Feminist Film Criticism* (Los Angeles: University Publications of America), 61–6.

Williams, Linda (1984b), 'Something Else Besides a Mother: *Stella Dallas* and the Maternal Melodrama', *Cinema Journal*, 24:1, 2–27.

Williams, Linda (1991), 'Film Bodies, Gender, Genre and Excess', *Film Quarterly*, 44:4, 2–13.

Wilson, Emma (2007), 'Miniature Lives, Intrusion and *Innocence*: Women Filming Children', *French Cultural Studies*, 18:2, 169–83.

Winterson, Jeanette (2019), *Frankissstein: A Love Story* (London: Jonathan Cape).

Woolf, Virginia (1992 [1925]), *Mrs Dalloway*, ed. Stella McNichol, introd. Elaine Showalter (London: Penguin)

Woolf, Virginia (1999 [1937]) *The Years*, ed. Hermione Lee (Oxford: Oxford University Press).

Woolf, Virginia (2001), *The Mark on the Wall and Other Short Fictions*, ed. David Bradshaw (Oxford: Oxford University Press).

Woolf, Virginia (2004 [1927]), *To the Lighthouse* (London: Vintage).

Woolf, Virginia (2008), *Selected Essays*, ed. David Bradshaw (Oxford: Oxford University Press).

Woolf, Virginia (2015a [1928; 1938]), *A Room of One's Own* and *Three Guineas*, ed. Anna Snaith (Oxford: Oxford University Press).

Woolf, Virginia (2015b [1931]), *The Waves*, ed. David Bradshaw (Oxford: Oxford University Press).

Woolf, Virginia (2018 [1928]), *Orlando*, introduced by Tilda Swinton (Edinburgh: Canongate).

Xu Jia and Kevin B. Lee (2013), 'Interview with Yang Lina, Director of *Longing for the Rain*', *Degenerate Films*, 24 May, <https://www.dgeneratefilms.com/post/cinematalk-interview-with-yang-lina-director-of-i-longing-for-the-rain--i> (last accessed 27 March 2020).

Yamato, Jen (2017), 'Ana Lily Amirpour Shoots from the Guts with Dystopian Cannibal Love Story', *Los Angeles Times*, 25 June, <https://www.latimes.com/entertainment/movies/la-et-mn-ana-lily-amirpour-bad-batch-2017-story.html> (last accessed 27 March 2020).

Young, Lola (1996), *Fear of the Dark: Race, Gender and Sexuality in the Cinema* (London: Routledge).

Yountae, An (2014), 'Beginning in the Middle: Deleuze, Glissant and Colonial Difference', *Culture, Theory and Critique*, 55:3, 286–301.

Zimmerman, Bonnie (1984), 'Daughters of Darkness: The Lesbian Vampire on Film', in Barry Keith Grant (ed.), *Planks of Reason: Essays on the Horror Film* (Metuchen, NJ: Scarecrow), 153–63.

Index

CPSIA information can be obtained
at www.ICGtesting.com
Printed in the USA
JSHW040234140922
30495JS00002B/5

9 781474 466967